CHANGING THE GAME

Wilbur S. Shepperson Series in Nevada History

D1268321

Changing the Game

Women at Work in Las Vegas, 1940 to 1990

Joanne L. Goodwin

 University of Nevada Press / Reno & Las Vegas

Wilbur S. Shepperson Series in Nevada History
Series Editor: Michael S. Green

University of Nevada Press, Reno, Nevada 89557 USA
Copyright © 2014 by University of Nevada Press
All rights reserved
Manufactured in the United States of America
Design by Kathleen Szawiola

Library of Congress Cataloging-in-Publication Data

Goodwin, Joanne L.
Changing the game : women at work in Las Vegas, 1940–1990 /
Joanne L. Goodwin. — First Edition.
pages cm. — (Wilbur S. Shepperson series in Nevada history)
Includes index.
ISBN 978-0-87417-960-6 (paperback) —
ISBN 978-0-87417-961-3 (e-book)
1. Women--Employment—Nevada—Las Vegas—History—
20th century. 2. Sex discrimination in employment—Nevada—
Las Vegas—History—20th century. I. Title.
HD6096.N35G66 2014
658.0092'5209793135—dc23   2014012343

The paper used in this book meets the requirements of American
National Standard for Information Sciences—Permanence of Paper
for Printed Library Materials, ANSI/NISO Z39.48-1992 (R2002).
Binding materials were selected for strength and durability.

First Printing
22   21   20   19   18   17   16   15   14
5   4   3   2   1

For Laurie

Contents

Illustrations

Preface

I began to conduct research on the lives of women in Las Vegas in 1995. That research began with the creation of the Nevada Women's Archive (NWA) in the Department of Special Collections, Lied Library at the University of Nevada, Las Vegas (UNLV). Many individuals, including community supporters, faculty, graduate students, and library administrators, brought the archives into existence and collaboratively created a resource for generations to come. In particular, the leadership of Jean Ford, Eugene Moehring, Sue Fawn Chung, Carol Corbett, and Myoung-ja Lee Kwon made our work possible. Since its creation, the professional guidance of Sue Kim Chung has helped expand the resource and keep it accessible for researchers. Out of the NWA came the impetus for an oral history center. Claytee D. White has built that center's collection into a remarkable resource for Las Vegas research. My work with the NWA started me on the path that led to this book.

Research that spans more than a decade garners more debts than I can adequately acknowledge. At the top of my list of people to thank is the large group who collaborated in the creation of the Las Vegas Women Oral History Project under my direction at the Women's Research Institute of Nevada at UNLV. More than ninety women have generously contributed their narratives to the project, even though they modestly wondered why we were interested and what their lives had to do with history. The eleven women whose narratives are presented in this book deserve my particular thanks. They allowed us into their lives, offered us their experiences, shared photographs as well as memories, and trusted in the greater good that this collection of oral histories would produce. This book focuses on women in the gaming and entertainment industry, but all the collected oral histories have helped to shape a new history of women in post-1945 Las Vegas.

The project would never have grown beyond a handful of oral histories had it not been for the students, collaborators, and colleagues who worked with me to collect the interviews. Initial ideas for narrators and much-needed community support came from Thalia Dondero and her daughter, Judy Habbeshaw, who knew the community that I had recently entered. Kim Beach Bach and Joyce Marshall Moore worked in the hotel-casinos and had the initial idea to interview women workers. Claytee D. White joined me and Marshall Moore, Barbara Agonia, Catherine Bellver, Caryll Batt Dziedziak, Layne Karafantis, Brigid Kelly, Myoung-ja Lee Kwon, and Kay Long to collect the oral histories. Angela Moor played many roles in the project and digitally archived the collection. As the project moved into video interviews, Kristin Guthrie played an important role.

Oral histories are a remarkably labor-intensive enterprise. The Las Vegas Women Oral History Project received important early support from Carol C. Harter, president of UNLV at the time. She saw the value of the project for its potential to contribute to Las Vegas history, to build strong faculty-student research relationships, and to strengthen university ties to the community. Financial support came from the UNLV Foundation, the Nevada Humanities, and a significant gift from Emilie N. Wanderer. I am indebted to the history department for offering me a graduate assistant for several years and facilitating the project in numerous ways.

For many years I had the sustained support of colleagues who kept alive the generative ideas and writing. Alice Kessler-Harris's foundational work in the field of women's labor history is matched only by her mentoring of others in the field. Annelise Orleck shared with me her own perspective and wise advice on the antipoverty movement in Las Vegas and its impact on the struggles to open nontraditional jobs. Rickie Solinger encouraged me to make room for my voice in this book while the project was in its infancy. She also counseled me to let the contradictions in the narratives stand on their own. Elizabeth Jameson shared her vast knowledge on women in the West and oral history as well as her sense of humor. My participation in 2006 in "Women's Narratives, Women's Lives: Intersections of Gender and Memory," one of the annual summer institutes sponsored by the Columbia Center for Oral History Research, proved crucial to my interpretation of oral histories. I am grateful to Mary Marshall Clark, Ron Grele, and the participants of the institute for their support and ideas. My gratitude extends to Bob Hogan, the director of the Nevada Community Enrichment Program. The assistance given by Bob and his staff made my progress on the book possible. A national network of friends and scholars discussed the varied and diverse aspects of this book over meals, online, in conference papers, and in publications. My thanks to Eileen Boris, Nancy Busch, Susan Chandler, Nupur Chaudhuri, Sue DiBella, Elizabeth Faue, LeAnn Fields, Sherry J. Katz, Virginia Nelson, and Mary Elizabeth Perry for their help as I shaped my thoughts.

My colleagues in the UNLV history department offered significant questions, ideas, and prodding. I am especially indebted to Eugene Moehring, whose knowledge of Las Vegas and urban history laid the foundation for new scholarship on the city. Andy Fry led the department and provided important institutional support during crucial years in the project's development. Sue Fawn Chung offered a positive example of combining university research with community engagement. Elspeth Whitney and Marcia Gallo provided gendered analysis as well as good friendship. Greg Hise, Andy Kirk, David Tanenhaus, and Paul Werth supported me through my academic process in varied and numerous ways.

One of my communities of support over the past fifteen years has been the staff, advisers, and students associated with the Women's Research Institute of Nevada (WRIN). Founded in 1999, WRIN has been a center for research and education programs based in gender analysis at UNLV. The institute found a home in the College of Liberal Arts and received much-needed office space and varied forms of support from Dean Chris Hudgins. The shared vision of my coworkers and colleagues Caryll Batt Dziedziak, Venicia Considine, Juliana Ormsby, Angela Moor, Crystal Jackson, Diana Thu-Thao Rhodes, Roberta Sabbath, Alma Castro, Barbara Agonia, Lorri Jackson, Deborah Campbell, and Tamara Marino provided the positive context in which I could ultimately complete this book.

The final details of getting a book published can give anyone aches and pains. I am grateful, therefore, for the fine assistance of the photo curators who made my job less of a burden. Ginny Poehling and Alex Hutchings at the News Bureau Archive of the Las Vegas Convention and Visitors Authority, Dolores Brownlee of the Special Collections Department of Lied Library at UNLV, Annie Segan of the Arthur Rothstein family, and Geri Kodey of UNLV Photo Services offered timely assistance. Several individuals included in the book loaned us their personal photos to benefit the oral history. I am particularly grateful for the generosity of Carolyn McClure and Carole Crew. Joanne O'Hare and Matt Becker of the University of Nevada Press patiently waited for the manuscript, and I am pleased to have chosen the press to publish the book. The anonymous readers of the manuscript went beyond the norm with comments and suggestions that have improved the book immeasurably.

Through my entire academic career, through the highs and lows, I have had the constant support of my life partner, Laurie Lytel. Her wit, patience, and love always make me a better person.

CHANGING THE GAME

Eleanor Roosevelt (*center*) joined the Las Vegas tourists in 1958 at the El Rancho Vegas Hotel and Casino. The owner, Beldon Katleman, is on the right. Roosevelt's involvement with the United Nations led the Clark County Chapter of the United Nations Association to invite her. Courtesy of Special Collections, University Libraries, University of Nevada, Las Vegas.

INTRODUCTION

Discovering Women in Post-1945 Las Vegas

In 1996 the *New Yorker* magazine published a portfolio of photographs of Las Vegas showgirls by internationally renowned photographer Annie Leibovitz.[1] The portfolio paired images of the women in their full performance regalia of rhinestones, feathers, and very little else with images of them offstage, as we might find them at the bookstore or grocery, without makeup and in simple clothing. The commentary that introduced those images—as well as the reactions from the general audience and my colleagues across the nation—revolved around the ordinary women behind the extraordinary presentation of women in the city known for its extravagance, consumption, and fantasy. This comparative presentation of representation versus subjectivity has been revisited numerous times in local and national press coverage of women in Las Vegas. The coverage tends to remain at the level of description, though, with little discussion about the women or their roles in the city's labor force.

Being immersed in my own study of women in Las Vegas, I found it fascinating that these diametrically opposed images captured the public imagination. Why do we find it fascinating to see a mother holding two daughters across the page from an image of her at work as a topless showgirl in a headdress? Why are we amazed that the short-haired, average-endowed woman wearing eyeglasses is also the traditionally glamorous performer? We are not similarly entranced by the magicians who perform in Las Vegas, and we do not expect them to release birds from their sugar bowls over breakfast. We understand the magicians are entertainers who perform for a living. And yet we are amazed when the veils of illusion are lifted from the showgirl to reveal the person beneath, as in the Leibovitz photos.

I begin with the portfolio of Leibovitz photographs because understanding women's lives in Las Vegas in the decades after 1945 is to engage with the entangled concepts of representation, subjectivity, and lived experience as well as to interrogate the era's changing ideas about gender and sexuality. As a tourist attraction, Las Vegas is all about leisure and fantasy. In the 1950s Las Vegas casinos promoted themselves as a resort attraction with something for everyone. They gave postwar Americans a way to enjoy their leisure and to break social conventions at prices within the range of the middle class. Casinos created a sense of security and safety for people vacationing in properties owned and operated by mob bosses. Las Vegas was called Sin City, but it became a tourist destination for dignitaries, families, and Americans from across the country. While the Las Vegas hotel-casinos became known as the entertainment capital of the world, the metropolitan area grew into a major city with a population of slightly more than 2 million in 2012. This dynamic city deserved a fuller understanding of its people and its history.[2]

The interplay of representation and lived experience also created unique problems for the historical study of women in Las Vegas. The female body has been ubiquitous in the city's entertainment publicity, yet women or gendered analysis has been invisible until recently. Furthermore, when the Las Vegas showgirl emerged as a female icon in the middle of the twentieth century, she did so when mainstream American society shunned public nudity and intimate relations outside marriage. The perceived ills of gambling, drinking, and naked ladies led Americans to assign meanings to women who performed nude—meanings that attributed sexual availability with the promotion of the city's entertainment. This attribution followed long-established attitudes toward public performances by women as well as the widely accepted, sexualized images of World War II pinup girls and Hollywood starlets. By the mid-1960s the Playboy culture had gained a foothold in America and heightened the debates over and the visibility of public nudity, sexuality, and commodification of the female body. While the master narrative of women in Las Vegas featured a sexy subject and an avaricious popular appetite for more, why challenge those stereotypes to explore the complexities of working life in the second half of the twentieth century?[3]

There is much to learn from the way workers represent themselves. While the master narrative produced a successful business plan that portrayed women as a sexual object of male desire, it did little to add to our knowledge of women in the city's history. Furthermore, the subjective experiences of dancers or showgirls would be a fruitful project from which to understand how women managed their lives and careers in a cultural context that limited pathways to success. Ffolliott "Fluff" LeCoque, the manager of Las Vegas's longest-running showroom spectacle, "Jubilee," pointed to the significance of alternative narratives when she said the showgirl "has an attitude. She knows who she is. She is communicating her mystique to the audience, yet remains a bit aloof." A viewer should look but not touch, as the performer remained in control.[4] Leibovitz tapped into these cultural messages when she mixed up images and gender meanings in her photographs of showgirls on- and off-stage. She disrupted our public relations–saturated understanding of *showgirl as hooker* when she illustrated them as moms, students, and workers. The narratives included in this book are from working women across the industry. *Changing the Game* challenges the well-crafted representation of women in Las Vegas and goes beyond the best-known, yet superficial, images to offer new perspectives and counternarratives of women's lives in the second half of the twentieth century.

Although tourists know Las Vegas as a fantasy land, it is also a workers' city.[5] At mid-century the city attracted men and women to work in the rapidly expanding hotel and casino industries. Women came to Las Vegas and worked at higher rates of employment than they did in the country as a whole.[6] These narratives are sometimes heroic and sometimes common, and all are a part of the changing gender and racial landscape of those decades. They uncover the areas of employment that attracted women to the desert resort town in the years after World War II as well as reveal the desires, thoughts, and actions of both well-known and relatively unknown women.

This book began with simple questions: Why did women choose to come to this city, a town in the middle of the Mojave Desert in the years after 1945? What types of work did they do? How did they develop their own potential in a city that commercialized most things, including women's bodies? The book not only puts women back into Las Vegas history, but also expands what we know about women in general during those years.[7] These stories encompass the transition in US history from the end of World War II, through the subsequent decades of economic and social transformation, to the platform of new possibilities that women had begun to experience by the 1980s. As Jacqueline Jones wrote of African American women, "Las Vegas might seem an unlikely place to gauge gendered transformations in the post–World War II United States outside the South; but the city, with its preponderance of service-sector jobs, has served as a bellwether of the forces shaping the national labor market over the last sixty years."[8] In addition, to the service work Jones studied, the hotel and casino industries captured the shifting boundaries of women's employment in the postwar decades. In this most unlikely place, the experiences and life choices of women who came to Las Vegas expands our ideas about women's lives in postwar America and its most famous resort town.

Why Las Vegas?

Las Vegas offers a complex site from which to understand many of the anxieties and desires of postwar Americans. The national preoccupation with military defense and the power and horror of atomic weaponry found its ultimate symbol in the creation of the Nevada Test Site located just ninety miles north of the city.[9] The focus on social order and conformity in the 1950s contrasted sharply with the presence of organized crime and the central role of mob finances in the development of early casinos. The benefits of the expanding consumer society rested uneasily alongside the increased commercialization of American life. Las Vegas's streets and casino showrooms provided the stage from which Americans witnessed changing attitudes about sexuality. This disquiet found its lightning rod in legal gambling and the sex industry in Nevada. Even the social and legal changes in race and gender relations played themselves out in a unique manner, although they were similar to other civil rights struggles of the period. In sum, Las Vegas offers an excellent site to study changes in American culture. The city continually attracted a wide swath of Americans to its increasingly popular attractions.[10] The themes of anxiety and desire, social order and social change, as well as transformations in the economy, shaped the background for this study.

Las Vegas lies in the Mojave Desert, midway between Salt Lake City and Los Angeles. The natural springs in the desert made the site attractive to the Paiutes, early Spanish and US explorers, Mormon settlers, and the railroad, which gave the original town site a foundation for growth. Aside from railroad, mining, and ranching, no major economic resource made the place attractive for expansion. As historian Eugene Moehring has argued, it was the infusion of federal funds for the Hoover Dam (1931), the gunnery school (renamed Nellis Air Force Base in 1950), and light wartime industry during the 1940s that kept the area stable.[11] The expansion of casinos (Nevada relegalized gambling in 1931) and resorts south of town on old Highway 91 (now known as the Las Vegas Strip), beginning in the 1940s and exploding in the 1950s, brought economic growth and corresponding jobs to the region. That growth continued through the twentieth century, to be stopped only during the Great Recession of 2008.

Unlike earlier mining booms, the growth of the area included the migration of large numbers of women. The population of greater Las Vegas expanded along with the economy in every decade since 1940, stopping only with the recession. Las Vegas (the urbanized area) had nearly 10,400 residents in 1940, 89,427 people in 1960, and 462,000 in 1980.[12] While other areas of the United States gradually lost jobs and population through the second half of the twentieth century, the hotel-casino industries in Las Vegas offered employment in the service jobs created by tourism. The employment of women was encouraged to fill the labor demands of rapid development and its related industries.

The story of Las Vegas's development from frontier town to international tourist destination has been told often. A warehouse could be filled with publications that explore casinos, but very few of these works are interested in any examination of women as historical actors. A few studies have used the perspectives of the workers to inform their analysis. Fewer have focused on the work performed by women in the *development* of the city.[13] One explanation for this omission in the history of the city's growth was a relatively weak base of historical sources necessary to write women into history.[14]

What Do We Know About Women in Las Vegas Post-1945?

What we know about the experiences of women in Las Vegas can fit into a proverbial thimble. The record is strongest in the early twentieth century—a period before Las Vegas distinguished itself as a gambling mecca, a tourism destination, or a fast-growing metropolis. We know that women helped build every part of Las Vegas, from the small town's ranches, businesses, churches, and schools, to the wartime industries, and to the casino resorts that have defined the city as a tourist destination city since the 1950s. Yet most of that knowledge was gained from working with primary materials and is just beginning to find its way into print. The archival record on women after 1945 was disorganized and sparse as recently as the 1990s.[15]

At the same time, much of what we think we know about women in Las Vegas came from constructed commercial images that I call the *master narrative*. Beginning in the 1930s, casino publicists and city business leaders shaped the fantasies that we identify with classic Las Vegas: the last frontier, resort fun in the sun, and the entertainment capital of the world. By the

1950s city boosters collaborated in their public relations spin, and the Las Vegas dancer or showgirl always figured prominently in that image. Young women in bathing suits (often dancers from the showroom) stand by the hotel pool in poses reminiscent of the World War II sweater girl. In the 1960s partially nude European shows played in several showrooms and the publicity machine featured the entertainers. To veterans of hotel-casino publicity like the Sands's Al Guzman, the appeal was obvious. "Pretty girls sell," he told a journalist. "You need to do something to get people's attention. A pretty girl will get an editor's attention."[16] In addition to the publicists, writers of fiction and screenplays pushed the commodification of women and drew attention to the wild side. Larry McMurtry's novel, *The Desert Rose,* described an aging Las Vegas showgirl whose daughter replaced her in the show. When the 1995 film *Showgirls* played in Las Vegas, many in the community expressed their outrage at its sleazy portrayal of the performers. The narrative of this business agenda remained the dominant trope defining women in Las Vegas well into the 1990s. It continued because the tourist destination drives the development of the economy and because the fantasies have become a part of American culture.[17]

Historians' analysis of US women in the decades after the war pointed to the conflictual social messages women received. As early as 1972 William Chafe claimed that a major transformation in public attitudes about women and their workplace opportunities would need to occur before women's status could improve.[18] Elaine Tyler May adapted the Cold War foreign policy word *containment* to describe the ways in which society viewed women's changing roles as a threat to family life. In her 1988 book *Homeward Bound,* May described the desires of Americans to start families following two tumultuous decades of economic depression and war. These desires, however, existed within the context of proscriptive efforts by institutions from religions, businesses, and the law to contain women's sexuality and thus their lives during the Cold War years. The presence of powerful restrictive messages that attempted to control women's behaviors existed, but abundant evidence of resistance to social norms also existed. As May suggested, containment did not succeed.[19] The decades following the war laid the foundation for what Barbara Bergmann called the dissolution of "the ancient system of sex roles under which men were assigned a monopoly of access to money-making and mature women were restricted to the home."[20]

Since the 1970s, historians of women, labor, and social movements have exposed the many avenues of women's public engagement and disaggregated any notion of one path for women. Research has emphasized the ways in which intersectional categories (gender, race, class, region, sexuality, religion, and ethnicity) create different women's experiences. Gender and policy, sexuality, race and ethnic differences, labor force participation, and women's union activities became significant areas of research advancing knowledge on twentieth-century women. Joanne Meyerowitz's 1994 collection of essays, *Not June Cleaver,* presented a compendium of this research and demonstrated how varied and complex a study of post-1945 women could be. More recently, dozens of books have explored women's public activism as well as changing cultural values toward women.[21]

All of these areas of research inform the Las Vegas case, yet it is the history of women's workforce participation that intersects all the narratives included in this book. The research of Alice Kessler-Harris, Jacqueline Jones, Eileen Boris, and numerous interdisciplinary scholars made clear years ago that women have had long histories in the labor force. Following the Great Depression, women from all family types joined the labor market during World War II and continued to work outside the home as either part-time or full-time workers throughout the twentieth century. Today we have a fuller understanding of women's workforce patterns, their entrance into manufacturing, their struggles to unionize, and, by the end of the century, their battles for economic justice.[22]

The history of women workers in Las Vegas has more in common with workers across the country than may be thought.[23] In 1940 approximately one out of four women worked outside the home in both Las Vegas and the nation. By 2000 the Las Vegas and national rates were similar again, but the ratio of working women increased to nearly one out of two. Yet, the Las Vegas women's work experiences varied in two important ways: (1) a higher percentage of women had worked in Las Vegas in the decades in between than in the nation on average, and (2) the main industry was tourism. Women who moved to Las Vegas to look for work in the postwar decades could find plenty of jobs in traditional lines of so-called women's work. They could serve food or drinks, type letters, or clean rooms and laundry in a small city that offered more jobs and better tips than they could find back home. Jobs remained race segregated into the 1970s, and women of color worked in back-of-the-house jobs in housekeeping or food preparation. Nevertheless, women continued to move to the valley for the jobs it offered.

This study covers the transition that took place in the years between 1940 and 1990 in Las Vegas. Those decades included a significant population increase. They were also the decades in which Las Vegas had a higher proportion of employed women than the national aggregate: In 1960 approximately 33 percent of women worked outside the home in the nation. That proportion was 44 percent of all working-age women and 55 percent of women of color in Las Vegas. By 1980 the US aggregate increased to 46 percent and Las Vegas had nearly 56 percent of women employed. Furthermore, the workplace had diversified. Reforms in national immigration laws added workers from Latin America and Asia, whose proportion in greater Las Vegas grew through the end of the century.

A 1980 comparison of women workers by race and ethnic groups showed that the historic pattern of higher workforce participation by women of color existed in Las Vegas. Well over half of working-age women worked: whites (55 percent), African Americans (62 percent), Latinas (66 percent), Asian Pacific Islanders (69 percent), and American Indians (61 percent). Although not disaggregated by race and sex, the data show that in every family status —whether married, single, with children, or without children—Las Vegas women worked at higher rates than did women in the United States overall. The census did not disaggregate employment by sex and race-ethnicity in a uniform manner for Las Vegas, making the trends difficult to track over time. Yet, as the figures above suggest, those communities had significantly higher rates of employment for women. Latinos grew to 29.1 percent of the Clark County population in 2010 and, according to a recent study, nearly one-third worked in the gaming industry.[24]

Until further studies on postwar urban rates of employment are undertaken and comparisons between cities can be made, we know that the Las Vegas tourism economy stood out as a magnet for workers. The city took its place in the national (and now international) economy because of its near-constant employment opportunities and its unabated capitalist fervor.[25]

The second characteristic that distinguished women's wage-earning in Las Vegas was the gambling-based tourism industry. Women worked in similar occupations as did their peers across the country in the postwar decades, but they did so in hotel-casinos. The most prominent exception would be the overrepresentation of artists and dancers. To better understand the employment context and the ways in which women negotiated their work, a brief description of the organization of gambling and its transition to corporate gaming follows.

Hotel-casino development exploded on the Strip during the late 1940s and 1950s, yet banks hesitated to make loans during the early years.[26] Developers used other methods to accumulate sufficient capital including leveraging resources from other businesses, bringing in other investors, or using the hidden interests of crime organizations. The last option funded the development and operation of many Strip casinos in the first decades. The mob bosses received the return on their investment from the casino skim—the money taken off the top of the winnings and returned to the bosses without being declared for tax purposes. In 1955 the Bank of Las Vegas (subsequently merged into Bank of America) began making loans for construction and expansion of resorts. Beginning in 1959 the Teamsters Central States Pension Fund financed businesses where union members worked, including Las Vegas resort casinos. Eugene Moehring has discussed in detail the reasons that led to greater state regulation and the establishment of the State Gaming Control Board and the Gaming Commission. These units had the respective responsibilities of investigating and licensing casino operators. In 1969 the liberalization of licensing laws, which limited the licenses to only the major stockholders, opened the doors for corporations to own casinos.[27] This transition in ownership began a shift in terminology from gambling to gaming, and from the last frontier to a resort destination for Las Vegas.

Legitimate business people owned, operated, and worked in casinos throughout these decades as well. They took opportunities as they arose as sole proprietors or in business partnerships. Chapters 1 through 3 of this volume discuss examples of legitimate ownership. These business people relied on relatives or trusted associates to handle money at the gambling tables or in what is known as the count room. They built relationships with community institutions. Some of the entrepreneurial ventures in casino development demonstrate the evolution of corporate ownership. During the 1960s Howard Hughes and Kirk Kerkorian were major investors in casinos, buying up existing properties or building new ones through their corporate enterprises. Claudine and Shelby Williams sold their first Las Vegas property, the Silver Slipper, to Howard Hughes. The Williamses invested their profits from Hughes into the Holiday Casino and raised additional capital from investors who held small percentages in the company. Since the Corporate Gaming Act

(1969) required licenses of only those with greater than 5 percent ownership, the Williamses held the license, yet additional investors held small positions. Claudine Williams described the Holiday Casino as a "mom-and-pop operation," one that she eventually sold to Harrah's.[28]

Many people who worked in the casinos from 1950 to 1985 have said, "The town was better when the mob ran it." Some of the narrators in this book made similar comments. The formality of the corporate structure, its rationalized work, and cost efficiencies radically changed the work culture and environments, according to the narrators. In his study of labor in Las Vegas, James P. Kraft measured worker dissatisfaction through the number and length of labor strikes. Relatively short-term labor disruptions took place in the 1950s and 1960s, Kraft claims, because of an informal agreement between owners and organized labor. In exchange for improvements in wages and benefits, union leadership maintained relative stability. The benefits provided, particularly through the Culinary Union, such as medical, retirement, and some forms of insurance, helped the union grow. However, the increasing size of casinos and the shift in management style to distant ownership and bureaucratic measures created a new phase in labor management relations. By 1976 tensions erupted when four unions went on strike against fifteen resorts. The sixteen-day strike involved thirteen thousand workers and resulted in a compromise in which both sides received something. In 1984 another strike of four unions led to seventeen thousand workers walking out. By 1984 fragmentation characterized both the unions and the Nevada Resorts Association, which worked on behalf of the owners. The strike ended with some properties decertifying unions and other properties making individual deals.[29]

The Culinary Union responded to the fragmentation in the mid-1980s with an organizing campaign to build and revitalize its membership. The constituency of the union also changed. African American women had comprised a significant portion of Culinary membership during the postwar decades and worked in a context of labor segregation by race and sex. Some, like Lucille Bryant (see chapter 6) and Hattie Canty (see chapter 7), praised the union for its support of workers like themselves. Between 1989 and 1993, Culinary membership increased substantially as the union organized new hotels and set union contracts. New workers from Latin America and Asia joined, and the unification of workers would be one of Canty's challenges as president.[30]

Unions played an important role for workers, as mentioned above, but they also maintained occupational segregation by initially failing to send women and people of color out for all jobs for which they qualified. Following the 1960 Moulin Rouge Agreement, which opened public accommodations regardless of race, National Association for the Advancement of Colored People (NAACP) members James McMillan, Sarann Preddy, and others met with the Culinary leadership about ending discrimination, but little changed.[31] Charles Kellar, an attorney for the local NAACP, pressured unions to send out African Americans for all types of work and to uphold the Civil Rights Act of 1964. He filed a complaint with the National Labor Relations Board in 1967 against the Bartenders, Culinary, Stage Hands, and Teamsters Unions and eighteen hotels. In 1971, having seen little change or progress, Kellar filed a complaint in US Federal District Court in Las Vegas against the same parties. That same day the unions and hotel-casinos signed a consent decree agreeing to open employment.[32] Jobs were to be opened to all qualified candidates and reports submitted to the Nevada Equal Rights Commission that showed who applied and who was hired for job openings.

It did not take long for female job seekers to realize that the elimination of race discrimination still barred all women from applying for a number of better-paying jobs. Casino dealers, bartenders, stagehands, and parking attendants all brought in more income than did housekeepers or kitchen aides. The antipoverty activists of Operation Life, about which Annelise Orleck has written so beautifully, made the connection between low-wage jobs and poverty for mothers supporting children on their own. The executive director, Ruby Duncan, made the point on many occasions that poor women wanted good jobs rather welfare.[33] D. D. Cotton, one of the dancers featured in chapter 5, became one of the individuals who continued to apply for previously segregated jobs and who helped to build the case against hotel-casino properties. The NAACP, women from Operation Life, and Legal Aid attorneys raised the same concerns on sex discrimination as they had on race inequity. In 1975, following an investigation into discrimination charges that lasted two and a half years, Equal Employment Opportunity Commission (EEOC) commissioner Raymond Telles filed a commissioner's charge against nineteen hotels and four unions. As a result, the hotels and unions signed the 1981 Consent Decree that promised to correct a "pattern or practice of employment discrimination" in areas of recruitment, hiring, assignment, transfers, promotions, and union referrals on the basis of sex and national origin. The decree set hiring goals for previously male-only occupations. For example, 15 percent of bartenders and 20 percent parking attendants needed to be filled by women and Latinos. The

Culinary Union, which previously had said it could not find qualified candidates for the formerly male-only jobs, set about to improve the skill level of its members. Despite ongoing complaints of discrimination, the 1981 decree was dismissed in 1986.[34] Two of the beneficiaries of the decree were D. D. Cotton and Carol Gerardi, the subjects of chapters 5 and 9, respectively.

Recovering the histories of working people is challenging. Archives rarely hold their papers. The census is helpful to a degree, but the texture and detail of workers' lives is best found in their own narrative histories through the collection of oral histories.

Oral History as a Source and a Method

The field of oral history has shifted from the recovery projects of the 1970s, which added marginalized people to the historical narrative and consumed their accounts as data, to a critical cultural assessment of the product and process. Interdisciplinary and international narrative theory focused on the context in which oral histories take place. Luisa Passerini, in a groundbreaking 1979 article, called on oral historians to reassess what she called "facile democratization" (taking the words of "the oppressed" as the plain truth) and to recognize "that the raw material of oral history consists not just in factual statements, but is preeminently an expression and representation of culture, and therefore includes not only literal narrations but also the dimensions of memory, ideology and subconscious desire."[35] In brief, the subject does not recount her life history in a vacuum, but in a historical moment. That moment shapes the particular forms of speech used, and, more importantly, the frameworks through which the subject understands herself, her opportunities, and the meanings that she attaches to ideas. Among those ideas are the intersectional experiences of gender, sexuality, race, and class. Consequently, the oral history offers events, but it also offers the ways in which narrators make meaning of their lives. Alessandro Portelli underscored this point when he discussed the use of oral history and the ways in which it differed from conventional sources. Oral history "tells us less about *events* than about their *meaning*," Portelli wrote (emphasis in original). "Oral sources tell us not just what people did, but what they wanted to do, what they believed they were doing, and what they now think they did."[36] The introduction of cultural context and meaning led oral historians to consider not only the narrator as subject, but also the relationship between subject and interviewer, memory, performance, and power relationships in the entire process.[37]

The critique of power relationships, authority, and subjectivity within oral history made it an attractive method to those developing new fields of social history and women's history in the 1970s. Practioners in those fields shared an interest in challenging the existing explanations of social relations and in finding new methods for understanding histories of groups previously untold.[38] Furthermore, it allowed the collection of sources in areas where few existed. Historians of women in the US West became early practioners and advocates.

Working alone initially, then in conversation with each other, historians of Western women plumbed oral accounts for clues to the history of women's lives. As Sherna Berger Gluck recounted in the first journal issue dedicated to the topic, "[W]e are affirming that our everyday lives *are* history. Using an oral tradition, as old as human memory, we are reconstructing our own past" (emphasis in original).[39] *Frontiers: A Journal of Women's Studies* dedicated an entire issue to the topic of women and oral history in 1977 and again in 1983. The second publication recognized the rapid change in the field's evolution and its move "beyond discovery to better project design, more useful analysis of the interviews, accountability to the interviewees, and, finally, to finished products that will be seen, heard, and read by a wide audience." Susan Armitage emphasized the importance of addressing subjectivity, intersubjectivity, authority, and context, which are issues similar to those emphasized by Passerini and Portelli.[40] By 1998, when *Frontiers* published a two-volume exploration of the state of the field, Armitage expressed frustration with the ways in which postmodernist critiques had stalled progress. As she discussed the importance of shared authority and not imposing interviewers' world view on the oral history, Armitage wondered, "[W]hat are the legitimate ways to draw meanings and generalizations from interviews?" While the exploration of power had added much to the historiography of oral history, she wondered how the historian could balance meaning and interpretation without imposition.[41]

Changing the Game began as a recovery project; in the years since its origins, however, it has grown to include not only the content offered by narrators, but also an interpretation of the meanings attached to their stories and the manner of their presentation. My initial thought on the collection was to leave intact the narrators' accounts and let them speak for themselves, and yet all of us tell our lives to others with a high degree of selection and reinterpretation. Similarly, oral histories are widely understood to be a creative product between the individuals involved. The interviewers' role, while not

always apparent, is nevertheless, always present. By inviting certain participants to be interviewed, shaping the core of the questions, and facilitating the
narrators' stories in the process, the interviewer interweaves her presence into
the product. In addition, the selections presented here are a fraction of the
entire narrative, a fraction selected and edited to form the book. In the end,
the book balanced the narrators' interpreted experiences with my historic and
analytical commentary to better situate the narrative within the larger context
of twentieth-century American women's lives.[42]

Collecting the Narratives

In 1995, as I completed my first book and struggled to find my balance teaching at UNLV, two graduate students approached me with an idea to collect
the life stories of women who worked in the gaming industry. Both students
were mature women who worked in hotel-casino jobs, one as a dealer and the
other at the registration desk. This was the great untold story of Las Vegas,
they claimed, and they needed to learn how to do oral history. I had been
working with a group of faculty to build a manuscript collection on women
in southern Nevada. That project made it very clear how important it was to
collect oral histories if we wanted to diversify the holdings of the archives. The
more I listened, the more I wanted to encourage the students' ideas and assist
them with their master's theses. I offered assistance in the research design,
including questions on the life course of women, but I found experts in the
methods and theory of oral history to teach us all.

Within a few months, there were four of us sharing notes, discussing
themes, and learning about equipment as we proceeded with the research for
the interviews.[43] I have described that process in detail elsewhere; the following excerpt describes our first steps:

> Since our original plan was to learn about the work experiences of women employed
> in the gaming industry, we divided our project into the four geographic areas of
> work. These were 1) the back of the house (service workers in food preparation
> and housekeeping), 2) the floor (dealers and cocktail waitresses), 3) the showroom
> (dancers, entertainers and showgirls), and 4) the management. We compiled a set
> of core interview questions covering the world of work as well as social, familial,
> and cultural experiences. Because so little was known about the women who came
> to work in Las Vegas, we added questions about their early history—their families
> and education—to get a better sense of who they were and how they became a part

of the city. This set of questions provided the framework for each interviewer, while allowing for flexibility and individual differences. We hoped that it would enable researchers to make comparisons between groups over time. In particular, the interviews sought to better understand the life course of women's work lives. By asking our subjects why they came to the city, how they combined work and family, what opportunities they saw for women, and how employment changed over time with the shift in ownership from families, individuals, or small groups to corporations, the interviewers began to reconstruct the narratives of women's lives.[44]

The breadth of this project on women workers (from managers and office workers to entertainers and housekeepers) differentiates it from other post-1945 labor studies that focus on one sector of the labor force.

We initially consulted community advisers for prospective narrators, then relied on our narrators' recommendations. Our criteria included the degree to which the narrator's experience contributed to a clearer understanding of women's employment in the gaming or entertainment industries. The advanced age of many of our narrators made it necessary to consider their general health. Also, the oral history needed to align with other well-documented sources. We attempted to gain a pool of narrators who had come to the city from the earliest days of development in the 1940s through the major building of Strip casinos in the 1950s and 1960s. We looked for overlap of their work experience with the emerging corporate gaming structure of the 1970s and 1980s. Finally, the narrators had to agree to the interview and allow its deposit in a public archive.

Within two years the students who had originated the project with me had finished their work and moved on with their lives, yet the potential for building a collection had just begun. Other students and community members expressed interest in working on the project. After a few years, the collection process was formalized into the Las Vegas Women Oral History Project, which to date contains nearly ninety interviews divided into three series: the original on gaming and entertainment, the second on Las Vegas valley pioneers, and the third on women community builders. The completed interviews are transcribed, minimally edited, and bound with photos provided by the narrator. Selections of the audio narratives are available online at http://wrinunlv.org, while the bound volumes can be located at the WRIN. The entire collection will be housed permanently in the Special Collections Department of Lied Library at the UNLV.

Interpreting the Narratives

Several themes emerged from the narrators' accounts of life and work, themes that hold significance for understanding employment in the postwar era. First, high levels of internal migration for employment characterized the early decades in particular. None of our narrators claimed Las Vegas as her birthplace, and only one had grown up in the region. A boom town for most of its existence, Las Vegas grew exponentially because the in-migration continued to surpass the out-migration. The married women came with their families, recently divorced women came with their children, and some came alone to take a job. Our narrators' migration stories ended in Las Vegas as they made their adopted community their home.

The centrality of employment in the narrators' lives became the second theme. Narrators expressed the importance they placed on working as a need, a challenge, or for self-fulfillment. Las Vegas's service economy emerged early in the nation's economic transition from the production of goods to service industries. The combination of a service economy and a boomtown created an employment environment that had low entrance requirements. The job opportunities also applied to other employment sectors. Rapid growth in the Las Vegas valley corresponded with large proportions of women taking professional, managerial, and administrative positions. Nevertheless, the expanding opportunities for employment existed alongside barriers of race and sex segregated jobs.

Persistence to overcome barriers, either as individuals or collectively, emerged as the third theme found in the interviews. Racial segregation in employment, recreation, and housing continued through the 1970s and sex discrimination in employment persisted in some areas until the early 1990s. The informal system of finding jobs through *juice* created a closed employment network limited to friends, associates, or relatives.[45] The system reinforced homogeneity rather than open employment to all groups. In addition, the Culinary Union had a mixed legacy in that it helped workers by gaining job security, but hindered them with lax initiation of equal employment practices. Sorting out the varied influences of these postwar years is an ongoing process.

Behaviors that would be considered discriminatory today presented their own cultural and, eventually, legal challenges. Yet, the narrators repeatedly stressed that the overtly sexualized business environment that surrounded them had little negative impact on their views of themselves. Some parlayed conventional gender roles to open doors. Many reported that they relied on professionalism and a relentless work ethic to move ahead. Some knew that their network of family and friends would offer shelter from a prejudicial work context. The Culinary Union provided a level of protection and economic security when respect and collegiality failed. A majority of narrators took pride in their own ability to "take care of business" in situations when harassment or discrimination occurred in the years before legal protection. In brief, women working in the gaming industry before there were antidiscrimination laws negotiated methods of survival and success that met their individual situations. The topic of women's methods of accommodation and resistance in Las Vegas and across the country calls out for more analysis.

With few exceptions, the narrators of the larger study wondered aloud why we might be interested in their lives and what their lives might have to do with history. Taken at face value, this may be seen as a self-effacing comment about their experiences or as a clear-eyed assessment of their class, race, or gender status. In contrast, some of the individuals whose narratives are included here had a different sense of their lives and its place in a larger history of social change or economic progress. Their willingness to give their accounts reflected what Sidonie Smith has called "talking back" to the official discourse of scholarly fields.[46] This book contains both types of responses.

Several factors went into my selection of the individuals for *Changing the Game*: the richness of their narrative, the detail of particular experiences, and their story's ability to convey a key aspect of women's lives at mid-century. All the narratives are part of the Las Vegas Women Oral History Project.[47] Instead of a book of "great women," this collection includes some well-known individuals and others who remain unknown outside of their family and community. Moreover, it includes women who made Las Vegas their home. Regardless of fame or fortune, my priority in selecting these narratives remained to show how working-class and middle-class women reflected on their work lives and to show the ways they dealt with them. I would have liked to include a broader representation of women's ethnic, racial, and religious diversity. Specifically, I would have liked to add the narratives of Latinas, but these narrators either did not agree to being interviewed, worked in areas other than gaming, or were unavailable. I hope that new projects promise to correct that problem. Thus, *Changing the Game* should not be construed as a comprehensive history covering women's experiences, but rather as a beginning work that will stimulate more research.

After selecting the individual narrators, I reread the texts, interpreted their meanings, and compared them with other sources for themes. I contextualized the source and interpreted the narratives' significance and meaning within larger historical themes and postwar US women's history. My goal was to present a fluid narrative that retained the original voice and content of the narrator, while at the same time succinctly conveying core aspects of her perspective.

Organization of the Book

Changing the Game covers the years from the earliest development of the hotel-casinos on the Las Vegas Strip through the transition to corporate ownership, and concludes with the enforcement of equal employment laws through federal involvement. That national transition from job segregation to equal opportunity comes to life through these accounts. The study ends in 1990 for two reasons. First, the steady increase of women into the labor force stabilized in Las Vegas and the national percentage of employed women matched that of Las Vegas for the first time since 1940. Second, by 1990 the impact of equal opportunity laws could finally be seen in employment. Despite the fact that the 1964 Civil Rights Act made race and sex discrimination in employment unconstitutional, it took several years for the hiring patterns of hotels and casinos to change. Two consent decrees in 1971 and 1981 prodded the corporations to make serious efforts to comply by 1990.

The book covers a wide swath of workers and follows a chronological trajectory as well as the spatial location of work within the hotel-casino. It opens with women who either owned or managed hotel-casinos, then moves to the showroom, housekeeping department, and administrative offices, and concludes on the casino floor with the newer jobs opened to women. Because women might move from one physical area of work to another (from the showroom as a dancer to the floor as a beverage server, for example) overlap occurs.

Chapters 1 and 2 contain two narratives from women who grew up during the Great Depression and became significant entrepreneurs. The classic characteristics of women entrepreneurs, defined by Jeannette M. Oppedisano, are intelligence, decisiveness, persuasion, and independence.[48] These narrators possess them all. Claudine Barbara Williams's need to help support her family led her to work in private gambling houses in Texas. Rather than becoming a victim of circumstances, Williams turned the cultural assumptions of poverty inside out as she developed and then owned her own clubs. She moved to Las Vegas with her husband, Shelby, in the mid-1960s to renovate and operate casinos. Although one of a tiny group of female owner-operators in a male-dominated culture, Williams took charge of her opportunities as they presented themselves. Williams's story is contrasted with that of another casino owner, Sarann Preddy. Preddy came to Las Vegas as a young married woman, but found the racial segregation of the 1940s South extended west to Las Vegas. Her narrative offers an explicit depiction of barriers shaped by race and gender bias that existed in Las Vegas before the success of civil rights. It also introduces the presence of entrepreneurial African Americans who worked within boundaries and nevertheless succeeded economically and helped to sustain a strong and resilient African American community.

The paths by which mid-century women developed professional lives is reflected in two contrasting narratives given by Bernice Jaeger and Ffolliott "Fluff" LeCoque in chapters 3 and 4, respectively. Both women had risen to top positions in their chosen fields (hotel management and showroom entertainment) by the 1980s. Each offers an example of career advancement for women before the practice of employment equity policies opened doors for women and people of color. These chapters also provide a view of the gaming industry as a business, one in which these women achieved early advancement.

As Las Vegas developed its reputation as the entertainment capital of the world, it relied on the labor and talents of thousands of dancers, showgirls, and musicians. Chapter 5 explores the showroom as a workplace, and looks at the experiences of the showroom's dancers through three narrators: Gail McQuary, Janet Kravenko, and D. D. Cotton. Entertainers came from around the country as well as around the world to dance in their chosen careers. In the early days a young woman "only needed to be beautiful," in the words of one entertainment director; the majority, however, had professional training. Despite the relatively short careers and the anonymity of most dancers, their work played a central role in creating the attractions that tourists came to see. Furthermore, the showroom venue became the site for the perception of new sexual mores, a perception that parallels in time the rise of the Playboy culture.

Service workers are the backbone of the operation of the hotel-casino

industry. During the 1940s and 1950s the predominantly gender-typed categories of housekeeping and food service relied on the abundant and inexpensive labor of African Americans to work in the back of the house. By the late
1980s the demographics had changed to include two new groups: immigrants
from Latin America and immigrants from Asia. Chapters 6 and 7 offer a view
of life from the perspectives of two women: Lucille Bryant and Hattie Canty,
who came to Las Vegas from the Deep South. Canty came around 1970, nearly
twenty years after Bryant, yet the steady demand for domestic work in the
hotel industry gave both newcomers consistent employment. Both women
give credit for their economic security to the Culinary Union. Canty became
a union activist and president during the Frontier strike, which began in 1991
and lasted six and a half years. Both women combined their jobs with raising
their families while participating in other community institutions.

By the 1960s the antecedents of change in gender and race relations had
been sown and would develop over the next decades. Through the narrative
of Florence McClure, chapter 8 explores the office employment in casinos,
as well as the transformation of middle-class women into agents for social
change. White women of her generation and background found that secretarial skills promised a sure path to self-support before marriage. McClure
continued to seek out work while she relocated with her military spouse. One
of those jobs, in office work, brought her to Las Vegas in 1966 to open a hotel.
She worked in the executive suites of the Frontier Hotel and Casino and the
Desert Inn Hotel and Casino. However, she had a passion for education and
community engagement, which she fulfilled by joining the League of Women
Voters (LWV, or the League). Through the League, McClure, like thousands
of other mid-century women, learned the way to move reforms through the
political process. McClure became a passionate advocate for the rights of
those who survived violence, especially those who had been raped. Her efforts
shaped Nevada's modern legal treatment and defense of rape survivors.

Chapter 9 returns to the workplace of the casino floor and explores a local
example of the national campaign to open up traditionally male-only jobs to
women. Carol Gerardi arrived in Las Vegas most recently, in 1980. Like many
of the narrators in the Las Vegas Women Oral History Project, she had not
participated in sex equity battles in employment. However, she did know that
she had entered a brave new world by crashing the men's club of dice dealing
at the craps tables. This final chapter traces one woman's journey to employment equity, while setting her narrative within the context of wider local,

state, and national issues. Ending job discrimination by sex and race removed the barriers against equal employment in the hotel-casinos, as it did in other workplaces across the nation. Yet, cultural and ideological resistance receded more slowly.

The conclusion explores the major findings drawn from the eleven oral histories and their contribution to our understanding of women's experiences in the post-1945 workforce. It contextualizes the narrators' stories within the shifting boundaries of employment opportunity beginning in the 1960s and continuing for three decades. While historians have noted the collective action of labor unions and rights organizations, this book looks at both collective action as well as individual strategies utilized by women in the years before legal equal opportunity. The conclusion also examines the benefits of oral history methodology. Analyzing the context and meaning offered in the oral histories presents new interpretations of women's workplace strategies during an era of segregated labor. It also frames the sexualized portrayal of women in Las Vegas as a measure of the shifting balance of power between men and women in the four decades following World War II.

The Las Vegas that most of us think we know escapes its own mythmaking in these narratives. The women who came to Las Vegas at mid-century help us understand the period in universal terms despite the unusual industry of gaming.

Chapter 1

CLAUDINE BARBARA WILLIAMS

Casino Owner

I was always kind of a take-charge person.
—Claudine Barbara Williams

In the world of gaming, few women have made it to the executive offices.[1] Claudine Barbara Williams is the exception. She spent most of her time since her teenage years learning games, working in gaming, and owning and operating casinos. Williams's experiences span the decades from backroom private gambling clubs of the late 1930s to corporate ownership beginning in the late 1960s until she stepped down as chairwoman in the late 1990s. She flourished in this unusual domain for women during the second half of the twentieth century.

Like many of her contemporaries, Claudine Williams learned the value of money during the hard years of the Depression. She started earning as a young girl alongside her mother, who worked in a cafeteria a few hours a week. She first witnessed the excitement of games of chance a few years later and discovered the work she wanted to do for life. Before she was out of high school, she worked in a supper club in Louisiana near her home and helped to support her family. She learned everything she could about the games as fast as she could, made lifelong friends with some of the masters in the Texas gambling world like Benny Binion and Jake Friedman, and met her future husband and business partner Shelby Williams.[2]

Claudine and Shelby Williams moved to Las Vegas in 1963 to pursue a business opportunity with the Silver Slipper casino located on the Las Vegas Strip. Within a few years they had turned that property around, sold it to Howard Hughes, and prepared for their next venture—building the Holiday Casino. Claudine Williams described herself as intimately involved in the daily casino operations working side by side with Shelby, even as they raised their son. The size and scale of the casino operation allowed her to manage the business in a personal way. She took pride in knowing her employees. She also knew every game in the casino and was able to step in to deal if the situation called for it. She called it a mom-and-pop operation, and it competed successfully in Las Vegas during the final era of mob-controlled properties and skimming scandals.

As Shelby's health failed, Claudine assumed more of the duties and eventually took over entirely. Respected for her knowledge of the business and for her business acumen, her transition to president and general manager of the Holiday Casino (later Harrah's Hotel and Casino) in 1977 went smoothly. Business associates invited Williams to join in ventures that facilitated the growth of the Las Vegas economy. She was not only the rare female executive of a major casino, but also the first woman to serve as chair of the board of directors of a bank in the state of Nevada (American Bank of Commerce), and the first woman to serve as the president of the Las Vegas Chamber of Commerce. In 1992 she was honored by her peers as the first woman inducted into the Gaming Hall of Fame. In these roles and many others, Claudine Williams became a pioneer for the generation that followed.[3]

She explained her successes in a male-dominated field as being willing to do what needed to be done. "To have equality, you've got to give equality" Williams said about the first step for women in the workplace. She acknowledged the challenges faced by women workers today as they attempt to reach the upper levels of management. Yet, the discrimination she felt most dearly was that of society's scorn placed on men and women who tried to support their families and make a living in gaming. Reading more closely, Williams's success also came from relationships she valued and developed from her earliest days. Whether it was coworkers who taught her games, friends who looked in on her as a young business owner, or bank officers who gave her loans to open a club, cultivating relationships as well as her work ethic proved to be an essential strategy for her path-breaking success.[4]

Williams sold her final holdings in the Holiday Casino to Holiday Inn Corporation in 1983 and became chair of the board of directors. She saw the move as a positive change that allowed her to stay involved in policymaking without the demands of ownership. This change allowed her to devote more of her time to community philanthropy. A firm believer in giving back to the community that had given her so much, she made numerous substantial gifts to the UNLV, and endowed scholarships for Harrah's employees and their children.

I was born in DeSoto Parish, near the little town of Mansfield, Louisiana. It's about eighteen miles outside of Shreveport, Louisiana, which is in Caddo Parish. Shreveport is not a big city, but it was a big city compared to where I was born. That's where we lived in my very early years and that's where I have my earliest memories. It was big farming country with cotton, peanut, sugar cane, and all kind of farming down through Louisiana.[5]

Shreveport is very close to Texas where the Texas oil fields were—Longview, Kilgore, Gladewater. There's a thirteen-mile triangle, which is twenty or thirty miles in some spots from that area. The Texas border was in and out of the whole area. Back in the oil booms, people followed those towns. Wherever there would be a boom, they would go there to work. That's why my mother moved there—to be able to work as a waitress. She also had lots of sisters and some brothers and they all lived right around in the area of Shreveport. She was close to relatives and close to where her mother was and she could get help with us, I suppose.

My mother was by then a single mother and I had one sister two years older than I was. My mother married an oil-field worker and when she showed up pregnant with me it must have been more pressure than he could stand. He left and we never saw him again. I thought it was his loss.

When I was about twelve years old I got a job in the same restaurant she worked in. My mother worked the split shift. She worked the noon rush and then she was off four hours and went back and worked the dinner rush. They gave me a job during the rush hours after school and on weekends. I would work just putting ice in the glasses and putting butter on the little butter plates. We had a lot of oil-field workers that carried a lunch and they would put in the order and I would put them in the brown paper bags and that sort of thing. Sundays didn't matter in the oil field. They worked Saturdays and Sundays too. They had different shifts that worked all the time. Those oil wells had to keep pumping. So I started to work very early, right along with her.

The wages weren't that high. It wasn't fabulous, but it was great that there were jobs. There were so many years that there weren't any jobs during the Depression. The good salaries and the good jobs didn't really come on until after World War II started. People began needing new appliances that were hard to get. That's when jobs began to get more plentiful.

I was always kind of a take-charge person and my mother was a wonderful, generous lady. The tips that she'd make during the day, her sisters would come by and get them and our rent would come due. Once I started working I took charge of all the tips and I'd hide them where they couldn't get them. So that's one of my early memories working with my mother. She was just very childlike and she'd say, "They need it. We have to give it to them." And I would say, "No, we don't. Not until our rent is paid." So that's the early part that I remember.

I went to a Catholic boarding school in Marshall, Texas, which is in between Shreveport and Longview. We were eighteen miles from home. My mother would always come on the weekend and that sort of thing. But with her working at night and as we got older, she had us both in boarding school. My sister loved it. I didn't. I wanted to come home all the time. Then as I grew a little older I went to St. Vincent's Academy as a day student. That's when I went to work at the Caddo Hotel, which is in Shreveport.

They had a little newsstand and I was hired to keep the case full with the magazines filled up and the cigarettes brought forward from out of the storage. . . . They had a little dice board where you threw dice for double or nothing, for cigarettes and cigars and magazines. One day the lady went to the restroom and let me watch her board. Well, I was in love, then. That's what I wanted to do. It was dealing with people and it was amusing them—seeing the fun that they got from winning and the thrill I got from just being a part of it. There hadn't been a whole lot of excitement in my life up until that time. There was no cash involved—double or nothing. I'm sure they did it just for entertainment. They didn't do it to try to win a whole bunch of cigarettes. It was magazines, cigars, cigarettes, candy, and chewing gum, anything you rolled double for. So I worked there until they let me work it one day a week. Other than that, I just relieved her, which I really don't remember how long that was.

Then some people from Dallas came up and opened a big, beautiful supper club called the Forty-One Club in Bossier Parish just across the river from Shreveport. They had big-name bands and just an elegant place. In the back was a private club where they had casino-type gaming. I went out and told them I knew how to deal dice. Well, I didn't know what odds were because double or nothing was all I'd ever seen. The man said, "Yeah, you're eighteen years old and you know how to deal, don't you?" And I started crying. I said, "I've quit my job and I need this job." So he said, "Well, shut up. If you want to learn, be out here tomorrow at two o'clock and I'll help you." His name was Claude Williams and my maiden name was Williams, also. So I think that made him take a little special interest in me. I went out every afternoon at two o'clock while he taught me. Then I'd go home and go back in the evening to work. I was supposed to work from six until midnight. But sometimes it would be six 'til one or two in the morning before you'd get home. So it was pretty hard to do. But I managed somehow to hang on to the job.

I was still going to St. Vincent's Academy, and if I had tests I could tell them and take off and not go to work. I finished the ninth grade and started in the tenth grade, but I don't think I went to the first report card. The job had gotten harder, so I got behind. Then I said, "I've got to quit and get caught up. Then I'll go back next year." I never did; that was it. I think it was in January, before I was sixteen in March that I went to work out there at the club.

You've got to remember they didn't have Social Security and things like that in those days, so they just asked you how old you were. You could get a driver's license at a service station. You just filled out a paper and they mailed them in and mailed your license back to you. I told them I was eighteen. A number of young women worked there, but they were a lot older than I was. I'm sure the only reason I got the job out there was having the nerve to go out

Claudine Williams as a teenager in Louisiana around the time she started to work at her first gambling club. Courtesy of Special Collections, University Libraries, UNLV.

and tell that man I knew how to deal, and that his name was so close to mine, and him being amused by my starting to cry and telling him he had to give me a job.

But I did everything in that club. I worked on the door, looking at people's cards to be sure that we let only people who were members in. I took care of the equipment, putting in all the chip boxes, and I put the money away. Then, as I learned to deal, I got to deal a little more. Back in those days, by being a private club, they didn't have dealers going on every forty minutes as they do today. They had one dealer for every table and then one relief person who took over when you needed to eat. I helped relieve them as I learned. There were other women who worked in all the departments—they worked as cashiers and they worked as cocktail waitresses. There were a lot of showgirls there because they had a floor show. But no other women dealers, at all. I was the only one.

The Forty-One Club was a supper club with a show and dancing. People came to dance in those days. Back in those days when you had all of the different big name bands, that was a show within itself. They all had vocalists and special numbers that the bands did. People would drive from all over. Dallas was like 130 miles away and a lot of people came from Dallas and all of these towns around to see these big-name bands. The ladies dressed elegantly. Men had to be properly dressed just to get into the supper club, much less into the private club. You had to be a member to go into that backroom. It was a private members' club. Usually, part of the party would be in the front dancing and a member of the party would be in the backroom gambling. It was never legal in the state. It was just that the local government said, "As long as it's your private club and it's just club members, then it's fine." That's why they had someone on the door checking memberships all the time. It wasn't a big room. You'd have maybe two craps tables, one twenty-one table, and maybe a chuck-a-luck.[6] That was just accepted in those days before you had the Kefauver investigation. As long as it's not open to the public, private clubs could operate.[7]

There were a lot of lovely people that worked there; some were so good and took care of me. Anything that they knew I wanted to learn, they worked with me. There were some people you wouldn't want to associate with, too. Basically you had the mixture that you would find in any nice club today—good people and bad people.

Eventually the club sold and I left Shreveport. I went to Houston, Texas, where Herman Williams helped me find a job. I was about sixteen or seventeen. I might have been a little older because I moved to Houston in late 1939, just before New Year's of 1939. That was like I was going a long ways away. It was about 140, maybe 160 miles away. I still went to my grandmother's every Sunday for dinner. I left on Saturday night. I moved my mother to Houston with me.

I worked two jobs in Houston during 1939 and 1940. In the daytime, I worked in a place called the Majestic Grill where there was a big sporting place upstairs. And then at night I worked at a place called Abe and Pappy's that had a dance hall with bands and all. They had a dice board, a small board that you could put up. . . . Then I took care of the cash registers and did the hiring of the cocktail girls and cigarette girls. One of the owners was Abe Weinstein. His son works for Harrah's in Shreveport now.[8]

When the war started in December 1941 I had been working in Houston for about four or five years by then. I opened a little place with a partner called the Bonita Club. It means "very pretty" in Spanish. We rented a little building in Galveston County just outside Houston at Kemah and served food and mixed drinks. Houston had to close up at twelve and people came down and we could sell drinks after midnight. And we had a little dice game, by then a little single-layout dice table. We ran that club for a long time and then sold it and moved out to a place on old Main Street Road. We bought a piece of property and built a club called the Western Bar. We had Western music and dancing.

A girlfriend and I fixed up a building in Dickinson, just outside Houston, and we were going to have a steak house. I'd saved up about $5,000 or $6,000 and then I had to go borrow some more and we were going to open this steak house. But we didn't realize the rationing had started. You had to have stamps in those days to get sugar and to get gasoline and all that kind of stuff. And we got the place fixed up so cute. We were going to have a high-class steak house. We went to call in and check what we had to do to get delivery for the kind of steaks we wanted and all of that, and a man said, "Well, what's your allotment now?" And I said, "Oh, we're new. We're just opening up." I was dumb. I didn't know. And he said, "Well, we can't take any new customers. We're just giving allotments to the people that are already getting allotments." So my partner got a bit hysterical because she had borrowed money. And I said, "Don't worry. I borrowed money, too. We're going to work this out." We couldn't get steak, but we could get hamburger meat. And we just made it a fancy hamburger place. We had them lined up outside because we did all kind of cute little things on them that other places didn't. We probably made more money there than we would have if we put in with steak because they were in and out quicker.

The man that loaned me the $5,000 became president of the Bank of Houston—Bill Traylor. I still do business with him. His uncle was the biggest owner in the bank and he was a young man and a bank teller. I'd always take my money in to him. He was my banker as far as I was concerned. Those other people, I didn't know anything about them. So when I got ready to make a loan he asked me, "Claudine, what have you got for security?" I said, "Bill, my word. You have my word." He says, "But I don't think they're going to take to that too well." And I said, "Well, you just let me come and talk to them." He said, "What if you lose this money?" I said, "I'll just get two jobs and pay it back. But I'm not going to lose it." So we talked three or four times and it took him about three days, but he finally let me have the $5,000. And that's what it took to open a place in those days.

We had men working for us, but I never had any trouble with people. I've always been very good with people and people have been so good to me. . . . There was a big club down the street, and when it closed all of the dealers and everybody that worked there would come to our club. It was after hours. The others closed at twelve. The man that owned the [club] would always come down to see about us and everybody knew that he was looking out for us. There was always somebody in there. When people ask me about being discriminated against as a woman, I really never was. I've had men to be just great friends and to help me all through my life. I think they would try you and see if you really wanted to work and really intended to do what you said. And you'd better keep your word. Don't tell them you're going to do something that you can't. It was always pretty easy for me.

I met Shelby when I worked at the Majestic Grill. He worked in the sports book that was just upstairs. Then later he was at clubs down in Galveston County. I knew Shelby seven or eight years before I went out with him or anything. We were good friends. Of course, during that time he served four years in the Navy. The day Roosevelt announced that the Japanese had hit Hawaii—Pearl Harbor—he signed up. I remember the club had closed up and everybody was standing over the radio—that was before television—and some of the guys including Shelby had had a few drinks while we were staying up all night waiting for these speeches and the information and to hear the planes coming over and a lot of stuff like that. And they went directly over and joined the Navy. So, I don't know if they would have been as patriotic if they'd have waited till afternoon or not, but they did [sign up]. We drifted apart. I'd hear occasionally about him from some of his friends. And I was gone from Houston and we kind of lost touch for a while. He was gone about four years. When he came back, we began seeing each other and talking and working together in a big club.

Shelby was different from most of the other gamblers that I had met in that a card man usually just knows cards. A dice man knows dice. Shelby was one of those people that knew the food operation. He knew how to be with people. He knew all about sports and horses. Cards and dice he learned very quickly. He didn't know cards and dice until we melded together but it wasn't thirty days until he knew a lot more than I did. He was just a very bright man.

We made very good partners. I was more conservative and he was one that would put it all out on the line. I would have had a smaller place and held a little money back for hard days and he'd say, "Oh, you can't do it that way. Just put it all in." I think that he always knew that I had a little money tucked away somewhere. Even though I didn't hide it from him, he knew there was some there. He never knew just how much, but he knew something was there. He knew me as well as I knew him.

Our first business together was a little place on Main St. in Houston after the war. He bankrolled the sports book. I owned the club and had the dice game and the drinks and the things in this club, and I would run it. But Shelby would have a man running the sports book who answered to me. I would let [Shelby] have the sports book in the club for a percentage of the profits. See, there wasn't any way to get capital, because nobody would finance those things. That's why you usually had several partners. . . . There was no such thing as borrowing money to open a gambling house.

It was a small world of people in the same business that we were . . . because it wasn't something that was accepted readily. A lot of people thought, "A girl working in that gambling house. Lord, gamblers and prostitutes and all that going on there." I knew better, but the general public didn't. So there weren't many people who wanted their wives or youngsters to work in those places. When you think of it that way, it wasn't so unnatural that there weren't many women working as dealers.

People had a lot of negative associations with gambling. That's what makes me so very happy to see what's happened in Las Vegas, to see my industry accepted as entertainment and a choice made by millions and millions of people. That makes me think I made the right choice. . . . Most people that haven't been to a legal casino jurisdiction where it's accepted by the community think, "I wouldn't want my wife in there." They think about casinos like they saw George Raft with a holster on and his snap-brim hat—as a gangster. Even the people that came into Las Vegas that were very bad people, some of them were real mobsters, but there were other people that were just dealers and workers that came in from Cincinnati and from different places. But they called them mobsters too. They had nothing to do with being a mobster. They were working for a living to feed their families. But you get thrown in this bucket. So as I was discriminated against by society, so was that bartender man that was making a living working at the Log Cabin in Cincinnati or somewhere [else] in Ohio, or anywhere. Then they came into Las Vegas and some might say,

"Oh, that's the Cleveland mob." Well, maybe one or two of those people might have been a mobster but others were just working men. . . .

During the war everything changed. See, the port in Houston was one of the biggest ports in the country—that and the one in New Orleans—they compete back and forth, who's the biggest. . . . So, there were a lot of service-men around the whole Houston area. As the war went on and they brought in more people—the Coast Guard and Marines, the sailors, the regular Army—they were stationed all around Houston . . . that's when we closed the Houston place. All of the private clubs closed down there. Now, I had moved my whole family down there. So, I went to Herman Williams, the man who had helped me get located in Houston, and I said to him, "I have to have a job." And he said, "Well, honey, let me think. I don't know where. Everything is closed up. None of us have a job." And I said, "Well, I have got to have a job." Then he said, "Well, I know a man in Dallas. Let me get him on the phone." So that's when he called Benny Binion. Herman said, "I've got a little girl here that really needs a job." And Benny said, "Well, what can she do?" And he said, "She's really smart." He said, "Well, send her on down here. I ain't never seen one of them." That's when I went to Dallas. I went to work for Benny Binion in Dallas after Houston closed up. . . .

Benny Binion was good to me. I'd been around a sports book, but I'd never been in one. In those days, you wrote tickets. People would come up with the bets and you wrote them down. He said, "You might as well learn to write tickets." I'd get up at four in the morning and go pick up all the literature and come down and he thought that was incredible. He said, "You're the only gal I ever saw that would get up and do that." Because then I worked at night at the craps game. He had about four clubs at that time, I think, I don't know. You don't ask Benny many questions. . . . So he thought I was really different because I didn't mind working any hours. Whenever he needed me, I'd go.

In the evening I worked on the door in the beginning and then later on I dealt all the games, whatever anybody wanted. I had learned to deal games in Louisiana and was still the only woman dealer at the time. Remember the old wooden Coca-Cola boxes? I couldn't reach the craps table, so I took that Coke box and had it carpeted on top, and I'd keep it under the table and pull it out so I could reach the line across the table. You have to deal whatever anybody wanted. In a private club, to really have a steady job, you've got to be able, because it's whatever the people that come in want to play. It's not like our casinos here that they just come in and want to play everything. . . .

I also worked for Jake Friedman in Houston.[9] He had a huge, beautiful, big white colonial-looking house that was the club. He would send out invitations: "Mr. Friedman is going to have a game dinner on such and such night; a special chef from somewhere will create the dinner. I'd like for you to be my guest." That was the way it operated. It wasn't a private club that was open all the time. You got invitations to come. He didn't hire a lot of people. . . . You'd get dressed up and go out and he'd have a nice dinner for you. And there'd be ten, twelve, fifteen people show up to work. And then after dinner he'd say, "Well, I hope everybody enjoyed their dinner. I'd like for you to stay, Claudine, and help entertain my guests." That was the way it was put. He was a man of small stature, but he was very prominent and he always dressed in fine Western clothes.

I first came through Las Vegas in '46 with some friends going to California. Shelby wasn't with me. . . . So there were the two hotels here then, the El Rancho Vegas and the Last Frontier. We stayed at the Last Frontier. Oh, it was fun. Sophie Tucker was playing and a comedian, I think Joe Lewis was his name, played with Sophie Tucker. . . . And the next time we came back we stayed at the El Rancho Vegas because they had horses there and I rode a lot of horses back in those days. You could rent horses there and ride all of them. Then Shelby and I came back. I married Shelby in 1950 and we came to look at taking part of the Sands. Jake Friedman was starting the Sands and Shelby had done business with him in Houston and I worked for him there. But after coming out here . . . I decided I couldn't live out here. I couldn't leave my mother and sister. And I knew my mother wouldn't want to come out here. And our son Michael was born November 20, 1954. My mother was there to help me and I had a girl who was with me. . . . So, we stayed in Texas, but spent time in Las Vegas.

People that worked out here [Las Vegas], by that time, they'd either worked for us or we'd worked with them, and we knew a lot of people in Las Vegas. We came out at least four times a year and we'd stay a couple of weeks, mostly at the Sands or the Dunes. Well, coming out and realizing how many friends you have in town and getting to know things. And then of course, Jake Friedman and the people from the Sands took over the Dunes. And I knew most of the people that worked over there. Then the Silver Slipper property became available.

The Silver Slipper was part of the Last Frontier's Village. There were other little restaurants and shops there. The people had a lease with an option to buy the Silver Slipper. And in that lease it said if anything against the law took place then the contract was null and void. Well, they got accused of some cheating in there and so one of the partners that was the owner of this land and the Frontier, T. W. Richardson, was a good friend of ours, and he called and we came out and put a bid in for it. . . . We bought the Slipper and twenty-two acres of land, a narrow strip that went back to Industrial Road.

So, we moved out here and I had, like, forty-five days to find a house and get moved before school started. Michael was nine years old when we got here [in 1963]. I had help with Michael, but even with the Silver Slipper I stayed at home in the daytime and did the purchasing and different things like that. Then I didn't go down until late because I'd wait till Michael went to sleep. We would sit down and eat dinner with Michael before we went to the club most of the time. And even if we had some guests who we had to have dinner with, we'd sit down and make like we were having dinner at home. . . .

The Silver Slipper was just a casino—no rooms. It was the darling place of all of the entertainers. The minute their shows were over they went to the Silver Slipper. They had "Minsky's Follies" and that kind of burlesque entertainment. Actually, we had the first buffet on the Strip. Now, they had what they call chuck wagons and they'd have them in the showroom or outside. On Sunday they'd have a brunch and things. But I saw how the buffets did downtown and everything, so I put one in and it did well. We built a wing onto each side of the Slipper. And we were working on plans to build the hotel in the back and have nice rooms and all of that, and we thought we could probably give a better price on the rooms than they were getting in the hotel. Those were the plans. Of course, Shelby's health began to fail.[10]

Well, he had trouble before we came out here. He smoked and drank too much. And his cigarettes—he'd play cards two or three days and nights and have one cigarette right after another. He had emphysema, bronchiectasis. That's when you cough and you lose all the cilia hairs. So he had to have treatments for that. He had broken a leg and his hips went bad. The operations then were seven and a half to eight hours and he had a bad heart; [he had] a heart attack. You know, he just—everything was wrong. The poor man was in misery. The last five years of his life he spent most of them in intensive care in Sunrise Hospital and he had twenty-four-hour oxygen. He had a big tank right in here at the office and one at home.

As Shelby's health deteriorated, they considered selling their property and returning to Texas. Howard Hughes played an important role in this decision: He had visited Las Vegas for years as a young man and enjoyed the party atmosphere. When he took up residence at the Desert Inn in 1966, he began a spree of hotel and casino purchases that became a forerunner of corporate ownership. The Williamses benefitted from this with the sale of the Silver Slipper. Hughes's top adviser in the early years was Robert (Bob) Maheu, a former FBI agent. The story that Williams relates below indicates the deteriorating mental health of Hughes. He feared that the revolving Silver Slipper on the casino marquee would come off and go through his window. After the sale the Williams returned to Texas for a short time, but realized Las Vegas had become their home. They returned and began to develop the Holiday Casino on a piece of land directly across Las Vegas Boulevard from Caesars Palace.

Then we went back to Houston and the doctor told me, "It will be a miracle if he lives over six months, maybe a year." So he told Shelby, too. We talked about it and talked about it. I said, "Well, Howard Hughes had come to town in 1966 and he wanted to buy the place." And so I said, "Well, I'll talk to Bob Maheu again," because I felt like if he was going to pass away, that his family and my family and all were in Houston, and there was a brother and sister and all. He said, "We need to go home." So I told Maheu, I said, "Well, sweeten that pot a little bit and you might convince me." And so we sold it to Hughes, but later found out—I kid Bob Maheu about it all the time—I said, "If you'd have shown me that telegram, I'd be a rich woman without having to work so hard." Because Maheu showed me the telegram that Hughes had sent to him—to "buy that thing. It's driving me crazy." And I was under the impression that it was just the sign going around, because his suite was right across at the Desert Inn, on that corner. And they interviewed Maheu and he said, "No, it wasn't just the slipper going around, he was panicked. Hughes thought the slipper might come off and be thrown into his suite." So, see, if I'd have known all that, I wouldn't have had to go through all of this. I would have had a big price on it.

Well, we came back and we found the land for the Holiday Casino.[11] At that time, on the Strip for a small down payment, you could buy land all up and down, then, and a friend of ours had tied the land up and he couldn't make payments on it. So he came to see us and we talked a little bit and then I said, "Well, let's just go look. Maybe we'll just take a little piece and we'll put it together." But we had to have controlling percentage of it to do it.

Everybody thought we were crazy. They said, "You're going to try to compete with Caesars Palace?" and I said, "No, there's a lot of people that would rather be in a family-run place than over at Caesars Palace." They said, "Well, you won't get any high players." I said, "There're a lot of them out there. I've had them before. They might have been a truck driver once and own a truck company now." So, it wasn't easy to convince them.

Well, Hughes had a motel and we bought that from him and put parking over there, and then on this side, Irwin Molasky's father had a motel.[12] That side, facing the Strip. He had a little motel over there and we bought that, besides the piece of land. And I bought some more land; I had to beg for it. The Hughes people didn't want to sell anything. They weren't using it; it was just there. And I kept after them 'til we got a little more land in the back. And Caesars was across the street. Where it started was just about—it set back. You know, we thought it was way back, then. And it's a little, a little south; it set back and had the water sprays going up . . . this was the end down here. There was nothing. The Flamingo was still there but I think Hilton had finally bought it, or anybody could have bought it to just take up notes on it. It had hardly any business at all.

We opened a casino only.[13] Holiday Inns ran the hotel. Kimmons Wilson with Holiday Inns was a friend of ours. And he had a partner—I think the man's name was Johnson. When he first put in Holiday Inns and went into the business, he promised them there'd never be any gambling there. And so, when we put this in, he said, "You're the only people in the world I'd trust to do this."

I had to be right with Shelby all the time because he was in a wheelchair most of the time. By the time we got the place open and all, he was in pretty bad shape. I did what had to be done. I let him [do things] when he felt like it. . . . We ran the Holiday Casino like a mom-and-pop business. You know, like a couple that runs a store. It'd be the same thing, because one of us was here. Sometimes, I'd go home early; we would stay to meet the graveyard shift. But most of the time, I was here sixteen hours a day. I'd go home around five thirty and lie down and take a little nap, and refix my face, and maybe change clothes. And come back, because you wanted to be able to contact all three shifts. Well, we had shift managers and things like that, but it's better, if it's your money, to know what's going on.

When Shelby passed away I took him home to Texas. When I came back, I realized I had kind of neglected the Holiday Casino during his illness. So

I realized I had to get moving and get some more games in the casino. So, I went to Ken Sullivan who was at the time president of Valley Bank. I went to Ken and borrowed $10 million to make the place bigger.

Even though Claudine Williams ran the property without Shelby, she continued to refer to her management as *we*.

We had liberal slots and they made a lot of money. I think most every place has high-roller gambling. Benny Binion downtown used to have high limits. And, we'd have a big limit. So that makes people that want to play high know they can make big bets. You can't bet over $200 or you can't bet over $1,000, or something like that. We realized that we could make more on the liberal slots and it got to be known all over town. Everybody loved our slots. I mean, they'd come from Caesars Palace to play the slots 'cause we had the reputation of them.[14]

Right across there was the bingo room. Anybody could play bingo that went in the bingo room. The ladies loved it. Well, then, they played the slots in between the sessions, too. They'd have a ten-game session or a five-game session and you buy your cards for that; and then when that's over, sometimes there's a break. You didn't make any money with the bingo room but it brought in slot players. They'd play bingo a little, and go play slots.

Well, we had the Riverboat theme. Riverboat was a working name; it was never named the Riverboat. That's what we used because we had to get permission to use the word *holiday* from Holiday Inns. And it took a long time to get that through. We had Rocky Sennes as the entertainment director—he was a sweetheart. He actually bought about three points in the place. His brother Frank was at the Stardust. He was in charge of entertainment, but we had to okay it. I mean, when he would come in, he would tell you what he had, but we'd want to listen, too, so he'd have them come in and then we'd do a contract if we liked it. Or if we didn't, we'd stall around some way.[15]

I like being hands on. I would pick out the wallpaper. I'd know the prices. It's a kind of a world out there. If somebody else picks it out, they're liable to get a couple dollars a yard on the carpet for their pocket, you know. If you're not hands on. . . . Anyway, when I was spending my money, I wanted to know what I was buying. That goes for everything in the casino.

Well, you know, it goes back [to] when I first came here. . . . It's like the gangster years, I guess. I thought they were just hotel people. But the big thing at the Stardust, if you remember when Lefty Rosenthal was there and then they came in . . . but they were skimming money off of the top and sending it back East. So I don't know what all those things were. But I know that if you've got a grocery store, people can only use so many cans of tomatoes and a couple of steaks and a chicken maybe. But if you've got a casino, your merchandise is money and you'd better be on top of it.[16]

Of course, I had a casino manager. Then you had shift bosses. And you had to have trust in them, but they also knew that you might be in any time. But the size of these places now, that would be impossible. You could not do that in this place today. It's huge. Harrah's owns about forty-seven casinos with one hundred thousand employees [at the time of the interview]. I knew all my employees by name. I knew who their families were and—it's passed me by. . . .

I like knowing all of the people. I'm a small operator. As president I had always run the meetings and met with the different groups. I used to have a training session with all of the young people that came in. . . . I don't think my style's changed very much. I learned very young—the way you treat people, that's the way they're going to treat your customers. I had an open-door policy. Sometimes I was a marriage counselor, anything, but if they needed me, I thought I should give them my time. On the other hand, when I wanted something done, they knew I wanted it done. And I found by treating them the way I did, that they'd go through hell for me. I've sat and listened to the women cry 'cause the husband was triflin' and things like that. I had other things to do, but I felt I owed them that. And I got kids all up and down the Strip that still say, "That's my mom."

In 1979 Holiday Corporation purchased 40 percent of Williams's interest in the casino. The company that never wanted any involvement in gaming had changed its position. In 1983 it purchased the remaining 60 percent from Williams and took over the casino business. Williams became chair of the board of directors of Harrah's Las Vegas.

I asked Williams why she thought she was one of the very few women who had risen to the position of president of a casino. Her answer and her thoughts on the present opportunities for women in the industry demonstrated the boundary breaking that she had experienced and her pride in legitimizing the business for men and women today.

Well, I had the experience. Very few women did. Listen, I was a wanton woman in the eyes of all of my Louisiana relatives for going to work in that place out there. And I had to. But I didn't let it bother me because I knew what I did was honorable. You just have to remember, not too many years ago

Claudine Williams on the floor of Harrah's Las Vegas Hotel and Casino, formerly the Holiday Casino, 2007. She built and operated the property with her husband, Shelby, until his death. At the time of the photo, the property had been sold to Harrah's and she served as chair of the board of the Las Vegas property. Courtesy of Geri Kodey, UNLV Photo Services, UNLV.

women that went out to work were considered bad if you weren't a nurse or a school teacher. That's the reason I left Louisiana and went to Houston, away from all of them. But the men that worked there, the old-time gamblers, if you will, they always treated me like a lady.

One thing we girls have had a hard time with is to understand that to have equality you've got to give equality. If you want to say, "I'm just a little girl," then go sit down somewhere in the corner. So many of the girls, they wanted the same pay, now, but they didn't want to do the same work. They would say, "Well, I've got children. I need that weekend off." Well, that man has children, too. And we say, "We can rotate, you can take turns with it." I'd try to explain to them. But it's been very hard. Women need to show they're willing to work. I mean, don't look at your clock at five o'clock and say, "I've got to run."

It's happening now, though; you see women out there. They're doing it. They're doing their job. Some of these ladies that work for this company can work as hard as any man you've ever seen. And they know that they're making a big salary and they're going to earn it. It pleases me so much to see the women learning they've got to give equally, because you're never really going to get anywhere if you don't.

There's a lot of very smart young women in gaming now but there are not as many of them that are actually involved on the floor—the casino part—the workings of it. They're in the support system of it rather than knowing table games, and knowing this, and that's part of it. So it's such a big industry now and there's so much more to it.

There are some girls that work for this company that just amaze me. It just thrills me to death to see how smart they are, and when they take on a job, nobody has to tell them what to do. They know how to go—"Tell me what you want done, what you want the end to be, and I'll get it done."

I think maybe that's one of the things—I've been able to change from the way it was to the way it is. And a lot of the people that were in this industry were unable to do that. They say, "Well, it ought to be like it used to be. Those were the good old days." But *these* are the good old days. *These* are the days that the people get so much for their money and there's so much to see and so much that they put to attract people and it's just marvelous the way it's come together. And it's a big beautiful entertainment industry now.

Having a family remains a challenge for women and mobility in the corporation. If you've got a sick child and the man gets a call that the child is sick at school, he calls his wife to go pick her up. But a lot of these young girls are in positions that they can afford to have children and have a nanny or something, where years ago you couldn't. But they're really executives and have salaries that allow them to do that.

Women also come to enjoy Las Vegas. You know it's so interesting—there are a lot of tours that come into Las Vegas for fine dining and shopping. I mean, it's not like years ago when they came just to gamble. That's no longer true. Women love the slots. You see equally as many women playing slots as men, maybe more. They love blackjack. But they're also the consumers, they come here for this. We've got the finest shopping. You couldn't go to a big city of any kind that would have any better shopping than you have in Las Vegas. And that's what women like to do on a trip as a rule. Even though they play some, sightsee some, they want to go shopping. Maybe they want to take something home to the kids or something, but they want to spend part of their time shopping. As do men.

Back when I started, it was different. As I say, some of the old timers say to me, "Mmmm, this ain't like it was." No, because we gave our rooms away, we gave our food away. That was our marketing program. We didn't have a marketing program, except, "Come on out and be my guest. Go to the show." That was it. Now we make a profit and that's what an organization is supposed to do. You've got shareholders and you need to make a profit for them. . . .

In addition to Williams's experience in the casino business, she took major roles in banking in the state, became the president of the Las Vegas Chamber of Commerce, and joined the board of the Las Vegas Convention and Visitors Authority. Among her numerous philanthropic interests is the UNLV. She worked with others on the founding board of the UNLV Foundation, which was incorporated in 1981.[17]

I didn't have an education. I know how hard it is in business without one. I had to stay up late at night and study something when the others went on to sleep because they already knew it. I had no choice. I want to try and help anybody that wants an education.

I'd like for the young people to realize that without an education they may be working for minimum wage the rest of their life. It's a different time and everything is electronics and engineering. Listen, even to be a waiter you've got to work a computer. And young people a lot of times want to quit school 'cause they're making a good bit of money bussing. I would like to try to convince them how hard it is out in the world without an education. You've got to work twice as hard.

I've supported UNLV for over twenty-five years. I've tried to get people involved in the university—people that come into town, people that have built businesses here. . . . Well, I tried to raise money and give some. I bought the first uniforms that the marching band had. . . . I wanted to build that dorm out there because what mother would want to send her child to Las Vegas and let them get out in an apartment? We only had those old torn-up buildings and mostly athletic people lived in them. Anyway, there just weren't any dorms. Now they have nice ones. . . . I set up a foundation for Harrah's employees to be able to send their kids to college—to any school for four years, if they keep up their grades. I contribute to UNLV scholarship funds. . . . Why wouldn't I want to help them?

You know, the world's been good to me. It really has. And the greatest gratification I get is helping out people that are trying to make something of their life. . . . I'm trying to do something with what I have to make it a little easier for somebody else. That gives me a lot of gratification. . . . And I love this business. I guess I haven't got sense enough to retire. They treat me well. I've said two or three times, "Maybe I should give up my office. You need it." And they say, "No, no, no, we want you to stay." And, if I can just add a little something, that pleases me; maybe something that somebody didn't think of, I might think of, in the industry. Or maybe giving background on how something started will help somebody else in the industry. I love this business.

Claudine Williams kept her office at Harrah's until her infirmities restricted her to her home. She passed away on May 13, 2009, at eighty-eight years of age. I met her at the casino office on several occasions and two memories have remained with me. On my first visit, as I waited for her outside the office, I heard an enormous rumble or roar, one that I couldn't place, but one with sufficient energy to raise my curiosity. Since no one else seemed troubled, I took their cue and ignored it. Our interview proceeded and I forgot about the noise until I left the office and took the elevator to the main casino floor. Then I realized that her office was situated immediately over a craps table in the casino. The roar was that of a group enjoying someone's good luck. How fitting for her office to be placed there and that the noise that had startled me was simply part of the background for the experienced.

My second image of Claudine came many months later. As I walked through the casino floor, earnestly trying to pay attention to the directions and tune out the stimulus, I realized I was walking a short distance behind her. Dressed impeccably, she walked confidently between the game tables and the slot machines, through the casino that she had built with her husband decades earlier. I watched as floor workers—security, beverage servers, and dealers on break—recognized her and greeted her warmly. She returned their greetings, stopping to talk briefly with each individual. I realized those exchanges reflected a time that had nearly passed, when owners and workers knew and valued each other.

As a researcher attempting to understand my new environment of a gambling economy and women's experiences in Las Vegas more generally, I believe these images have lingered for me because they epitomized the strangeness or unfamiliarity of the Las Vegas gambling culture. Not only would I need to understand the history of the town, but I would also need to unwind the imbedded morality lessons learned about the city and women who worked there. Claudine Williams reflected the success of a self-made woman in a field that was not only dominated by men, but also was understood as an illegal activity until recently in any other state in the nation. Her greatest experience of discrimination, she said, was when people disrespected her and other working people who were trying to support their families.

As important as they are for women's history, Williams's experiences also represented a mid–twentieth century women who achieved heights in the business world without college degrees and before government affirmative action policies. We know little about this group.

She came out of a childhood characterized by work at an early age. Education was a luxury, not an expectation. Family, not government social services, provided the safety net. Her experiences and insights, to the extent that she would talk about them, revealed an approach that did not reject ideals of equality as much as accept the necessity to maneuver through a work world defined by survival of the fittest. She used relationships with workers and owners, lenders and consumers, to shape her success.

Chapter 2

SARANN PREDDY

Casino Owner

Finances is what kept us from going any further.
—Sarann Preddy

The transition from family-owned to corporate-owned casinos had little if any impact on ownership for Sarann Preddy.[1] Rather, the difficulty of obtaining investment capital had the greater significance for her business. She owned and operated a number of businesses in Las Vegas, yet she loved gaming the most, and one casino in particular. She had an all-consuming desire to bring the historic Moulin Rouge Hotel and Casino back to its glory days. Las Vegas's first, albeit short-lived, hotel-casino on the segregated Westside stayed open for only a few months after it opened in 1955. Nevertheless, the Moulin Rouge served as a symbol of the best in talent, artistry, and economic prosperity for African Americans in Las Vegas. Preddy's commitment to economic entrepreneurship and civil rights merged alongside her efforts to rebuild the resort. That she, and others, failed to do so only highlighted the risks and challenges faced by an African American woman club owner.

Growing up in Oklahoma, she remembered her father's experiences with small business. Carl Childs owned a few businesses when Sarann was young, and later worked in construction. Her mother Hattie, who was Creek Indian, took care of the family and worked in those family businesses. Preddy attended a small country school with about twenty-five students, including American Indians, African Americans, and whites. To continue school, she moved away from home and boarded in a nearby town. Shortly after graduating and getting married in 1942, Sarann came to Las Vegas from Oklahoma. Her husband secured a job at a war industry plant called Basic Magnesium, Inc., in neighboring Henderson, Nevada. Preddy had a harder time finding work. She spent six months in Los Angeles gaining office skills, yet she found no place to use those skills once she returned to Las Vegas.

Blacks made up less than 1 percent of the population in 1940. The thousands of African Americans who moved to Las Vegas during and after World War II met an informal segregation process that restricted black housing and business to the Westside. This undeveloped area was adjacent to the downtown district, but a world apart. De facto discriminatory business practices stunted black businesses with restrictions on loans to build homes or start businesses. Preddy's narrative tells us not only about her experiences in gaming, but also about the community life located within the largely segregated Westside that she remembered warmly—a vibrant community of black-owned businesses, clubs, and churches. It also introduced a small but persistent group of civil rights activists who had been pushing to end discriminatory practices since the 1920s.

Among the new residents of Las Vegas during the 1950s were the middle-class professionals who moved to Las Vegas from more racially progressive areas and who assisted in moving racial equality forward. The first arena was in public accommodations. Not only could black residents not enjoy the resort casinos, but even internationally acclaimed African American entertainers such as Sammy Davis Jr. and Count Basie would have to rent rooms on the Westside while they played the major casino showrooms. In 1960 an agreement was reached between hotel-casinos and the NAACP to open public accommodations. Over the next two decades the organization continued to work to eliminate racial discrimination in housing, education, and employment.[2]

When Sarann Preddy looked for office jobs in Las Vegas after her training in Los Angeles, she encountered occupational segregation that limited her options. African Americans could work in the back-of-the-house service jobs or in private domestic service. Preddy addressed the situation by dealing cards in the small Westside clubs and running her own businesses. She also decided to work to improve the situation and joined with others to form the Black Chamber of Commerce to support business people.[3] She held an active membership in the NAACP and ran unsuccessfully for public office. Her discussion of women's involvement in the civil rights campaigns is a rare record of their involvement. Along with all of these activities, she raised four children. More details on these parts of her life may be found in the original transcript of her oral history.

Then, in 1985, "I got the bright idea about opening up the Moulin Rouge," Preddy said. She viewed the revitalization of the property as a means to reenergize the West Las Vegas economy. She and her family poured everything they had into it. They obtained a lease for the bar, bought the property, and attempted to get a full gaming license. The once-bright prospects for financing with partners never materialized, however, leaving the family to sell their investment to a developer. Regardless, Sarann Preddy's name remained synonymous with the Moulin Rouge Preservation Association, a group that helped get the property listed on the National Register of Historic Places in 1992.[4]

Preddy was a contemporary of Claudine Williams, although Preddy had moved to Las Vegas twenty years earlier. Both women came of age during the war years, learned how to deal the games of chance, and loved working in gambling. Beyond those similarities, their lives diverged enormously. For Preddy, postwar race dynamics shaped her business opportunities and her narrative detailed the challenges she faced accumulating sufficient capital to build her dream. Nevertheless, Preddy engaged actively in building business opportunities and in creating better opportunities for her family and neighbors through her civil rights work.

My father came here first and he bought a lot and built a small house. And then in the next year he built a larger house. Then the next year he built a larger house and that's the place that we lived, at 512 Madison, for forty-some years. . . . My mother still speaks about the house—that it was so much better than the one she has now and it was so insulated. . . . In the early 1940s and the 1950s there wasn't much home buying. You had to build little houses out of your pocket. There was no way to get any financing. They would not finance anything in West Las Vegas. The first financing that happened in West Las Vegas was from people that moved here from out of Utah. They had a little mortgage company because I remember distinctly that my father had built some apartments and this is where he got his financing from. When he built his first house right after he came here, he built it for cash. There was no financing to be gotten in West Las Vegas. That was a no-no. That's why it took the places so long to build up and why there were so many shacks and half-built places, because they couldn't get any money. . . .

It was fun during those times because in West Las Vegas is where all the businesses and all the churches were in one little small community and every-body knew everybody. When you washed, you put your clothes on the line and leave 'em for two days and we didn't even have a key to the door. And where I worked at the Cotton Club, it was two blocks and I could walk. I went out of the back way down to the alley to the street and then walked to work. And I have gone to work like at twelve o'clock at night. I worked the graveyard shift and I would walk out and walk down there by myself and there was no problem. . . .

Unable to find work outside the clubs, she went to Los Angeles and took a six-month busi-ness course, only to find no business opportunities upon her return to Las Vegas.

When I came back here, then I got started working in the clubs. I was a dealer and you had to be twenty-one, so I had to wait 'til I was twenty-one years old to start working in the clubs. I started out as a keno writer. Then after that I went from that to twenty-one, and I've done everything in the clubs that they were doing during that time. They are a lot more sophisticated now, but I kind of learned to do everything. . . . During that time, they didn't have any [dealer] schools or anything here, so you were taught by other people who had been taught earlier than you. The people that owned the clubs and older dealers would teach whoever wanted to learn how to deal. . . . So when I came, every-body was excited about the gambling and I think I tried it a couple of times and I lost my money. So I never tried it anymore and that gave me the idea of pursuing to be a twenty-one dealer because that was what I wanted to play. So I learned to be a twenty-one dealer and I was on the other side of the table, so I never wanted to play. . . .

A lot of the Westside clubs were owned by blacks at one time. The Brown Derby was owned by blacks. The Cotton Club was owned by blacks, and the El Morocco was owned by blacks. The Town Tavern was owned by a black. At one time the Louisiana Club was owned by a black. Basically they were all kind of owned by blacks, not at the very beginning, but right after that. When I first came, the only club on the Westside was the Harlem Club. It was owned by a white person. Then the Cotton Club came and it was owned by a white man, but it wasn't long before he turned it over to a black man and then he formed a little group [with other investors]. There was two or three of them that owned it. And then a black man originally owned the El Morocco and then black people owned the Town Tavern. People only stay in gaming for so long and they start selling out or turn it over to somebody else. Then Chinese people started coming to West Las Vegas. I think they were the only ones that actually owned the clubs. Now they did build a hotel over here, the hotel on Jackson and D Street, Carver House. White people built that and they owned it. Then they changed the name from the Carver House to the Cove. . . .

I worked in the Cotton Club. The Cotton Club is still there on Jackson Street, the building.[5] . . . [The table limits] were much smaller on the Westside, and downtown they weren't as large as they are now. They might have been $25,000 during that time. I really can't remember because we didn't frequent downtown. It was so prejudiced here and so segregated, so blacks did not go downtown to gamble. But white people did come over in the area, on Jackson Street. That was like the Strip in the black area. I think the payoff was a little different. . . .

Tips was great because during that time money was plentiful and people really spent their money freely. A lot of times people would be playing and I've had people say to me, "I'm playing this ticket and if I hit, I'm going to give you half of it." And that actually has happened . . . and they gave me half of it. . . .

I met all the entertainers who were coming to Las Vegas during that time because they could not stay on the Strip. So when they finished working on the Strip they came to the Cotton Club. So when I was dealing keno—I was a keno writer—I wrote for all the people like the Mills Brothers, and the Ink Spots, and Sammy Davis, and Pearl Bailey, and you name 'em—all the people that was coming here during that time came to West Las Vegas. Most of them lived in West Las Vegas. . . . So I had a chance to meet these people and know them on a first-hand basis because when you're writing keno it's almost a personal contact. People hand you the ticket and you give it back and you're dealing and you learn these people. We used to have parties in the back and they would participate. . . .

Sarann Preddy moved from working in clubs to owning one herself within a short time. Her first entrance into the business side was a much simpler process than she had imagined.

After I worked at the Cotton Club, I left and went to Hawthorne [Nevada] and opened up a club at Hawthorne.[6] . . . I was married the second time to a fellow that just got discharged out of the service. . . . And for a short time he was working as a substitute teacher here in Las Vegas and he wasn't on steady. So they were doing a lot of hiring in Hawthorne and a lot of people was moving to Hawthorne, so he went to Hawthorne and he liked what he was doing up there. And we moved and went up there. . . . When I went back up there, he [Woody Lofton, owner of the Lincoln Bar] practically gave me the place. I remember that I had to have $600 to go into the place and I came back and got the $600 from my father. And that's how I got in that club, and I stayed there for seven years. . . . We had keno, we had twenty-one, we had a crap table, we had [a] poker table, and we had slot machines. . . . The name of the club was Lincoln Bar. That's what it was when we took over and later on through the years, and I don't know where I got the name from; I named it the Tonga Club.

So I stayed there for seven years and it was quite an experience because I worked in the community organizations there. I was president of the NAACP and I did a lot of traveling. And, of course, I made a lot of money. We bought a big house there and the first house we bought we lived next door to the banker, the president of the bank. And most people cautioned us about, "You know it's dangerous to live over there, because you're black. And people might do this, that, and the other." And I remember when we moved in, it was a nice big house and we had big picture windows . . . and we were doing some things and I didn't have any curtains over the windows. People would come by to tell me that, "Oh, don't you think you need to hang something up. There might be a drive-by shooting." But I didn't pay that any attention because I found out that the people were very nice.[7] . . .

We had a minister who along with some of us organized a branch [of the NAACP] in Hawthorne. . . . He was president for a couple of years and then the next year I was elected president. It was a lot of fun because it was a small town and it was a lot more involvement and people really got along. . . . I had a lot of support and we used to bring some of the speakers in from the national [NAACP] to come in [to] Hawthorne to speak. And when they came there and saw how prejudiced it was, well they blasted things and it helped somewhat because finally they integrated Hawthorne. It did give us something to do and it gave us an outlook on going further in life—myself, too. I had not been really involved. I came from a small town in Oklahoma and Las Vegas was a small town, also. So it was something that was very much needed and I think it really did help. . . .

■ Preddy considered Las Vegas home; she visited nearly every weekend because her parents lived there and took care of all but one of her children. In 1955 her father worked on the Moulin Rouge Hotel and Casino. The property quickly became a topic of fascination to her.

My father was building the Moulin Rouge and I heard him talk about it all the time; when I came [to Las Vegas] I visited and saw it being built. So, for the grand opening, naturally working for myself, I was able to take off. So, I came back and it was so exciting, I came down here and stayed a whole month and I worked about three weeks of that month as a dealer. . . . I didn't work in the Moulin Rouge. I worked in another [place, a] Chinese place. There were several Chinese that had places on the Westside. . . . They had the El Rio and that's where I worked. And while I was here, working to me was always a pleasure because then you got to see everybody and got paid, too. I was never a partier to go out and party, so I liked to be in the midst. So, I would work and then when I would get off of work then I would mingle with the people somewhat. It was just a lot of fun, working and being around the people.

The Moulin Rouge made such an impact over in West Las Vegas because they got all of the whites started coming. . . . People was there from all across town and people from out of town would frequent the Moulin Rouge. It was going to be *the spot*. . . . I met Alice Key during that time and Bob Bailey and Dr. West and Dr. McMillan and all those people—Ann Bailey. . . . Well, having people from different parts of the country, and especially where they had been involved in entertainment and were doing a lot more things in other larger cities than they were in Las Vegas, I think it certainly added to Las Vegas having these professional people move in town. It gave it a different look, a different atmosphere. . . . And of course a lot of these, being entertainers, these were a lot of classy people. So they added a lot to the atmosphere of West Las Vegas.[8]

Sarann Preddy as a young woman at the opening of the Moulin Rouge Hotel and Casino,
1955. Courtesy of Sarann Preddy and the Las
Vegas Women Oral History Project, UNLV.

▨ Preddy continued to operate her club in Hawthorne until 1957 when the ammunition
depot, the largest employer, started laying off workers. She sold her club and returned to her
family, and worked at the West Las Vegas clubs.

When I first came back I went to work at the El Morocco. . . . A white man
from Reno had bought it and he'd redone the club and it was absolutely beautiful. . . . It didn't stay open very long, maybe a year. When it closed, I went
to work at the Louisiana Club working for the Chinese people who had it.
Then Chinese people bought the Town Tavern and it was a little nicer club so
I migrated over there. I worked there for maybe a year and then they stopped
the women from dealing [in 1958]. . . . They passed a resolution at the city that
no more women dealers [could work] in the city of Las Vegas. I think the men
thought that women were going to take over like they were doing in Reno.
So when it closed I was the last person that worked, because I was working
the graveyard shift; so they laid everybody off and then when they got to the
graveyard shift it was my last time.[9] . . .

And all of my experience was in that field and I really didn't know what I
was going to do because I had no experience in anything else. I went downtown and worked at a dress shop for a couple of weeks, but I was used to
making all this money in the club and it was in tips more or less. Then, downtown, I think I was making $9.00 a day down there doing something and you
work three days and I had four kids, so that wasn't hittin' on nothin'. So then
a friend of mine was a dealer and we got the bright idea of going to Reno, so

we went to Reno and worked up there. B[ut] me having kids, I went up there and stayed about three or four months and then I came back to Las Vegas to be with my family. . . . You could only deal in the Chinese and the black places. They didn't hire any blacks as dealers in the white places. [Reno's segregated section was] maybe a block from downtown, but it was clubs owned by Chinese people and they hired blacks to work in there because most of their customers were black because they could not go to the other clubs. They made a lot of money off of black people so they hired blacks. So I worked up there and, being from Las Vegas, I wanted to come back to Las Vegas.[10]

When I came back here I did various little things.[11] . . . Then I got the bright idea about going into the bar business. . . . I went into the Playhouse Lounge, opened up the place. And that was in the Cotton Club where I started out working, in the same building. . . . I spent a fair amount of money in there fixing it up real pretty. I had marble-top tables made and all the bright, hot-pink furniture that was in there, fixed it up really nice. . . . Well, I didn't have the finances during that time and probably the know-how to get gaming licenses in Las Vegas. . . . They were becoming to be a little more sophisticated. When I was in Hawthorne, you didn't have to go through all that red tape. It was almost like getting a minor business license. . . . So I didn't stay in that place, maybe a little better than a year.

▨ For Sarann Preddy, no line separated business opportunity from civil rights. Her narrative blends discussions of both. While always a businesswoman at heart, she worked with other women and men to open job opportunities.

I got started with the NAACP when I lived at Hawthorne, Nevada, and became president of the chapter. Then when I moved back here, Lubertha Johnson was in the NAACP and I can remember that I always wanted to be like Lubertha Johnson or Mabel Hoggard.[12] Lubertha Johnson was connected to some housing program out in Henderson. I was very young when I heard her speak and I never will forget. She was so flamboyant. She gave this dynamic speech and it just blew my mind. She was a very articulate woman. This was something new in Las Vegas because during that time we didn't have many prominent people involved in organizations. She had a lot of respect from the people in town. If she spoke, then they listened. Being a woman and a very educated woman with the drive, she certainly made a mark here because people really looked up to her. It's strange how all these things happen and now when you get a new city these people are lost. Nobody knows about her anymore. I guess somebody else come along and take that place. But I don't see any impact that anybody's doing that was as great as it was when she was doing. After working with Lubertha for so many years, I just got attached to working with her and thinking that she was such a neat lady. I wanted to be like her.

With the NAACP, I kind of like started at the bottom. They used a group of us out of the Gamma Phi Delta sorority as hostesses whenever we'd have an affair.[13] So I started with that and I kept going and going until I formed an organization through the NAACP, the Women's Auxiliary, and then that branched out.[14] At that time it was very effective because it was a mixed organization. It wasn't just black women. It was white women as well. We did a lot of things together like having voter registrations and we had teas to raise funds to support the NAACP and to support some of the other organizations, like some of the students. Hannah Brown, Ida Crockett, Eleanor Walker, and a host of others were involved. We were kind of like an arm to support the main branch. I served as vice president under Dr. McMillan and I served as treasurer. Gwen Weeks Rainer was the person that was involved in politics. She was like a grassroots recruiter and her thing was getting all black people registered to vote, which was very important. If you don't get out and get involved and if you don't vote, then you don't get much. Sarah Hughes was very much involved and connected with the Culinary Union. She was the head of some department in the union and she worked very hard recruiting blacks and also getting them involved in joining the NAACP so that movement could be furthered along. Alice Key was very much involved in the movement. She was a writer and always stayed on top of things and brought all the issues out and pushed them. She was very knowledgeable about what was going on because she had come along with these things in California. I think Alice played a big part because she studied all the bills and she kept up with everything and reminded everybody what they were supposed to do.[15] And Bernice Moten was involved at that time. Bernice was involved with the school district and she was elected to the school board. So she was in a position to have some influence on a lot of things changing. Eleanor Walker was the president of the NAACP at one point and she grew up here. She also was in politics a little bit.

▨ Las Vegas valley's first major breakthrough on desegregation came within the context of major national challenges to race segregation laws. Landmark US civil rights cases such as *Morgan v. Virginia* (1946) and *Brown v. Board of Education* (1954) successfully challenged race discrimination in interstate public transportation and education, respectively. Nevertheless, local groups, often supported by NAACP chapters, needed to fight to end discriminatory practices locally. Peaceful demonstrations throughout the South drew national attention to the refusal of local governments to implement the Supreme Court's decisions. Las Vegas business owners wanted no such publicity. In 1960 representatives of hotel-casinos, government, and business met with leaders of the NAACP to forge the opening of public accommodations in Las Vegas in what is known as the Moulin Rouge Agreement. Four years later Congress passed the 1964 Civil Rights Act, which provided the legal foundation to end race segregation in all arenas, including employment.

The local NAACP asked the US Department of Justice to investigate job discrimination in the hotel-casino industry, and in 1971 the department secured a consent decree with eighteen properties that promised to hire more black workers. To the dismay of the African American women activists, sex bias continued. Legal actions continued throughout the 1970s in an effort to broaden the antidiscrimination laws and open formerly male-only jobs to women. In 1981 another consent decree, this time focused on sex and national origin, theoretically opened up all hotel-casino jobs to anyone who was qualified. Preddy's comments below refer to the changes that the 1971 Consent Decree made in the lives of African Americans in greater Las Vegas.[16]

Las Vegas had its problems. I remember downtown at the Sal Sagev Hotel—that was Las Vegas spelled backwards—they definitely didn't want any blacks to come in there when they integrated. He said he would close up before he would let any blacks come in his club. I remember way back during the war when they were bringing the Japanese through here. They brought a convoy—they had trucks coming through for days—and they stopped off in Las Vegas and they housed the Japanese people downtown and most of the drivers was black. They had to come on the Westside and find them a place to stay, but they let the "enemies" stay downtown. And the Sal Sagev Club, I think the man had an experience with his wife and a black man, so he never wanted any blacks to stay in his property or have anything to do with them no more in life. So when they came up with the consent decree, and it may have been further back than that, but something came up to where they were making agreements with the places to open up, he said, "Never." He'd close up before he'd let any black people stay in his club.[17] . . .

The NAACP was busy working trying to get integration. They came to me and asked me—because one place, Jerry's Nugget in [North] Las Vegas told them they would hire someone if they could find someone that had any experience. They figured that they couldn't because nobody had been dealing. So, they came to me and asked me if I would take this job. They begged me to take the job just for six months. This way it would open up [for] people to be able to go into the other places to work. So I finally decided that I would do that and I went to Jerry's Nugget and I was going to work six months. I worked there seven years. When I started working there, they were such nice people to work for and there was no problem. And I was right at home dealing twenty-one. That's what I always wanted to do anyway. So when I went down there to work, I worked there for seven years.[18] . . .

Before that they didn't have any blacks in the gaming industry, period. That was such a lucrative field and such a closed thing, it was a surprise to me that they actually let blacks get involved. Handling all the money and that kind of thing and having access to it, I just couldn't see it happening before it did happen. When they had the consent decree there was a lot of the hotels who volunteered and really came out really strong for this. But it didn't last very long. They did all this because they were forced to do it. So they made a big grandstand entrance and then later on they kind of weeded it out. They need the consent decree to come back again because they do have a lot of blacks working, but per capita they don't. . . . You walk in a club and look at especially the dealers and you may see two [black] dealers out of two hundred. But you may see 10 percent as black customers. . . .

There's never been very many women involved in gaming until the recent years, and even now there's not an awful lot of them involved as far as owner-ship. There's some women that hold high positions in the gaming, but as far as ownership I doubt if there's been five women involved as owners of the places. There may be some that has a small interest, or maybe a large interest, in some of the hotels but I haven't even heard of any of those. I know some of them got top executive jobs but not many to say, "Women own a casino." I only can remember three women who owned casinos. Claudine Williams, I believe, was one of them that outright owned their business. Mitzi Briggs, I believe, from the Tropicana was the owner there. And then the lady [Margaret Elardi] that owned the Frontier. . . . Those are the only women that I can think of that owned a hotel on the Strip. In the early years there were a couple of women that owned some of the gaming places downtown. [Mayme Stocker] was the first woman that had a license. I believe she was the first *person* that had a gaming license in Las Vegas, period. . . . So there were very few women that ever held any license.[19]

After working as a dealer for several years, Preddy joined business partners to manage a bar and develop gaming in it. Located on H Street and Owens Avenue in the West Las Vegas neighborhood, she called it the People's Choice. She was able to get a gaming license for that size club with "three or four twenty-one tables, and poker, and slot machines." After about

Sarann Preddy (*second from left standing*) watching a game at her club, the People's Choice, ca. 1977. The clubs of West Las Vegas catered to the African American community and were small relative to downtown and Strip casinos. Preddy said her club had a few twenty-one tables, poker, and slot machines. Courtesy of Sarann Preddy and the Las Vegas Women Oral History Project, UNLV.

six or seven years at the People's Choice, Preddy undertook her dream to reopen the Moulin Rouge Hotel and Casino.

Then I got the bright idea about opening up the Moulin Rouge, because it had been defunct for so long. . . . A lot of people had talked about reopening the Moulin Rouge and tried to be interested in getting the Moulin Rouge. No one was successful in doing so. . . . I went by and talked to the [owner of the place]. I guess he took a liking to me and we sat down and talked and he made it possible for me. I had to have some money, but he made it possible for me to come in. . . . And I had a license already at People's Choice right down the street, a full gaming license. I was very naïve and I said, "I'm not going to have a problem, I already have a license and plus I know everybody in town. I know everybody on the gaming board [State Gaming Control Board]." . . . So, when I got ready to apply for the license and went in they told me, "We can't give you any license because of the landlord." . . . He has to be suitable also. That landlord had slot machines in the Moulin Rouge when I went in there and in another property, but the gaming board said that was a mistake. . . .

When we went into the Moulin Rouge, we were thinking we were going to move the gaming up there and that way we would make money and we'd grow into the place and maybe one day we would be able to buy it. But that didn't happen, so that worked a hardship on us because we didn't have anything but a bar and you don't make a lot of money on a bar with a place that big. So we stayed there and spent a lot of money. We didn't have lot of cash money but we owned several pieces of property. We had some property out on Desert Inn Road and some on Tropicana, so we kept selling off and selling off. . . . We kept going back and trying to do things to get the gaming license. . . . Each time you go back to the gaming license board, you've got to spend some more money to be investigated again. You might take them the same papers but you've got to come up and do it again. We kept spending all this money, so finally we did get the license. And then each time they gave us the license—which was so unfair—they gave them to us for like six months, I think, the first time. So in six months you couldn't go out and really do anything because people that was interested in getting involved say, "We don't want to put any money in here because how do we know what's going to happen after six months." . . . Finally, we arranged enough money to buy the place [in 1990].

Owning the property did not put an end to the difficulties of raising capital. The place needed remodeling and Preddy needed to acquire additional investors. She worked with the city and local banks, which looked promising at one point but fell through in the end. Then she pursued a number of out-of-town investors, including Black Entertainment Television and the Pequot Indian Tribe. The stress of the negotiations proved too much for the family. Her husband suffered a heart attack and her son returned to a job at a hotel-casino on the Strip. They recognized the investment had gone as far as it could and "returned the keys."

Gaming is so unique and the big-time operators, they don't want anybody to get involved in gaming. They certainly don't want any minorities to be involved because gaming—it's the leading thing in the world. As long as they can keep a lot of people out of it, money and politics is the only thing that counts now in America and maybe in the world. . . . We can't compete with these people. I think the intention was to never have any blacks to be success-ful in gaming beyond Jackson Street. Matter of fact, one of the guys on the gaming board told me when I went before the board—and it's public informa-tion because you can get a printout from when they have the meetings. . . . It took me so much money [and] time to get a gaming license at the Moulin Rouge and I questioned him about this. He said, "Well Sarann, you got to remember. You moved up. So as long as you're over there [on the Westside], then everything is easy. But when you start getting up in the world, it's going to be tougher." . . . Finances is what kept us from going any further. I think it was one of those things that I came along just maybe twenty years too early.

Since relinquishing the property, other owners have attempted to redevelop the Moulin Rouge. In 2003 a fire gutted the property and ended any such plan. Only the sign remains, and it's protected as part of the city's Neon Museum. Preddy's hope that the Moulin Rouge would revitalize the economy of the Westside dissolved again. This interview took place before the fire. Consequently, she continued to express her faith that the Moulin Rouge would rise again and bring the community up with it.

I think if the Moulin Rouge can get off the ground floor, it's certainly going to help the overall West Las Vegas because they're already building over there. . . . When it opened the first time it was a great impact with Jackson Street because it opened up and then brought awareness to people about nicer places to go. It brought more people into the area because people started coming to Las Vegas because of the Moulin Rouge. And Jackson Street, it made them take more pride in their buildings. They started fixing up more and they got more customers to come over into the area. It was just a tremendous help when it came over and it's too bad that it had to close. Because I think if it had stayed open, Las Vegas Westside would have been booming now like downtown. . . . I think the Moulin Rouge could be the gateway to West Las Vegas. And the Town Tavern is the only other club that is open over there, or probably could be. Like in the old Cotton Club, there's a church in there now. Then the Cove was torn down and there's a church in the Brown Derby. The El Morocco was torn down. Years ago they had another club across the street from the Town Tavern. Most people probably haven't heard of it, the Club Alabam. It was there but it's torn down. So the Town Tavern is the only open club. It's a nice building. It just needs some finances and it's just hard for blacks to get any finances in that area.

It's a shame that Las Vegas is the largest gaming city in the country, and as many blacks that comes here and as much money that is being made off of blacks, we don't have one gaming casino. I'm hoping that it does come and I would be still out there fighting, but I think I've reached the age, maybe now, that it's a little too strenuous for me to be involved.

In 1997 when Sarann Preddy recounted her life history she was approximately seventy-three years old. (She kept her birth date private.) She had raised her family in her adopted city and seen Las Vegas grow from a town of 8,400 to a city of 2 million. She worked for much of her life, and rather than accept the limits of job segregation, she created her own businesses. Preddy discussed the many changes that occurred during her years from the perspective of an entrepreneur and civil rights advocate. Those two identities merged for Sarann Preddy. She had the initiative and knowledge to build and grow businesses, and yet the historical timing of her efforts hobbled her at times with what she understood were race-based practices. Consequently, working to remove those practices became as essential to her life as her entrepreneurship.

Chapter 3

BERNICE JAEGER

Assistant General Manager

It was like we died and went to Heaven. . . . You didn't have to worry about being raided.
You didn't have to worry that your husband was going to end up in jail.
—Bernice Jaeger

At the age of twenty Bernice married Ivan Jaeger in Cincinnati, Ohio.[1] Like many young couples in 1955, they started a family right away. By the time they moved to Las Vegas in 1961, they had two young girls. A third daughter was born in Las Vegas. In many ways, Jaeger resembled the classic homemaker of the era. She stayed home to raise the children and participated in community activities like Girl Scouts. Her life differed on a central point, though: Bernice's husband and the men in his family had worked as dealers in gambling establishments in Kentucky; when those clubs closed, they moved to Las Vegas.

Cincinnati was too conservative for gambling, but across the river in Kentucky a number of gambling clubs existed. The Lookout House and the Beverly Hills Country Club were two of the nicest. The underground nature of gambling made for close-knit relationships between the workers and their families. The closeness served as an informal referral system allowing only those who were known to each other to enter the system. This was a necessity when operating in an illegal environment, but remained a practice when the jobs moved to Las Vegas. As a young adult in this environment, Bernice developed a respect for "the boys" who made lives for themselves and their families when they came out to Las Vegas.

In 1961 Kentucky law enforcement cracked down on the clubs, as law enforcement was doing around the country. The Jaegers were one of the first families to decide to pack up and leave the Midwest to relocate in Las Vegas. About fifty families from that specific area followed them over the next few months. Women helped each other settle their households while the men helped each other find jobs in casinos. There weren't many people in the United States who knew the gambling business when Las Vegas started, so the casino people had to come from places where gambling was underground. Her mentors, both men and women, had learned their business in those areas.

In addition to detailing the migration of families, Jaeger's narrative offers a description of community and childrearing in 1960s Las Vegas when it was still a small city. She describes the type of activities available to her children, the role she took as a room mother at her children's school, and the volunteer service she enjoyed as a Girl Scout troop leader. The glimpses into family life here and in the other chapters provide a rare perspective of Las Vegas as a residential community.

Jaeger had not intended to join the hotel-casino industry, but then an opportunity arose. She still had older children in school and was finishing her college education when she was offered a job in convention sales. As she took on tasks with greater responsibility, she gained an understanding of the structure of the hotel-casino—the separate components that made up the entire enterprise. Jaeger understood that all the parts had supporting roles to the casino business. The casino was the heart of the operation; all the other areas, from the showroom to the dining room, supplemented the main attraction of the casino.[2] Gender structured the hotel-casino workplace during the 1960s and 1970s, according to Jaeger. The hotel and its workers provided services to the patrons of the casino. Correspondingly, these areas employed more women than men as front desk clerks, food service workers, and clericals, and people of color as housekeepers. In contrast, white men dominated the casino floor—not only as dealers, but also as pit bosses and floor supervisors. These jobs frequently brought in the highest pay and tips. The only women who worked on the casino floor were beverage servers and change girls.

Jaeger moved into management and had worked up to assistant general manager of a small hotel-casino (four hundred rooms) by the early 1980s. She admired the old-timers' hands-on approach to management and what she referred to as a family feeling between workers and management. Businesses were smaller and personal service for hotel guests reigned supreme. When she had the opportunity to manage a property herself, two reference points guided her: (1) the personal style of her mentors, and (2) her prior job—running a household.

In 1997 Jaeger left the hotel-casino industry. She returned to the university and completed a master's degree in counseling in 2003. The career change was one she never regretted.

G aming had been in northern Kentucky for years and years. It was underground, but everyone knew it was there. Cincinnati was a very conservative city and all the fun and entertainment was across the river in northern Kentucky. . . . There were posh supper clubs back there then. They were beautiful things. There was the Lookout House, there was the Beverly Hills Country Club, and various places. . . . [Gambling] had always been there and it was condoned. Everyone knew it was there. It was funny because every year they would have a grand jury, and so they would close down for ten days or two weeks for grand jury. That was the only time we would get a vacation. So the last time that they had the grand jury, they had a do-gooder who came in and was going to clean up everything. And that's what he did. He actually did.

They ended up running all of us out of town, so it was like we died and went to Heaven. We all came here.[3]

Most of my husband's family has been in the business all of their lives. . . . My husband's uncle would oversee an awful lot of the gaming activities in that area. My husband, when he worked there, was a dealer. His brothers were dealers. His cousins were dealers. When that closed down in 1961, actually we were one of the first families to come out. I just had a feeling that it wasn't going to open again, and where else would you go but Las Vegas, if that's the kind of business you were in.

Actually when you think about it on the whole grand scale of things, there weren't that many people in all of the United States that were dealers. Not like there would be truck drivers or something. . . . And the people that came out of Kentucky, it has been said, were the best dealers by far. They were trained well. They liked what they were doing. They were very conscientious about it and they were very good dealers. I've heard that often since I've been here, that the fellows who came out of Kentucky really were the cream of the crop. . . . [Dealers] did migrate around, almost like your lettuce pickers or something like that—a migrant worker. They would maybe go to Florida or go to a warmer climate. Or maybe they'd go up to [Lake] Tahoe. Maybe with the season, they would move around. It was like a circuit. . . .

So we packed up and came out here and then after a few weeks more and more people came. That whole summer [of 1961] they started to come out, and into the fall. There was a real colony of us. The fellows helped each other find jobs and the women helped each other. We had this box that we kind of circulated through the crowd. When we came, we didn't bring anything. We brought the kids, [the] electric skillet, my sewing machine, four dishes, and some silverware. That was it. We all had to start over, and so we had this box we'd circulate. It had some linens and some pots and pans and a couple of dishes and some old cups and things like that. I know that sounds crazy, but so many of us came without an awful lot until our things got here. So we all helped each other. . . .

We all knew that coming here, we weren't going back. I knew that coming down Boulder Highway. And it was terrible because there was nothing on Boulder Highway when I came down there, except this big tumbleweed that was in front of our car. It was like, "Oh, my God. This is Las Vegas?" I thought it was the Strip. I had no way of knowing, and I thought, "There's nothing even out here, just this dumb tumbleweed." I had this lump in my throat and tears practically coming to my eyes and I thought, "Well, I can't let my husband know that I feel this badly." I had two little babies in the car and this was going to be it and all I'm looking at is a tumbleweed. And dust blowing all over and it was just terrible. . . . There was nothing. But we knew we had nothing to go back to. So whatever we had and whatever we knew, we could do it well here.

Las Vegas was a very safe town. In those days, we really didn't even lock our doors. You could drive around at night and nobody ever bothered you. My husband was working a crazy shift and I remember I used to pick him up quite late behind the Riviera Hotel. I would sit back there and wait for him and nobody bothered me. It was in the summer and I had the windows rolled down listening to the radio. No one came along. No one bothered you. They didn't want any kind of static happening in this town, especially things that the tourists might ever see. If anything was happening, it was happening perhaps further out or whatever. But we never worried about the children. It's funny, in this town of all towns, there were always curfews here and the kids didn't get to stay out late anyway. And they really enforced those curfews.[4]

It was a small town and you did the same kind of things you do in other towns. You picnic and go to the lake and to the mountains, all those things. It was a wonderful town to bring up kids. It really was. Other people seemed to look out for your kids, too—a lot of neighborhood functions all the time and other mothers looking after kids that would stay over, or whatever. . . . I was a room mother so I was always running down there [to the school] for parties with the cupcakes and all that. There were always dances and swimming parties and slumber parties. I had a lot of slumber parties in my day. Camping. . . . I wanted to be able to spend time with [my children], so I became involved in Girl Scouts. I started out in Girl Scouts when the first one was a Brownie and went all the way through twelve years of Girl Scouts. I was even on the board, as a matter of fact. I was a Girl Scout leader for twelve years. It gave me an opportunity to know who their friends were and all these kids always ended up at our house for parties and meetings. . . . I don't think I would have been accepted as a Girl Scout leader had I stayed in Ohio. . . .

It was really strange to me because when we said we were leaving for Las Vegas, so many of our friends in Ohio had a fit: "[You're] taking those children to Sin City?" They really berated us for that and I worried about that, but actually we ended up having less problems with our girls than so many of them did in other cities. . . . My children were never interested in the casino business. It was something that was always around. . . . I think many of us had an opportunity to provide our children with the kind of education maybe we would have liked to have had. So they've gone on into other things. . . .

[The best thing was] you didn't have to worry about being raided. You didn't have to worry that your husband was going to end up in jail. You didn't have to worry about any of those things. You just came here and you were so happy to be here and have your job and not worry about all that stuff. No one was looking down their nose at you. You were just as respectable as anybody else. And that was the beauty of it. I think that's what kind of tied us all together, that we had this now which we didn't have before. We hadn't really changed much. We were still the same people, but it was like we had that [stigma] lifted off of us. Because where we did come from, so many of us, [gambling] wasn't permitted and so you didn't talk about it. You weren't as social as maybe you would have been because you don't want everyone knowing your business and knowing where your husband worked. It was a difficult existence that way. You couldn't even get an insurance policy; all those kinds of crazy things. So this was heavenly, when we got here.

As her children grew older, Jaeger returned to finish her college education. The Community College of Southern Nevada (later renamed the College of Southern Nevada) had opened in the early 1970s. She graduated with an associate of arts in liberal arts and an associate of applied science in hotel administration in 1973 and 1974, respectively. The final course she took was "Orientation to the Hotel Industry." The class required a field practicum in which a student spent time with a mentor in the hotel industry. Jaeger explained how that class changed the course of her life.

They had a difficult time with me because in the early 1970s there weren't very many women out in the industry and they wanted to pair me up with a female executive. They were able to select one at the Riviera Hotel, Inez Rambeau. She was the director of convention sales. So I went out to visit her. I would go out once a week and I really just sat there and observed. As time went on we developed a real friendship. Inez and I came from gambling families. Her father had owned a casino and my husband's family had been in the casino industry all of their lives, so there was great rapport between us. We seemed to really understand the business. . . . I do believe that we both realized that it wasn't the sales department that was filling the hotel, it was really the casino. That's where it all was. We sort of knew our place.

When Inez Rambeau's secretary left the job, Inez offered it to Bernice. She had not planned on taking a job, but after thinking about it and discussing it with her family, she decided it was a great opportunity. In 1973 she started her hotel career in convention sales. Rambeau had been working in the field for twenty-five years and Jaeger found an excellent mentor. The convention sales area gave her the big picture of how the hotel-casino industry worked and how all the areas worked to feed customers to the casino.

Certainly, years ago when our convention areas were smaller, we had to be very careful that the people that we brought in were going to be people that would stay and play in the casinos and not just be there for their meetings. I can remember one time at the Riviera we booked in a convention—something where they had household cleaners and mops and toilet mops and things like that. Well, it ended up that the general manager of the hotel just became livid because these people were not really the type that were going to be playing an awful lot in the casino. . . . So, I caught on that if you were going to book anything in a convention area it's going to have some repercussions on the casino. . . . We would book in things that would really take that conventioneer, after their meetings, out into the casino to play. . . .

But it gave me an opportunity to see how all the departments intermingled and how important they were to each other. You had to be sure when you were booking a convention that you had the backing of housekeeping and all the porters, and they were all going to be there to be sure that everything was set up properly. All of these things were so important. There had to be real communication between the departments. You could really kill yourself if you didn't have that proper communication . . . working with the food and beverage department, too, to be sure that all of the intermissions were handled, that all the coffee was there and the sweet rolls and everything else that they wanted to keep themselves happy. You're working constantly with the front desk to be sure that all the rooms are blocked. There's a hierarchy that you have, to be sure that the proper room is going to the chairman of the board and [to each] of his people. So there's a lot of things to keep on top of. . . . The casino needed to know if this was going to be a large convention, because they certainly would want to put on more dealers and more help. You don't ever want to be caught without enough help in the casino. The restaurants needed to know how many supplies they would need. Room service would need to know what time their meetings were going to be in case they needed to start up their room service earlier in the morning. Engineering had to know about extension cords and plugs and where they were going to set up things.

Porters needed to know to do all the set-up work as far as tables and chairs. And always things would change. So you thought you had it all down pat and maybe you'd send that off Friday thinking that come Monday of the next week was going to be wonderful and of course that never really happened. There were always changes. . . .

After I worked there for a few years with [Inez], I moved on to become assistant to the hotel director. This was really a plum of a job. It was probably the most social I job I've ever had. I thoroughly enjoyed it. I sat right in the middle of the hotel lobby and handled everything that came my way, literally. I loved every minute of it and I do believe that back in the 1970s the Riviera was a very nice hotel. We had an awful lot of VIP guests and they were very interesting, charming people from throughout the whole country—throughout the whole world, actually. I worked for a man [Dick Chappelle, hotel director at the Riviera] who was such an interesting guy. He was brought to town here by Bugsy Siegel and he, himself, had an interesting life. He knew people from all over the world and so I had a great opportunity to visit with all of them.

In many cases, guests would come and they had been sent out by Mrs. Thorpe's butcher and he had been here before and he had a good time, so, "Go see Bernice." So that's the way it always was in the old days. You'd have somebody's hairdresser showing up or whatever. You never knew who you were going to be dealing with when you unlocked that door in the morning. . . . If they needed to see a show somewhere else, we'd get on the phone and get them over to the Dunes or the Sands, wherever they wanted to go. We just took excellent care of them. If their eyeglasses broke, I knew who to call. I knew where to send them. I'd send them over to my dentist if they chipped their tooth. If they broke the strap on their purse, if they broke their high heel, if they needed to have their dress repaired or the hem taken up, those were the kinds of things that you needed to know. And it always worked. I would find babysitters or whatever else they needed. [Comps] were easy enough to do in the old days. . . . We would handle all of the show reservations for our guests and if they were going outside to see a different show and they wanted to not stand in line, I would call whatever hotel and it would be very simple. You would just say, "I need a pass." And they would say, "Oh, sure. Just have Mrs. Smith see the maître d'. A seat will be available." There never was a problem. . . . There was a band of us in those days, like executive secretaries in the hotels, and we handled all of that. The fellows didn't even need to get involved.

All we had to do was call Phyllis or Lois or Brenda, and we gals could take care of all that stuff. It was just so easy. It wasn't any big deal.

It was inbred in me, because I came from a gaming background, that the casino was running everything. Whatever they said was fine because that's where the money came from. So there wasn't a big deal about how much money you were going to make in your food and beverage department or the lounge. In so many of these areas, most of the things were comped off anyway. You were there just to service the player. . . . The same way with the showroom. You could spend a fortune employing a really good act, but you knew if you had him there, he would draw the gamblers and so it almost didn't matter. You knew what your goal was. . . . Of course, as years went by and the corporations came in, then all these departments had to start pulling their own weight. We never had that before. Today, nothing seems like it's reciprocated.

I do believe that, in those days, all of us who worked in the industry went out of our way to try to take care of [visitors]. It wasn't a job. It was something that we really cared to do, and throughout the years so many of these guests were repeat guests. [They] came back year after year. Families came back. Their children came back. Before you knew it, there were grandchildren. The list goes on.

During the course of the interview, Jaeger mentioned the multiple divisions within the hotel-casino and observed that the hotel and the casino had different gendered identities. She described the way in which a typical property was divided into smaller workplaces, and followed up with her assessment of the people who worked in those divisions.

The general manager oversees all of the departments. This is the way it was then. It was his job to oversee the casino and the hotel, see that they worked properly together. That's quite a large job. There's also, usually, an assistant general manager. There are the hotel managers and then there are the casino managers. They have a lot of people under them in two different structures. The casino would have shift managers, pit bosses, floor people, assistants, dealers, pit clerks. Your hotel would have a hotel manager or a hotel director and he would have an assistant. Then you'd have various departments under that: room reservations, housekeeping, engineering, and those types of departments. Then of course all of those departments would either have an assistant or, in those days, all those departments had a heck of a good secretary. We were still small enough in those days that a good secretary could handle those kinds of things. Then housekeeping broke down into the laundry and areas like that. The same way that food and beverage would break down into room service and catering and help's hall and areas like that. So each of those departments broke down into something smaller.

[The casino,] I'd say, was definitely a male world. There were very few women in the industry. In Reno they had women dealers and then it did start to finally happen here in Vegas. I can't remember, but it might have been in the 1970s perhaps. Might have been a little bit earlier, but when I came here we didn't have women dealers. I suppose it's like when women invaded anything—you know—it was like we were taking these jobs away from the men. . . . I really think up to the 1960s that the people who worked in any kind of gaming operation anywhere in the United States probably were put into that job or were given that job because they knew someone. They were trusted by the men who ran these places because, for the most part [outside Nevada, they] were illegal. So whoever hired them had to trust them. In many cases it was a relative. They felt they could trust a relative, or they came highly recommended by a relative. If any of these men were given jobs, say, as dealers, they were going to protect that job. They were going to do the best job they could and they were going to make that man look good. It might have been their uncle or their relative or cousin or whatever. They weren't going to screw up. So they were pleased to have the jobs that they had. . . .

Most of the time, to tell you the truth, our husbands didn't even talk about this industry around us. They just didn't think we should be involved. I think it was a shock to my husband when I actually went to work in the hotel. It wasn't anything he ever thought I was going to do. I always thought it was a pretty fabulous place. You know, these hotels were so glamorous in their day. It was an industry I was always interested in. And I've been very lucky in the industry. It wasn't easy, though, I can tell you, because starting out, if you were in it, then maybe they would let you be in room reservations or something like that. Maybe you could be behind the front desk. It wasn't that they were going to take you too seriously. . . . The men who ran it then, I don't think they thought we [women] could be in it. I'm speaking of the much older men who came up maybe as a bootlegger or in the numbers game. I don't think they could ever see a woman being in the pit or whatever.[5]

So, I think that people who worked in the casino in those days certainly felt like they were carrying the whole ball. And in many cases they were. . . . The status was also reflected in their salaries. Someone who perhaps would be in the accounting office, maybe in a fairly good position, would certainly not be making what a pit boss would be making in the casino. It wouldn't matter what kind of education they both had, either.

You often found women running personnel offices and in some cases payroll. Many times you'd have a female executive as a housekeeper. . . . Maybe they would work in the cage, if you'd like to think of that as the casino area. Or a few of them would work as dealers, but you wouldn't see too many that were on the floor—I'm speaking of the 1970s—as a pit boss or anything like that. You'd see pit clerks, but you're seeing more women as pit bosses now. That started to change in the 1980s.

Although working women in Las Vegas were frequently associated with sex work in the public's imagination, you would not know it from the interviews. Jaeger was one of the very few narrators who discussed the sex workers of the era. Her discussion points to an obscure relationship between prostitutes and hotel-casinos, yet even her willingness to discuss the prostitutes carefully avoided any direct association between management and procurement of sex workers for customers.

I can remember that I would see a lot of the call girls coming in to the hotel. We even had a spot where the telephones were, the house phones, and we used to call that hookers' haven. I don't know, maybe it was as I got older it seemed like all the girls going to the telephones were getting younger, but it was like some of these kids looked like they were like teenagers, even, very young. But I couldn't help but notice it. Now, I don't think a guest would notice it. I was just tuned in after a while, after passing and listening to their conversation or noticing them congregating around these house phones, when they would get into the side door of the hotel. I guess they would call the room and make the plans before they would go upstairs. . . .

I would guess that if a girl went into a property and really misbehaved in any kind of way, she would be escorted out—would be eighty-sixed—and her picture taken and all of these things so that if she returned, security would know her. They wouldn't want her back in there for a particular reason, perhaps something she did—if she rolled someone or whatever, those kinds of things. I'm guessing that probably in other cases, that there may have been women who went into the hotel and perhaps conducted themselves in a more discreet fashion and so maybe they looked the other way in those days. . . . I think it depends on the property. The last property that I was in, the Continental, was a small property and it was never condoned there at all. If we thought that there was a hooker problem, these women were eighty-sixed and they did have their picture taken and if they came in again, they were thrown out. That was the particular philosophy of that property. I've been in larger properties where you have to wonder if it wasn't condoned or made available to the guest that wanted the services. If you have a player and he's a high roller and this is the type of action he wants, the casino may feel it behooves them to try to make him happy. I'm not saying it's right or wrong, but throughout the years I think that certainly did happen. I would guess that they would bring in a girl that to them had a good reputation—that wasn't some kooky kind of person that would bring the whole house down on them.

The levels of different call girls is really something. . . . Your call girls that serviced the hotels at the very highest level, in many cases, those women were good conversationalists. They were very attractive, to say the least, very well dressed, the type of woman that you would want to take into a gourmet room, who you'd want to be seen around town with. And in many cases, the men seemed to like them for their conversation, even because they were well educated. It wasn't some little Lolita that you'd see out in the parking lot. It wasn't that type. It was a very classy-looking woman. . . . Well, there's a lot of hookers who do hang around the hotels. There's no doubt about it. You certainly see it, like when a fight comes to town and all these things. There's out-of-town hookers that come in. . . . For instance, a school teacher, secretary, or whatever in LA would come over on the weekends to Vegas to be a hooker for the weekend. They make tremendous money. Then they would go back and nobody knew about their second life over here.

Although Jaeger took a college course on the hotel business, most of her education about gambling came on the job. She had a fondness for the old-time gamblers and a sense of respect for the path they took to provide for their families.

Chappelle [the hotel director at the Riviera] had a bunch of people around him and I just loved a lot of these older guys. They had been here for years. They were some of the original people that came out here. . . . They all had followings and that's why they were still important to the hotel. They still had friends—usually a contingent of gamblers from wherever they were from—who would still come here. So they still brought business into the hotel, even though they were now getting up in years. A lot of times they didn't have an awful lot to do all day, so they would end up sitting in our office and I sort of babysat this whole crowd. They were fun, though, and I enjoyed that. I learned a lot from these older men. . . .

Many of them had been in gaming somewhere else—in Toledo, Hot Springs, or any of these other towns. You had gambling everywhere. You really did. It was underground, but it was still there. They were young men at the time and [they were] brought up in that industry. There's not a lot of people that can say that. That's really a small group of people who actually ran those gaming places in other cities. . . . A lot of these fellows didn't want to work in the factories or the mines or things like that [where they lived], so [gambling] was something that they preferred. . . . Gaming was everywhere and the men who worked here came from somewhere else and were a part of that. They knew how to run those places. That's why they were valuable here. They started this all up, here. We would never have any of this if they hadn't started it up and kept their thumbs on it and knew how to do it. Not everybody knows how to run a casino, believe me.

I have to say that I learned a lot from Mr. Ed Torres.[6] I really did. This man would spend fifteen minutes in the office. That's as much as I would see of him in a day. He'd come in the office and I'd have his personal checks all prepared for him and he'd sign his name. He had his finger on things. He had only one piece of paper [and] he would refer to that; it told him the whole story of what was going on and that's all he wanted to look at. He looked at the bottom line of that one piece of paper every morning and then I filed it. Then he went away and he spent the whole day walking around the hotel. You never knew where he was going to show up, so everybody was always on their toes. . . . Talking to people who have been in the gaming industry all the way back in the old days before they even came here, they all remark that in the old days when they worked in the joints the owner or his boys were always there on the floor. Somebody was always watching for the owner's interests. I'm sure they do that today, but it can't be quite the same. It's not the same as the owner actually being there, walking floors. I think that makes a big difference.[7]

Torres bought the Aladdin Hotel and Casino with Wayne Newton around 1980. Jaeger and dozens of other employees from the Riviera went to work for him. She became his personal secretary with the plan to learn as much as she could from him about management. However, it didn't work out as she hoped. Torres had no plans to promote her, she soon discovered, so Jaeger used the job to learn as much as possible for the next opportunity. It came when she was hired as the assistant general manager at the Continental Hotel and Casino where she stayed for twelve years. Her time at the property coincided with the implementation of federal affirmative action mandates, rules that sought to bring greater employment opportunities to women and minorities in the gaming industry. The measure met firm resistance and Jaeger offered her perspective on why that would be.

Well, you didn't have any choice. You had to do it. The government was going to make you do it. I think probably some of the old fellows really didn't like it at all. They worried that maybe some of these people that they would have to hire wouldn't be capable, even. Then on top of that you also had the advent of dealers' schools and things where they were just churning people out and sending people out there to get jobs. A lot of times, those people were not always real, real qualified either. . . . They didn't come from that same kind of culture that came out of all these little gaming areas throughout the country and had that background and philosophy. . . . You had the 12.5 percent decree. . . . You had to have a certain amount from the Spanish culture. You had to have a certain amount of women. You had to have all these things that you didn't have to worry about before.[8] . . .

At the Continental we always were real careful to include women. I especially pushed for women. I was a women's studies major, so whatever field, I was always trying to get them in there.[9] We didn't happen to have any [women] crap dealers at the moment and we didn't have very many women dealers at the moment. But it was that they hadn't applied. It wasn't that we would have refused them a position. We just didn't have that many [female] applicants, so that was just kind of a problem. There wasn't much that you could do about it. . . .

[Women] certainly could have made a lot more money dealing than doing any kind of clerical work. That's for sure. Many of the women were taught at dealers' schools; that's how they learned. My husband taught a lot of people, a lot of women to deal. . . . In my living room, usually, at the ironing board. I would set up the ironing board and he would teach people to deal until he got such a big following that he actually built a twenty-one table and we kept it out in the garage. He would teach people to deal there. It had the green felt on it and everything. But there was a lot of money to be made for women dealing, for anybody dealing. I think they may have made more money in the old days, to tell you the truth, than they do today. They do have to split tips up so many ways today.

The local organizing to end job discrimination by race, sex, and national origin led to federal action in 1971 and 1981 with two consent decrees. These agreements among hotel-casinos, labor unions, and the EEOC were the result of years of work on the part of local NAACP, legal aid attorneys, and aggrieved workers. The consent decrees set goals for hiring in types of jobs where women and racial or national groups were poorly represented (dealers, bartenders, as well as management). As Jaeger noted, the properties frequently promoted from within to fulfill their agreements.

They were coming up the rung. Certainly that did happen at the Continental. . . . The slot manager there started out as a change girl. I thought that was always really good, to take somebody that's come up through the ranks, because they know the problems on the floor. . . . These women turned out to be very loyal employees. They appreciated that someone recognized that they had some talent. I found women usually did their homework. They came to a meeting prepared. They don't rely on the secretary to have all the answers gathered for them. They know themselves. I always appreciated that. The women that worked for us were really top notch, just first class. I had a good mentor myself [Inez Rambeau]. To this day, the things I learned, the background I had, things that were important, I did learn from her. And I've always appreciated that and I've always told her that.

I've always felt that women are very good in these positions. I think women make very good hotel managers. I don't see any difference running a house from running a hotel. You do all the same kinds of things. You invite the guest in, you provide a nice bed for them, you make sure the linen is clean. It's all the things you'd do if you were having a visitor at home. You fix them a nice meal. You try to entertain them. You try to have your kids behave and all these kinds of things. That's what you do when you have a hotel. It's just on a grander scale. But if you have that principle—that this is your home and letting that guest know that you're treating them just as you would treat them if they would come into your home—that's it in a nutshell. . . . I've always found if you revert back to that commonsense thing like, "What would I do if this was my own house and how would I handle this?" If you've been a housewife, and boy I sure have been for years, that helps.

Jaeger continued her domestic metaphor in her philosophy on management. She emphasized individual service and an ethic of loyalty that she found similar to that of a family. The fact that she married into the older gambling culture of tradition and loyalty among casino workers influenced her perspectives on federal regulation as well as labor organizations. Both appeared interventionist and counterproductive to her. Yet, as she notes below, she was supportive of women moving into positions of responsibility.

Our business [gambling] was never unionized. In the old days, it was run by people who treated their employees like family. . . . They didn't have unions in any of the places like Hot Springs [Arkansas]. I have never been in a union. When I worked at the Continental, it was not unionized. I think if you can keep your place from becoming union it's much easier to run. . . . I realize that unions are necessary. However, we were able to manage the Continental without a union. . . . I'd worked in other places that had unions. The Riviera had unions. The Aladdin had unions. I know what difficulty that can be, too. I know the expense of the payroll when you had unions. . . .

I did have all kinds of things there to let them know that I really cared or that the company cared. . . . I had an employee emergency fund . . . [so] if they had a death in the family and they had to get on a plane, I was standing at the door with a check. . . . Whatever emergency came up, and there were evictions and there were all kinds of things throughout the years that they needed some extra money for. . . . I didn't see anything wrong with having some kind of matriarchal management there. I was sort of considered the mother hen, but I didn't mind that at all because that's what I wanted to be. I watched how in the old days these men did take care of their employees. . . . And we did the same.

I think it was after some of the older fellows moved on and maybe some younger people came in that you started to see the shift. For so many years, the gentlemen that ran the casinos were not real interested in having women in any kind of casino-oriented management. They really didn't put much credit to anything that we would say or think. They didn't feel that was our place. . . . So many of the women were really getting better educated in the hotel fields and there wasn't really any reason that they couldn't advance. There wasn't anyone really holding them back and more women were getting into a better position so that they were helping these younger women coming on—accepting them as their assistants and protégées and taking them under their wing and really helping them. So I think in the hotel end you did see that. It took a while for the casino end but it's there. . . . The industry is so open [now] and there are women in just every phase of the industry. You certainly see women pit bosses, certainly women baccarat dealers, floor people, no matter what. That wasn't anything that you would see in my day. . . . Never in my lifetime did I expect to see what we have here today. I think there's a lot of opportunity for women. . . .

When the Continental came under new management with the sale of the property, Jaeger decided it was time to change careers. The world of gamblers that she knew and loved had changed dramatically under corporate rules and management. "I just didn't feel like I was as needed as maybe I was once before," she said. In fact, the world of *gambling* had become the world of *gaming.* That transition brought a multitude of changes in regulation and accountability. Hotel-casinos grew bigger, went public, and hired MBAs to run them. Jaeger's style of matriarchal management, as she called it, no longer fit on the landscape of Las Vegas Strip properties.

I always like to go down to the Horseshoe. I think Benny Binion was the master.[10] I used to take my boss down there because I said, "This is 'Casino 101.' Whatever you want to learn about casinos, this is where you're going to learn it." . . . I used to stand there with my boss and say, "Just listen to this." And he'd say, "Well, what are you listening to?" I said, "The sound of the music, the music of the money falling into the slot drop-bins." There was such excitement down there, with the crap games and all of that. . . . You'd hear all those fellows playing at the crap table, and they were yelling. And especially if you'd get a junket in from Texas, they were lettin' out some kind of war whoops. That was such fun. Everything was always at a high pitch down there. And I liked that. That was the way it used to be. All casinos were like that at one time.

Chapter 4

FFOLLIOTT "FLUFF" LeCOQUE

Company Manager

They knew that I was about business.
—Ffolliott "Fluff" LeCoque

From the 1930s to the 1960s hundreds of small clubs and cabarets dotted the landscape of America's large and small cities.[1] Depending on their size and financial backing, the clubs might offer dancing, traveling musicians, and floor shows, but they all offered Americans nightlife entertainment. The Copacabana in New York City, the Cocoanut Grove in Boston; the Palmer House Hotel's Empire Room in Chicago; the Lookout House in Covington, Kentucky; the Latin Quarter of Miami Beach; and the Moulin Rouge in Hollywood are a handful of the clubs. They ranged in entertainment from burlesque to big bands. Some were private clubs, which offered gambling in a back room. Most had a chorus line, a staple of entertainment that offered dancers an opportunity to pursue a career in dance when the concert hall was not an option.

Producers of dance troupes had established networks that provided the entertainment. One producer could have several dance troupes working in numerous clubs at the same time by utilizing the circuit. Some producers had international circuits that toured Europe and South America. Dancers looking for work auditioned at the dance companies' main studios, such as Arden and Fletcher in New York, Moro Landis Dancers in North Hollywood, and Dorothy Dorbin Dancers in Los Angeles. Once hired, the companies sent the dancers where they were needed on the circuit. During the 1940s and 1950s Hollywood musicals offered another venue for dancers, and the talent moved west to follow the jobs and their dreams of stardom in the movies. By the mid-1960s the amount of work for dancers in musicals onstage and onscreen had declined. Las Vegas, however, was expanding its showrooms and creating showroom extravaganzas. All those production shows had jobs for dancers.

Fluff LeCoque's career spanned several decades in this competitive field due to her discipline in dance and her loyalty to a particular type of entertainment developed by her mentor, Donn Arden.[2] Dance and musical theater became the dominant focus of her life from an early age, and she worked continuously in those fields. She first visited Las Vegas in 1947 and returned several times before settling there in 1963. Her narrative discusses the changes that occurred in the organization of club entertainment during her career, the rigors of rehearsals and maintaining ones dance skills, and dancers' parts in the social fabric of the era. Throughout LeCoque spoke about the intersections of work conditions, race relations, and the public's views of women's bodies in the context of showroom entertainment.

LeCoque started when clubs were small and the format featured a line of chorus girls with a headliner. Ambitious and willing to work hard, she took on additional responsibilities with various companies as she moved around the United States and Europe. She became a principal dancer and choreographer within a few years and worked on circuits for choreographer and producer Donn Arden. When business took Arden to different locations, he gave her the responsibility to implement his vision with the dance troupe. LeCoque joined Arden in Las Vegas when the major hotel-casinos became the place to stage large-scale variety productions; eventually she became the company manager. Her story offers the perspective of a mid-century career professional who, instead of pursuing advertising or publishing, built a career in musical theater. The narrative also offers perspectives on the daily regimen of a dancer, the influence of organized crime in club financing, the rise of the showgirl era, and her loyalty to Donn Arden's vision of the showroom extravaganza.

Showgirls were an essential element of Arden's productions. Drawing on the work of Florenz Ziegfeld Jr. and Earl Carroll, Arden capitalized on beautiful bodies as an attraction for his shows. When he brought a version of the French production "Lido de Paris" to the Stardust Hotel and Casino in Las Vegas in 1958, he introduced Americans to the Bluebell Girls and propelled the shift to partially nude showroom entertainment. Arden and LeCoque teamed up again in 1981 on "Jubilee!"—a production that remained the standard for classic showgirl entertainment in Las Vegas. LeCoque said of Arden's use of women's bodies, "You can't say it's not for sexual attraction. But it's not meant to be pornographic like a strip club. . . . He wanted to beautify women."[3]

LeCoque remembers always dancing as a young child in Butte, Montana. Her formal instruction came later, when the family moved to Seattle. At the age of seven she began taking lessons from Ruth White, a devotee of Isadora Duncan, who had a school in Seattle. Her next teacher was Arville Avery, who had been with Fanchon and Marco, a big road company that toured the United States. She continued training in dance and theater during college.[4]

I went to the University of Washington on an Evergreen drama scholarship for four years. At that time they had two theaters there: the theater-in-the-round, which was conceived and built by Glen Hughes. It was the first theater-in-the-round in the entire country. It was called the Penthouse Theater and it's still operating today and my name is in flagstone in the courtyard. Then the other theater was a legitimate theater called the Showboat. . . . We used to work in those theaters all the time. If you weren't acting, you were doing props or scenery or costumes or selling tickets or doing something in the theater. It was really wonderful training because it was like a job. . . . Those two theaters were really, really great. Each play ran six weeks, six nights a week, in length. So during the four years I did a lot of shows.

I also had a dancing school when I was going to college. . . . I used to give the football players ballet lessons. . . . They came and asked me if I would give their football team dancing lessons for coordination so they could pivot fast, turn fast, and they could jump. So I said, "Sure." I had this dancing school right on University Way, but the football players would sneak in the back door because they didn't want anybody to know they were taking ballet classes. That didn't last very long. . . .

I left college to go on the road with a little road company called Embassy Company. We joined Junior Equity and we went first to Spokane. The guy that put this all together, he and his wife were old vaudevillians and they had done a lot of road shows, tap shows, things like that. So he got the idea of putting this company together and he had all these young kids, you know, his wife and himself included. We were all excited. I packed up my trunks and I thought, "I won't be coming home again." Now this was during the first years of the Second World War. . . .

It was the middle of winter and we worked in this theater on Skid Row and it was cold. You'd look up where the skylight was and all the glass had been knocked out and the pigeons used to roost in there. What would happen is all the alcoholics, all the winos, and everything on Skid Row would buy a ticket to this theater and then they'd go in and they'd sleep all day in there. Right next door was a whorehouse. Well, I didn't know anything. I was really dumb and stupid, very innocent in those days. . . . Oh, we had so much fun. We did *Arsenic and Old Lace,* and we did all the old things that you didn't have to pay any royalties on. It lasted about three weeks and then one day we went down to get our money at the box office and the woman said, "Well, there isn't any money here for you." So we went to find the owner of this company and of course he'd split. He just left us all stranded, high and dry. So I said, "I'm not going home. I made my decision. I'm going to go on with my career."

My girlfriend and I decided we would head back to New York. But in the meantime we would go stay with her family for a while in Montana and get rested up. We had enough money to buy a train ticket and it was a troop train going back East. There were only two seats available because all these kids were going back East to be shipped out. . . . They were cooking over Sterno in the aisles and everybody trying to sleep and oh, it was some kind of a trip. . . . Then I called home and said, "I think I'd better come home. I don't have any money." That was the first time I left home. I went back to school for another year, on scholarship again. I worked in quite a few shows.

I came to Las Vegas for the first time in 1947. I came here as a singer with a band, Chuck Gould's Orchestra, and we played at the Last Frontier Hotel for six weeks. At that time, there was only the Last Frontier and the El Rancho Vegas and a place called the Bingo Club, which is now the Sahara. And out on the highway [the Las Vegas Strip] there was the Red Rooster owned by Grace Hayes. She was quite famous. I got the job because I went with the orchestra leader. I really could not consider myself a singer, but I looked good and I could play the maracas. In those days every band had a girl singer. . . . My stint was playing the maracas and singing songs for the dinner show. . . .

Well, in those days they used to have dinner dancing. The Last Frontier Hotel had a dance floor and tables all around the dance floor. The band was up on a slightly raised platform about two and one-half or three feet. So the band would play music for the people while they danced. You know, they had their dinner and then they would ballroom dance on the floor and then after a certain period of time the main show would come on. Two shows a night. The show usually consisted of a line of girls and two acts. First a chorus line of girls, then an act, the girls did another number, and then the star would come on, like Liberace or somebody. That was the format. And that remained the format for a long, long time until the "Folies Bergere" came here and the "Lido de Paris." Then it changed.[5]

I was awed because it was a place where all the movie stars came. It was glamorous. I had never seen anything like a resort with a pool out there and gambling and all these people would dress in Western clothes all day long. Then at night they would get all dressed up in their gowns and be very, very elegant. I was impressed with that of course. But I would never gamble. I still don't gamble.

I never got involved with anybody. Once again, not consciously thinking about it, but having seen the girls that did get involved, it just didn't seem right to me. I wasn't a prude because I was living with somebody and not married, but I just didn't want to mix my business with pleasure. And you know that paid off very well in the long run because the gentlemen that I worked for—and they were always gentlemen to me—knew that they could trust me and they respected me. They knew that I was about business. I was about taking care of my business as a dancer or a company manager or whatever. There were lots of opportunities, but I just knew that was not for me. So it was a good policy.

After the Frontier, I went to California and worked in Hollywood. Then I came back again to do a show at what was then the Thunderbird Hotel for Hal Braudis who was the entertainment and publicity director. He and his wife had a production company. . . . I danced in the chorus. When I was at the Thunderbird, I got this call from some people I had met in Hollywood who were putting together a show to go to Paris called the "Hollywood Extravaganza." They said, "If you would like to do it, come to Hollywood, and talk to the producer." So I went in and they hired me right away. . . . He signed me up and then in November we went to Paris.

At the age of twenty-six years, LeCoque assisted the manager with arrangements for the dancers to get to Europe. The dancers performed three shows a day, seven days a week. After about a year, she returned to New York City.

I got off the boat in New York with $20 in my pocket and I headed for the Roosevelt Hotel, which was the only hotel I knew. I had to pay the cab driver $20 to get my trunk and my luggage from the pier to the hotel. So here I am in the hotel and I don't have a dime. So I get out my best clothes and I go looking for a job. I went to the Copacabana and they would have a job for me in twelve days. I couldn't wait that long. And I went other places. I finally wound up in the Donn Arden and Ron Fletcher offices in New York and I said, "I'm looking for work." . . .

The Arden-Fletcher Dancers were based in New York, but you must realize that there was a huge nightclub circuit in those days. Every major city in the country had one or two or three or four or several nightclubs where stars would perform. They'd put on a floor show, the orchestra was behind. Because they changed the stars like every week or every two weeks in order to bring customers in, they would hire these various choreographers to put a line of girls in there. With this huge network of nightclubs all over the country, the choreographers would have a home base. They would create the routines, do the costumes, hire girls, and send them out to the various places to work. At the time I started working with Donn Arden, he had productions at the Desert Inn in Las Vegas, the Riviera just outside New York, the Lido in Paris, he had shows in Italy and South America, the Lookout House in Cincinnati, something in Miami, Florida. He must have had about ten different places where he had dance groups working. . . . Frank Sennes booked the entertainment for most of these places. It was all mob connected; the mobs owned the nightclubs. So once you got in, you know, you had a pretty good working circuit. That's the way it worked. And of course you make a success one place and they want you someplace else. . . .

They asked if I wanted to go to Cincinnati in three days. I said, "I'll go." So I wired my dad for some money. I said, "I'll pay you 10 percent [interest] if you loan me this money." He did. And that's how I wound up at the Lookout House in Cincinnati.[6] . . .

LeCoque did not know that her professional career would be linked to Donn Arden for the next several decades. Arden had attended her show in Paris with another famed dance entrepreneur, Madame Bluebell.[7] At the time, LeCoque was the principal dancer for his Lookout House show, but only vaguely knew Arden and Madame Bluebell. Bluebell and Arden worked together after World War II at the Lido in Paris and formed a long partnership. She hired dancers and he choreographed shows.

So, the Lookout House in Cincinnati was a very, very famous nightclub at that time. Actually it was in Covington, Kentucky, across the river because Ohio didn't have gambling and Kentucky did. The Lookout House and the Riverside were both big gambling casinos. Of course they were run by the mob—the Cleveland syndicate. The Lookout House was typical of the nightclubs in that era. It had gambling and a big bar, and they had a dining room–showroom with the stage raised up so that people could have dinner [and then] dancing. . . . The band was on the stage and whenever [people] finished their dinner, usually when dessert was being served, then the show would start.

They had the same old format: a line of eight to ten chorus girls would do an opening production then they'd have an act, then the girls would do another production, and then usually the star came on. And that would close the show. So it was like two dance numbers that the girls did. We did two shows a night, seven days a week. We didn't have any days off. And we changed shows. Every two weeks they'd have a new headliner in. And sometimes it would be every week they'd have a new headliner in. So that usually meant that the dancers would be rehearsing in the daytime and performing at night. And if it was a change of show every week, that's what would happen. . . . I stayed there for about six months doing different shows.

While I was at the Lookout House, I heard that the Desert Inn was doing a new showroom.[8] . . . They were actually going to take the band off the stage and put them to the side. And there was going to be a revolving stage with staircases coming down from the sides. So you would go up the back and come down the side to make your entrance. . . . Donn Arden wanted to do more-elaborate numbers instead of just dance numbers. He was putting together a miniature production, meaning that he would have more diversification as far as dancers were concerned. . . . He wanted to know if I wanted to come out to Las Vegas to open the new showroom. And I said, "Well yes, of course." So at the end of the six months in Cincinnati, I came back to Las Vegas and started rehearsing for the new shows that were going to go in this room.

Now this was an innovation for Las Vegas showrooms. First of all, it was the first time the band would be off the stage. The band would be to the side of the stage. We would be able to have sets. We had props before, but you could never have sets. You could never have a backdrop thing. It was always the band in the background. We were going to do what they called miniproductions. Now instead of just a line of girls getting out and doing a dance routine to a certain song, these productions were going to have a little storyline, which had never been done before. And besides just having girl dancers, there were going to be boy dancers as well—and a principal girl singer and a principal male singer. So that was an innovation and that was the first time that was really done in Las Vegas. . . . The stage had a revolve in the center so you could have a set piece on it and it could revolve around. It also had a rain curtain—a very pretty effect. . . . There's a pipe running across the front of the scene and in the floor, on the stage, there has to be a trough to catch the water. There was a little area with a lid on it and they'd press a button and the lid would flip up and underneath there would be a metal tray to catch the water, and it would drain and it would be recycled and pumped back out. It literally is raining. It's very pretty.

Frank Sennes, the entertainment director, was in charge of hiring entertainment and the acts for the people that ran the Desert Inn. He also had the Frank Sennes Agency and worked with his three brothers all over the country. Frank was going to open a big theater in Hollywood, right off Sunset and Vine, the old Earl Carroll Theater.[9] So they were going to do productions there and Donn asked me if I would like to go. I would be a principal dancer, company captain, and production manager. And I said, "Yes!" . . . When Donn would do a show, he would come in and do the show and then he would leave it because he had to go someplace else to create another show. So a production manager was left in charge when he was gone. That's what I did. I put it together. . . . I had to hire the cast. I did the choreography. I got all the music together. I taught all the girls, all the boys, all the boy singers, all the girl singers, and I was the principal dancer and I had no understudy. . . . I was in Hollywood for maybe ten years at the Moulin Rouge. Six days a week. We did six production shows and they all ran about a year and a half or something like that. . . . Then Donn called me and said that they were redoing the showroom at the Desert Inn, putting in a bigger stage, and wanted to know if I would come to Las Vegas. It was about 1963, and I was divorced, so I said, "Yes. I'll come."

By the time I came back in the '60s, four hotels had the big extravaganza shows. There was the "Lido [de Paris]" at the Stardust, there was the Desert Inn, there was the "Folies Bergere" at the Tropicana, the Dunes had "Casino de Paris." . . . Well, the "Lido" was nude, the "Folies Bergere" was nude, "Casino" was nude. At the Desert Inn we didn't have any—yes, we did too, I take that back. We did too have nudes.

Miss Bluebell would hire the girls in Europe. Primarily she stayed in Europe because she was connected with the "Lido de Paris" there. So when they started bringing shows from Europe to here, Miss Bluebell would do the casting except for the principal dancers. Donn would usually oversee

Fluff LeCoque at the Lido in Paris, ca. 1960s. *Left to right:* Rene Fraday, Donn Arden, Margaret Kelly, Pierre Lewis-Guerin, Ffolliott "Fluff" Charlton (LeCoque). Courtesy of Special Collections, University Libraries, UNLV.

that. . . . There would be a lot of American dancers who would go over to Europe and then they would be rehearsed there and then they would come back here. But they were always billed as a European troupe. I was kind of awe struck with the glamour of it all. . . . I admired them. I didn't have any resentment. I didn't have any feelings that they were taking jobs away from me. But I was in a totally different field. . . .

In the early, early days, like when I first came to Las Vegas and was at the Last Frontier, [dancers] didn't mix. That was not required. It really didn't start to happen until they started building more hotels, like the Flamingo and the Desert Inn, and the El Rancho Vegas. . . . So then the whole idea was to have beautiful girls just for atmosphere, really. Just for atmosphere. It would be a draw. . . . Later, dancers had to mix. That meant that you would have to stay in between shows and they wanted the girls to sit in the bar. And you usually had to stay from one to two hours after the shows and dress the bar. Now if you wanted to gamble with somebody, you could do that, but they wanted you to stay there. So we all had to dress up. I mean it wasn't like coming to work in jeans or shorts and going home. You had to come to work dressed, like in cocktail dresses, and hang around. You weren't forced to mix but if somebody said, "I'd like to introduce you to," and "Have a drink with this [person]," you were expected to. There was never anything [like] you had to go to bed with him, but you were supposed to entice them to get to the tables. . . . When Bluebell came in she said, "I'm not going to allow my girls to mix. I will not let them sit out at the bar and I don't want anybody calling them out of the show to go out and meet somebody." . . . So Miss Bluebell put a stop to that [with her dancers]. . . . But as far as having out-and-out prostitutes or call girls, I'm sure all the hotels did. . . . It's a service. But it's very, very hush-hush. It's handled very well. Security knows all the girls that come in off the street and they eighty-six them right now. . . .

▨ The public perception of a showgirl was that she was sexually promiscuous and yet in interview after interview narrators refuted the idea. Since LeCoque was at the helm of creating shows that utilized both dancers and showgirls, she was asked how this misperception not only survived, but also thrived.

Truthfully, when people see a picture of a nude girl or know that you're working topless, because it's never totally nude, people think you're exploiting yourself. You're exploiting your sex. You're exploiting women. They think it's shameful. And they do think that, even to this day. You can't blame them for thinking that, "Well, any woman that does that is opening herself up for marketing." But we know that there are all shades of it. You have all the strip joints and I know a lot of those girls. They're married, have two or three kids, and they're making money. They make good money down there. Why is it we do this? It's because men want to see you. Men want to see you and yet they'll call you a prostitute even if you don't do anything.

In addition to mixing, dancers frequently were asked to partake in publicity events for the property at which they worked. From photographs to riding on floats, the dancers who dressed the bar also became models for public relations.

We all did publicity free. We posed for pictures. We did interviews. We did anything and were not paid for it. . . . I posed as Miss Thunderbird and thought nothing about it. I was never too concerned about how much money I was making in those days. I just loved to work. And the pleasure of having your photograph taken and being in the newspapers and all that kind of Hollywoodish thing that we all grew up with in that day and age. And you did get taken advantage of, if that's the way you felt. I personally never moaned and groaned about it because I enjoyed doing it. But there were other people who said, "Well, we ought to get paid for this." And that's when the union started coming in. Truthfully, they were right. . . .

Before there was any kind of a union or anything, if you broke your leg or something, you were out. They would replace you. They might assist you in some ways, but most of the time it was your tough luck. . . . I broke this big toe and I went on and performed. I painted my feet like ballet slippers, painted them, did my show and my toe was all swollen up. We had no understudies. Then I went to the doctor because I literally could not walk the next day, could absolutely not walk at all. . . . Stupid. Stupid in one way because I probably went through a lot of damage that I wouldn't have had to go through if I had insurance coverage. But on the other hand it gave me tenacity, well I had it anyway, but it was just my training. You just go on, you just keep going on. . . .

If you had a cold, I mean, what's a cold? I've danced when I had a 105 temperature. I remember at the Desert Inn, I came off from a number and I lay down in the hallway outside the dressing room on a bench out there. I was just burning up. Sam Tucker, who was the head of the Cleveland syndicate at that time, was at the Desert Inn. He happened to be walking down the hallway and he came over and said, "What's the matter, Fluff?" And I said, "Oh, I don't know. I'm just so hot." He put his hand on my head and he said, "You stay right here." He called the doctor and the doctor came and I had a 105-degree fever. He gave me a shot and said, "You go home." I said, "I have to do a show. I have to do the next show." They said, "No you don't. You go home." So they carted me home. I couldn't even walk. It broke the fever and I was back to work the next day. . . .

It's a godsend that there is insurance now, that they do have medical coverage. I think it's wonderful. And like I said, some people don't take advantage of it. But you have it there so you don't have to work when you're severely injured. And you do have some kind of disability so that you can survive if you are injured. I don't know, maybe I was just fortunate in those early days that nothing serious happened. . . .

We didn't belong to any unions when I started. There were unions. There was the AGVA, American Guild of Variety Artists. . . . When I was at the Moulin Rouge in Hollywood, I had contracts and AGVA was there. Everybody had to belong to the union. They would come around and everybody had to sign up. It was very successful. I mean LA was a very union town. . . . A lot of the acts belonged to AGVA because they all worked Hollywood, [and] they worked the East Coast. Remember, it was a big circuit so the union was beneficial because it set certain standards. . . .

AGVA was pretty strong in Las Vegas, because they sent their representatives up from California in 1963. . . . Even though Nevada is a right-to-work state, the union would put the pressure on you. They would come and say, "You need to belong." If somebody said no, well they didn't have to, but they usually wound up joining, because through AGVA at least you got insurance. As little as it was, you still got insurance. . . .

Of course, Donn never liked the unions because it put restrictions on him. For example, when we were rehearsing, someone would say, "Break." And he would say, "I'm not finished yet. You have to take your break later." And the unions would say, "You need a salary raise." They operated like all unions do. So for management it wasn't good because they couldn't get away with things. . . .

When it got to the point that the hotels decided that they were going to offer the dancers a better contract and more insurance and more coverage than the union could provide, that's when it started to switch over. And that's what the hotels have done. Now you have SIIS [State Industrial Insurance

System] accident insurance. You would never have gotten that if it had not been for unions. The unions set the standard and raised the living standard all over the country, but now corporations are offering better advantages than what the union could offer. But the problem is that even though that happens, if you're let go by the corporations or hotels or businesses your insurance and everything automatically stops. . . .

When LeCoque returned to Las Vegas, she performed in several Arden productions: "Hello America," "Hello America II," "1968 Pzazz," and "1970 Pzazz." She was a principal dancer when she was in her forties, then became company manager. She had been combining roles as performer and manager for years. Then the transition gradually occurred. She remembered, "As I got older, instead of being in every production number, I was in maybe two. And then I got to be in one. And then finally it got to be that I was more a company manager than a performer." Remarried again, she decided to hang up her shoes for good in the early 1970s. In a field where dancers are considered over the hill at thirty, LeCoque had danced until she was forty-five. Retirement lasted only a short time. In September 1973 Arden asked her to be his company manager for the productions at the MGM Grand Hotel and she remained in that position until her retirement in 2012. They opened "Hallelujah Hollywood" in the Ziegfeld Room at MGM Grand in 1978. "Jubilee!" opened at the MGM Grand on July 30, 1981.[10] Bob Mackie designed the costumes and Madame Bluebell assisted with the selection of dancers. The show became known as the spectacle to see for Las Vegas showgirl entertainment.

The rise of showroom extravaganzas coincided with the end of de facto racial discrimination in Las Vegas's public accommodations and employment. While African American acts had long been a staple of showroom entertainment, they worked within a segregated context. In 1960 an accord among civil rights leaders, politicians, and business people opened casinos to patrons regardless of race. Nevertheless, actual integration of many sectors of the workforce, including the showroom, took much longer to implement. LeCoque noted that when she returned to work in Las Vegas black acts played in the showrooms, but dance lines were not integrated. She offered her own explanation for the slow process of integration.

In 1974 we were doing a show called "Hallelujah Hollywood" at the MGM and Donn hired a line of black girls and two male black dancers, Allen Weeks and Winston Dewitt Hensley, and one principal black girl dancer/singer, Patrice Chanel. They were not integrated into the other line or other numbers. It wasn't mixed. They stayed in their own group. . . . They were stunning, beautiful girls. Most of them were at least six feet tall. It was exciting to see them onstage primarily because it was the first time that they had been used as dancers in a production show in Las Vegas. There may have been one or two scattered here and there throughout the years but this was a group of black dancers. And they were gorgeous.[11] . . .

The black girl dancers had their own dressing room. The two principal boys were in the principal's dressing room. Patrice Chanel was in the principal girl's dressing room. Then, as time went by and I had to find replacements for the black girl dancers, I hired a white girl, Diana Saunders, who was in their dressing room. The reason for that is because all the costumes that are alike stay in one place. So that the dressers who have to dress that group know exactly where they have to take those costumes or return the costumes. If you had them all mixed up all over, it would be too much for everybody to remember. Even now the topless girls are in one area and the dressed dancers are in two different areas because of the logistics of the dressing rooms. But they stay in their groups because that way the dressers know where the costumes have to go. . . .

When we started "Jubilee!" in 1981, then we had a line of black girls and a line of black male dancers, but no singers. It always depends on the people that come to audition for you. There was a big movement for integration and we had been criticized because we did hire black people, but we didn't integrate them. And we didn't start breaking up the lines until maybe eight years ago [1989], not out of prejudice or anything, but simply because of the way the show was set up. I could see how Donn was thinking about costuming—everything was geared to show off their beauty. It's a mindset that you have and it's very hard to break that pattern sometimes. You think of it as this way and then all of a sudden to mix it up, it throws the balance off. I mean if you have one black girl over there and none on that side, it doesn't balance. So that's the way we were all geared to thinking about it. Then once I started to change it, it doesn't make any difference at all. And that's the way it should be. . . .

There was a certain amount of pressure because at that time the NAACP was setting quotas. I mean, you have to have so many black people, so many minorities, in your show. And I was saying, "That's true and that's fine but what if I don't find somebody qualified? First of all, I'm responsible for the quality of the show, and if I don't find a black dancer that comes up to par, I'm not going hire her." You did feel pressure because you had a certain amount of black people in the show and you wanted to keep that quota but then as we started changing over and we started integrating I said, "Well now, wait a minute. If people are qualified, whether they're singers or dancers or nudes, they should be hired." And it made it easier, actually, because there were many times when wonderful black people would come and I didn't have an opening for them. I might have an opening in the white line, but at that time I wasn't given authority to hire somebody. . . . I always had to go to the bosses for approval of whoever I was going to hire. I had to take the pictures. They wanted to see them. I would audition. So I didn't have free rein. When Mr. Joel Fischman came in, he said, "That's your business, that's your department, you take care of it."[12] . . .

Entertainers don't really see color; they see talent—more than those outside of the entertainment world. But you have to admit that because of the prejudices that you grew up with, even though you were open minded, you were still a little apprehensive until you got to know the people. Once you got to know the people, all barriers were down. But it's the initial approach. Until you got to know them as people, even though you accepted them as people and appreciated their talent, until you got to know them, there was always a slight barrier. But once you were over that barrier, that's the right thing. But it's because of our childhood upbringing. It wasn't only prejudices against blacks. It was the Japanese, the Chinese, and before that it was the Irish and the Germans. Everybody had their prejudice. . . .

"Jubilee!" is classical now. This is the kind of show that people used to expect of Las Vegas when they came here with all the girls and all the dancers. As long as we keep it up and keep it fresh, it's the epitome of a Las Vegas show. . . . The "Folies Bergere" started it because they were the first ones to go topless. The girls used to wear pasties. But they only had one line of nude girls and that was something in those days. But now it's different. I've got thirty nudes out working in our show. Not in every number. And they dance. They're not just mannequins. They don't just parade. We have ninety-four people in the show. . . .

For a while everybody had to be skinny, but anorexic-looking women onstage are not pleasant to look at. You want to see slim, trim bodies. When I say trim, by that I mean you want to see tight bodies. Even with the boys. . . . We're in the business of when people look at you they want to admire you. They expect to see perfection. Nobody's perfect but we have to get as close to it as possible. . . . Some people, they put that pressure on themselves, but they're sick. They look at themselves and they see themselves as fat and [they] might just be nothing but bones. They have an emotional disorder, there. I have had anorexic dancers and I've had to let them go. It's sad. . . . I don't go by poundage anyway because everybody's frame is different. You have some very, very slender-framed girls. You have some larger-framed girls. I just say, "I don't want to see any bones and I don't want to see any bulges, so that's up to you." It depends on how the girl or boy looks. That is our business. . . .

When Hollywood was running a lot of musicals and there were a lot of musicals on Broadway, everybody wanted to be a star. They wanted to get in the movies. They wanted to get on Broadway. So they may not have been as well trained as some of the dancers are today, but they had more ambition to make something of themselves. Then all of that started to fade out. The Hollywood musical scene went downhill. Broadway started going downhill. There were no musicals. The generation of dancers that grew up in that era started to see that being in this business was not going to give them stardom. . . .

In the last ten years dancers have begun to see that very few are able to make a living after a certain age being a dancer. So they take advantage of the university and study something else that they can do after this career is over. That reality changes your work ethic in this respect—the show becomes a job. It's not a matter of love. It's a job. It changes your work ethic, your approach to theater. It changes the spark that you have onstage.

LeCoque's career offers a unique perspective on women's professional achievements in the long postwar era. She married, and she had a career in dance. She pursued musical theater and danced until age forty-five. Her move into management—a career achievement—came before the implementation of equity laws. In a business that focused on beauty and bodies, LeCoque remained staunchly unapologetic. She focused on the art form of which she had been a part for decades and saw the work of nude dancers as a way to earn a living. More than other narrators, LeCoque's experiences bridged the subjective and objective position when examining the way in which women's bodies were used to build the entertainment. Although many conclude that the naked female body represents the objectification of the female form, LeCoque argued that the dancer held the power. The dancer used her nudity to compel viewers' appreciation, while remaining aloof and unattainable, yet well paid. While some would liken that response to the expansion of strip clubs, LeCoque adamantly set the showroom performers apart from those in strip venues and declared those performers to be a form of art.

Chapter 5

GAIL McQUARY, JANET KRAVENKO, AND D. D. COTTON

Dancers

I knew what I wanted to do was be a dancer.
—Gail McQuary

Dancers gave Las Vegas showroom entertainment of the postwar decades its structure. The headliner may have brought in the people, but the chorus-line dancers gave the performance its structure by opening and closing the show. In the earliest years, physical appearance could replace professional training for a few. Jack Entratter, entertainment director for the Sands, advertised openings for chorines with an ad stating "All you have to be is beautiful." However, most dancers started in their youth with professional dance training and maintained their skills with classes. Performance standards rose steadily as the venues grew from small clubs of the 1950s to technically complex showrooms of the 1970s. Grueling rehearsal schedules and, at times, dangerous settings tempered the glamour of the job. Nearly every narrator recalled an example of working with an injury or illness, and remembered the challenges of navigating stairs and sets with heavy headdresses and shoulder harnesses. Dancers and showgirls brought the glamorous veneer that became the iconic visual symbol that attracted men and women to the gambling center, particularly in the decades from the 1950s through the 1970s. Despite their ubiquitous presence, our knowledge of showroom dancers and the roles they played creating the Las Vegas spectaculars has remained superficial beyond the dance community. The invisibility of such a visible feature of that era's entertainment provoked an exploration into the lives and experiences of women who danced in Las Vegas showrooms.[1]

The audience viewed dancers and showgirls interchangeably, but the producers and performers did not. The spectacle production shows produced by Donn Arden and Frederick Apcar, for example, built on the early-twentieth-century impresarios such as Florenz Ziegfeld, Busby Berkeley, and Earl Carroll with their use both of female mannequins and of dancers. Distinctions existed between the two since the 1958 introduction of showgirls to Las Vegas in "Lido de Paris." A dancer danced and a showgirl posed. The term *mannequin* aptly described the showgirl's primary role—to pose. Donn Arden, who brought the Paris show to the Stardust, insisted on a specific height and appearance and taught his performers what they called the Arden walk, which moved the pelvis in a sensual manner as the showgirl moved across the stage. The "Lido" differed from burlesque, which had been a mainstay in

Las Vegas with strippers like Candy Barr and Tempest Storm, according to Fluff LeCoque. The job of a showgirl, she said, was "to be mysterious. She has a certain mystique about her. The true showgirl does not sell."[2] Despite the public's correlation of nudity with sexual promiscuity, LeCoque made the distinction in terms of performance. Even though she was topless, the showgirl performed sexuality, yet remained inaccessible. The intent of the producer to idealize the female form and the perception of some viewers continued to be at odds. Local journalists pointed out that dissonance in stories. One article noted a survey by a local hotel that asked visitors to categorize women in Las Vegas. The two most-frequent responses were that Las Vegas women were showgirls and hookers. In contrast to the visitors' view, the local articles emphasized the people behind the performers.[3] By the late 1970s showgirls were everywhere in Las Vegas entertainment. Over time the showgirl also danced.

This chapter departs from others by including selections from three individuals' narratives. One single narrative could not convey the range and diversity of the dancers' backgrounds. Even then, the subject of dancers and showgirls deserves a fuller discussion than this chapter provides. These three narratives convey the variety of paths taken for dancers who came to Las Vegas during the era of rapid casino expansion. My commentary places those experiences within the wider historical context. Between 1940 and 1980 job opportunities for most women continued to be structured by gender, with a majority working as a waitress, secretary, or sales woman. These narrators chose the chorus line over those jobs because of their passion for dance, desire to have fun, and curiosity to explore the country (and the world) with their dance companies.

The first narrator, Gail McQuary, wanted to dance and started right out of high school. When she had the opportunity to dance at the Sahara Hotel and Casino, she jumped at it. After several years, McQuary left the stage and built a successful real estate business in Las Vegas. The second narrator, British-born Janet Kravenko, arrived with the second group of "Lido de Paris" dancers. One of the Bluebell Girls, Kravenko had no trouble finding jobs even after she married. When she left the stage, she opened her own dance studio.

The majority of images of dancers and showgirls of the postwar era portray white women, yet an influential world of showroom dance existed alongside the more frequently noted achievements of African Americans in music.[4] The development of Las Vegas as the entertainment capital of the world coincided with the transition from race discrimination to equal employment. With few exceptions, African Americans performed solo or in all-black groups, leaving integration of the chorus line until the 1980s.[5] D. D. Cotton, like other African American dancers, performed in cabaret and musical theater productions in all-black troupes and worked on racially segregated circuits. One of those stops for Cotton was Las Vegas, where she met her future husband. Without the opportunity to dance in any of the Las Vegas showrooms, Cotton worked in a variety of positions and assisted the NAACP to open all jobs to people of color and to all women.

In contrast to the differences among the performers, dancers shared many experiences in common. They all spoke of the physically hard work, the schedules without a day off, the

Headliner Pearl Bailey, 1958. Bailey made it a point to perform with a racially integrated line of dancers at a time when Las Vegas did not integrate chorus lines. Courtesy of Las Vegas News Bureau.

ingenious ways in which they combined work with family life, and the perpetual question of "What next?" when the stage career ended. These themes appeared throughout each narrative.

The popular representations of dancers and showgirls in advertising, fiction, and film have shaped our understandings of these performers. Since the first woman performed on the stage, society has labeled her a public woman, a woman of loose morality. These narratives take us to the other side—that is, the subjective experience of the dancer as a worker, an artist, a mother, and a performer. Most notably, the following narratives introduce dancers as they see themselves, thus adding to and challenging the dominant narrative that portrays them as others wanted them seen.

> We were the Saharem Dancers. "There's only twelve of us in
> the whole world that's on the stage, guys."
> —Gail McQuary

Between the early 1940s and the early 1960s, many Las Vegas showrooms followed a simple entertainment format. A line of dancers opened the show with a routine, a second act (a comedian, jugglers, or adagio dancers) followed, and then the featured entertainer performed. The show closed with another routine by the chorus line. A shift occurred in the 1970s when the large revues and production numbers became the star. Chapter 4 discussed Donn Arden's enormous stage productions at several properties. Some showrooms tried to introduce Broadway shows. All of these shows hired dancers.

Gail McQuary came from a musical family. Her mother played trombone professionally with Babe Egan and Her Hollywood Redheads, and her father played saxophone with a group that traveled internationally. She began dance instruction at five years old with tap and ballet lessons. The family moved to California around 1948 or 1949, and she continued dance lessons and performances through high school. In her senior year a dance teacher encouraged her to audition for Moro Landis Studios. The company had several dance troupes that worked across the country and they could offer her an opportunity to continue to dance. She followed her teacher's advice, and shortly after graduation received a call from the studio asking if she wanted to audition for the Sacramento State Fair. She got the job and started rehearsals immediately for a two-week job as a dancer in a sixteen-dancer tiller line.[6] McQuary remembered, "We did a routine before that and then we would end up with all the kicks—the tiller line. So we're kicking our little fannies off from morning till night. I lost weight, I couldn't move, my feet were all bleeding. It was just a gruesome thing, but I'm in show business. I've got my chance." Just before the Sacramento Fair job ended, a principal for the Moro Landis Studios approached McQuary and asked if she wanted to work in Las Vegas at the Sahara Hotel with the company. After consulting her parents, Gail agreed to become one of the Saharem Dancers in 1957.[7]

So I did it.[8] It was like, "Oh my God. Now I'm really in the big leagues." You know, you dream about this all your life. I knew that I was going to be a dancer from the time I was two years old. . . . I knew what I wanted to do was be a dancer. And I could care less where it was. But now the opportunity came and I could not throw it away, at all. I could not throw it away, so I took it. It was wonderful. . . . I was still eighteen when I was dancing in Las Vegas. . . .

[I] had to get there by seven o'clock because we had to get our makeup on and get ready. The show was at eight. We do eight to nine fifteen or nine-thirty show. Then we'd mix to eleven, and then we'd go back to the dressing room, get ready for the twelve o'clock show, do a twelve o'clock show which would be over by one, one fifteen, one thirty. And then we'd mix to two thirty and I'd say, "OK, bye." And I'd walk back by myself on the Strip—or it was Fifth Street, still is—to Boston, to my little apartment. . . . Then you'd get up the next morning and go to rehearsals. That's all I did was rehearse and do the shows. But it was exciting. My first job there at the Sahara, I worked five months without a night off. They had no swing girls. You worked all the time. I made $125 a week for working seven nights a week, rehearsing almost every day, and doing three shows on Friday and Saturday nights. Yes. And I loved every minute of it. . . . Not one night off for five months. . . .

Everything that you touched in Las Vegas in that era was nothing but class. Everybody dressed up. When people came to Las Vegas it was like going to a gourmet restaurant, you know, where you had to dress up and you had to act the part. And people did, whether they had the money or not, they dressed up because this was the place to come to dress up. That's it. End of conversation. You know, you wore the minks, the fur, everything. No matter what the weather was like out there, you dressed up. . . .

Every night I dressed up because between shows we had to look beautiful and pretty. And then after the show we always dressed up and we would go out and sit and mix until two thirty. And then, if we didn't have a rehearsal the next day, we'd go out and go to another club, you know, go hear Vic Damone singing or something like that. I mean, we had the opportunity to hear all these wonderful, fabulous entertainers and it cost us what, a dollar for a drink? I mean, it was amazing, absolutely amazing. . . .

The dancers frequently mentioned the added job benefit of being treated like a celebrity. Those interviewed took no umbrage when asked to volunteer to pose for public relations photos or special events that advertised the hotel-casinos. For many of them, it was a component of the prestige afforded to them and signified its own type of power. For McQuary, mixing was an element of that celebrity. In her view, it was a social aspect of the job with no strings attached. The requirement for dancers and showgirls to mix with the customers in between shows varied among properties. As we will see in the second narrative, some companies would not allow mixing in their contracts. African American entertainers were not allowed in the restaurants or casinos until after 1960. Unrelated to job requirements, the African American dancers and musicians, excluded by segregation, partied together in the clubs of West Las Vegas.

The girls, the dancers, . . . when we sign a contract, is that after the first show you would go out front, which meant the cocktail lounge or the corner bar or any bar, go to the coffee shop if you didn't drink and you just wanted to eat something. But it was the idea that you had to make a presence in the hotel, to look pretty, to make everything nice. And we did that and I never had a problem with that. In fact, I sort of liked it because we'd get dressed up and people would come up and sometimes they'd ask us for our autographs, sometimes they talked to us. We had a great time. And then after the second show we did the same thing until two thirty [in the morning]. We had to mix until two thirty. We did not have to sit with customers. What we did was pretty up the place and I saw nothing wrong with that. . . . A lot of the people thought that the girls had to sit with certain people or if the boss said, "Hey, Gail, come over here. I want you to sit with so and so, and he wants to take you out to dinner," you had to do that. That never happened. It never happened, and I was in the business for eight years. It never happened. At least it never happened to me and I never saw any of the bosses take any of my friends and say, "You have to do this or you have to do that." . . .

[In fact,] if we had a costume that was very low cut in the front, we had mesh sewn in so your breasts, your boobs, wouldn't show. You could see a little outline but we were never falling out of our costume, so to speak. The owners would get upset. They'd say, "Look at her." So we'd have to stitch some more mesh up because, "Gosh, it's too low for her." So no, it was very prim and proper, *very* prim and proper. . . .

The dancers were not topless, the dancers I'm talking about that had to mix, were not strippers. They were high-class dancers. They were the chorus-line girls that worked their little fannies off. They mixed and they went home, or they did whatever they wanted to do.

You have to understand, we never went out on dates. I'm working seven nights a week for months. If I wanted a date, I'd have to say, "Pick me up at two thirty in the morning and we can go have breakfast" or maybe an early dinner if I wasn't rehearsing. But I'd have to be at the hotel by seven o'clock because I had to get ready and get my makeup on and be ready to go at eight o'clock for the show. So my love life was nil, as were all the other girls, except for a couple that were married. But they worked seven nights a week. We'd never go out [on dates]. We could see them after the show. We could see them between shows. We could go out with them and have breakfast and stuff. But we couldn't go to a movie. We'd have to do it in the afternoon. We never had a normal dating life. We never did. You think about this and you think, "My God, how'd they do that?" But you know, it wasn't really that important to us at the time because most of us were my age, maybe a little bit older, once in a while we'd have a girl in her thirties, "Oh, my God," but it just wasn't impor-tant to us. . . . I think most of the women that I worked with that were my age at that time, in their teens and twenties, I knew when they were born so we all had the same values. It was different. We just didn't do things. We just didn't go around, pardon the expression, screwing guys. We just didn't do that. We were good girls. We were just good girls.

And you know, what was so nice about that era was everybody knew your name, and when I say that, I mean, Milton Prell who was the owner, he would go, "Hey, Gail. How are you doing? Carol, Mary . . . " He knew everybody's name. I mean, he looked out for us. We were like surrogate children to him. He said, "If anybody's messing with you, you let us know." We used to have people thrown out of the hotel because they would become obnoxious with us. They just looked over us. We were like little prizes to them. We were like a celebrity. We were the Saharem Dancers. "There's only twelve of us in the whole world that's on the stage, guys." So we felt pretty good.

I was very focused on being a dancer. I was not focused on being *the* best dancer. I was not focused on being a Betty Grable or a Cyd Charisse, let's say. I was focused on being a dancer. . . . My role models were the people that I wanted to be like but I guess my role model was my mother. She brought me up to be very independent, but [I saw] her as an independent woman, but yet married and having a career. And this was back in the '30s and '40s and the '50s.

I ended up at the Sparks Nugget, because of the production shows coming on board at that point in time—we're looking in the early '60s—our routines, instead of just being eight or twelve girls coming out and doing the kicks and tillers for about a very strenuous six or seven minutes, which is really very strenuous, our routines got longer. So our routines are like fifteen or twenty minutes. They were getting into the production-type show to compete with the big productions that were coming on, like the "Lidos" and things like that. . . . More singers now, more dancers, more showgirls, more change of clothes. . . . We couldn't compete in doing these production numbers and then just having a singer come on or a comedian come on as a star anymore. Because the big, nude production shows were coming on, the topless. It brought something new to Las Vegas, that's true. And all of a sudden people said, "Yeah, I want nude. I want to go to these production shows."

Gail McQuary's view of the world of dancers and showgirls in the early years, 1957 to 1964, may seem unbelievable today in a country where sexuality is a larger part of popular culture. Rather than a denigration of character, McQuary understood the showroom dancer as a persona that signified respect, beauty, and power.

It meant respect. I think that's the main thing, because when people saw the dancer onstage, or they saw the dancer rehearsing, or they saw the dancer between shows mixing, or whatever, they knew that we had to be treated with respect. We got respect from the people we worked for, we got respect from the

stagehands, from the musicians. It was just an era where we were eight dancers out of—in the whole world that were dancing . . . with the top entertainers,
the top stars of the day, then. You have to be good. You just can't be one of the
chorus. You have to be good. . . . You have to know what they're talking about,
because if you don't, then you're replaced by somebody because there're a
thousand other dancers waiting to replace you. Just like on Broadway, there're
a thousand dancers. So I think when they saw a picture of a showgirl then, I
don't know what they think of today, but I know then it was, "Oh my God, is
she beautiful. Oh, I'll bet this is a great line," if you had Moro Landis dancers
or you had the Dorothy Dorbin dancers or you had the Donn Arden dancers.
This was, "My God, you're a Dorothy Dorbin dancer?" "You work for Donn
Arden? How wonderful." There were people who were envious of you. I think
respect says it all. They just respected the fact that we were there and we were
working and we were good. And we looked nice. We looked great.

▨ Moro Landis had half a dozen shows in different places around the country as did Donn
Arden. In addition to the Nevada cities, their dancers might work in Kentucky, New York,
Florida, or California. This was the economy of scale for entertainment companies. McQuary
moved from Las Vegas to Reno to the Beverly Hills Country Club in Kentucky, then back to
Las Vegas with the company. She married, had a daughter, then she divorced. Gail successfully combined dancing with childrearing for a while, but then shifted into cocktails for one
and a half years. Then she met a trombone player and decided it was time to get married
again. By 1964 they were back in Las Vegas.

In 1976 McQuary went to school and earned her real estate license. In her first year, she
sold over $1.5 million in houses. Always interested in her career as well as family, she worked
up to positions of general sales manager and corporate broker.

The second narrative comes from a European who was part of the wave of professionally
trained dance troupes that changed tourists' entertainment expectations. From the intimate
showrooms of McQuary's Saharem Dancers to the larger revues, Las Vegas entertainment
continually reshaped itself. At the age of seventeen, Janet Kravenko joined the famed Bluebell Girls and began an international tour that would bring her to Las Vegas.

I fully expected to go back to Paris and another contract for Bluebell.
—Janet Kravenko

My aunt has a dancing school in England and always had it, so it's been a
dancing family.[9] My grandmother and grandfather were ballroom champions
of Great Britain and my aunt was a dancer with a group in Paris rather like
the Bluebells, and then—'cause it just follows down the family, so it's a family

concern. We never considered not dancing, or if you did, it was a strange phenomenon in your life.

She trained me to teach, so at fourteen I was teaching for her. She had a school in England. She'd always had her school with my grandmother's house. When she came off the boards, as they say in England, when she was in her twenties, she was teaching for another teacher in Birmingham, in England. And my grandfather was a very quiet man. He went down there [to the dancing school] one day and talked to the lady and he said to my aunt, "How much are you getting paid?" And she was working a lot of hours and I think it was like a guinea, which was a pound and a shilling or something, for a class. Well, he comes home and a few weeks later a big pile of lumber is delivered and he builds her a studio at the end of their garden and he said to her, "You're not teaching there anymore. You're gonna have your own school." And you didn't argue with your parents in those days. She said, "Okay, Dad," and she did, so that was the studio I was raised in.

And then my aunt and my grandmother and grandfather moved to this very old Victorian house and it's so big, this place, that we were able to have two studios in this old, old house. It had been a farmhouse originally, and then the Victorians had built this music room and a lounge room and it had stables outside and it was enormous. It doesn't stand anymore. They pulled it down because of taxes but now you can't even find it because there's apartment blocks there. But that's where we taught. They had wardrobes, or closets, so big we could all sit in there, where they used to hang up the big hoops from the dresses. So I started teaching on and off for her on Saturday morning by the time I was fourteen, so I figured that's what I would probably do eventually.

I always knew I wanted to be a Bluebell, and so it was an automatic that I would audition for Bluebell when I was about seventeen. I left school at fifteen, which was legal for the kind of school I went to, and my father insisted that I take secretarial courses, and I blessed him for it. I knew he was right. There was never any argument anyway. And he said he wanted me to be older before I went away to work in the theater, and he was right. I'd been doing night school and shorthand/typing, and then. . . .

I was a very bad secretary for about a year and a half, just waiting for the moment when I could audition. Then I did audition for Bluebell and got the job. That was in, oh gosh, '57, I think. I know I was seventeen. '56 maybe.

Madame Bluebell, her name is Margaret Kelly, . . . formed a dance troupe in Paris after the war. She's actually got a book written about her.[10] And the dancers are very tall, and at first British, because of the training. Very tall, very slender, a certain look about them. And then she had the troupe in the "Lido de Paris." And then we had touring troupes and there were eight of us on tour. There were about four different groups touring at one time in the '50s and '60s throughout the world. So I wasn't tall enough to go to the "Lido," but I was tall enough to go on tour with her. And that was a fantastic life for a seventeen year old, touring the world. [I was] very protected in those days. There were a lot of rules and regulations. You couldn't date anyone you worked with, you couldn't go out after a certain time, you had to adhere to rules and regulations, couldn't go out with stagehands, weren't even allowed to speak to them, with very good reason because we were on tour and we had a contract, we moved around Europe and India, South Africa, so you couldn't leave any girls behind, you know, that kind of thing. . . . I know I toured like that for about two years, around the world and then I came to Las Vegas with the second "Lido" show in '59.[11]

[When we found out we were going to Las Vegas] I said, "Okay, Las Vegas, where's that?" and someone said, "Oh, it's in a place called Nevada," and I said, "Okay." They said, "Well, it's in the middle of the desert somewhere," and we had no idea. . . . We were in the second "Lido" show, so the first "Lido" show had already been here, and when we were at the airport in Paris, the girls were coming in from Las Vegas—it was like a turnaround plane and brought us back—and they said, "Oh, you're gonna love it, it's wonderful," and so that kind of cheered us on.

But when we arrived on a very early morning in June, it was a hundred degrees already, I know that, and it was the old McCarran Airport, the one that's now the private airport, and we had come on a prop—it wasn't a jet, it was a prop—and we'd come from Paris to New York. . . . So, we arrive and they open up the door and of course the hot air hit us and it was like, "Oh my God, how are we going to survive this?" So we're out on the tarmac and we all go down the steps looking our best in our heels and—what a way to travel, heels and big skirts, can you imagine? And the photographers were waiting for us at the bottom. . . . And they put us in buses and started off down the Strip. Well, of course, in those days there were great gaps between hotels and it was desert, you know, and it got very quiet on that bus. We'd just come from Paris; you can imagine. . . . Very civilized, very small, busy city. Got very quiet. And we got into the Stardust and they said, "We'll give you breakfast and then show you your rooms," and we said, "Fine." So we went to the coffee shop and the food was wonderful, and [we] went to our hotel rooms. And they said, "You can sleep until noon and we have a rehearsal this afternoon." So we didn't know about air conditioning, so we kind of slept and got up and it was freezing in there. So we got dressed—I don't know what we were thinking—got dressed in our warmest rehearsal gear and stepped outside, of course, into a hundred-and-something degree heat. We couldn't believe it. So we quickly learned that inside was cold, outside was hot, and what to wear. But we were like, "Oh my God, we're here. Oh well, I'm not staying here. I'm not gonna pick up my contract. Six months, I'm back to Paris." . . . It was a very big culture shock to us. Of course, four months later we loved it and there was no talk about going home then. The contract was up and they offered us another year. Of course we all stayed and a couple of girls left because they weren't happy here, [or] because they had other obligations.

Many of us stayed and married Americans and I think mainly because we were at the right age—we were twenty—at the right time in our lives where we would start looking, not that I remember looking for anybody, but I think it was because it was the only time we had stayed in any one place long enough

Dancers of the "Lido de Paris" at the Stardust, 1962–63. Madame Bluebell auditioned dancers in Europe who performed around the world. Donn Arden brought the "Lido de Paris" to the Stardust in 1958. The costumes of the early productions are modest compared to those two decades later. Courtesy of Las Vegas News Bureau.

to meet other people. So a lot of us did stay and got married. . . . I think what happens is you get on with your life and you start making a life and it grows on you and time goes by and you don't even think about it, you know. I mean, I fully expected to go back to Paris on another contract for Bluebell and, of course, I met my husband-to-be and that took care of that. . . . And after my "Lido" show finished, I went to England and my husband followed me and we got married in England.

And I came back and we hadn't got a job between us. . . . And we went, that first night we were home, on the Strip to get jobs. It was that easy in those days. Bill, my husband, he knew people. And I walked into the Dunes and I bumped into a girl that had been in the show with me at the "Lido" show and she said, "Oh my God, you're back." She says, "Come and see Ronnie Lewis. He's putting a show in for Major Riddle."[12] So I go over to the table and he says, "I'd love to have you." He says, "We start rehearsals in a week or so and the salary is such-and-such." So bingo, I had a job. So, the next night we went out and Bill talked to a maître d' at the Riviera and bingo, he had a job. That's how it was in those days.

Actually I worked at the Dunes a lot. I was pregnant with my eldest daughter Alison when I was at the Tropicana in the "Folies Bergere." And that particular show closed and the new one was opening that Christmas and I was about four months pregnant, and it was obviously a good time to stop because I could have perhaps got another month but the costumes began to get a little tight here, so I couldn't.[13] . . . In fact I worked for [Lewis] after my first pregnancy. That's another story. I was still nursing and he called me and said, "I really need you. Could you come back to work?" I said, "I'm still nursing." I think Alison was about four months old, my baby, and he said, "Well, we'll work it around your nursing." So I had Alison partly on a bottle and I would go to work and halfway through the afternoon, of course, I would start leaking through the leotard and he'd say, "Oh, time to go home. Janet's leaking," and they'd send us all home because I was leaking [laughing]. . . .

Then I worked the Dunes a lot, too, for Frederick Apcar in "Casino de Paris." . . . This was in the early '60s, . . . I know I worked until both my children went to school full time, not just kindergarten but when they went to first grade, then I kind of stopped. . . . It wasn't a decision. It was probably a show finished and I just didn't go back, do you know what I mean? Because of the hours. But when they were little it was actually perfect, because like the first daughter, I'd have someone take care of her, I'd go do a show, then I'd come back between shows and put her to bed. [I could do that] in those days and then I would go back and do a second show. And my husband worked at night too, he was a waiter and maître d', so we'd both come home around one, two in the morning, and I'd give her the last feeding at two in the morning and then she'd sleep through until about eight in the morning, which seemed very early at the time. So you adjusted that way. And then I would just rest with her in the afternoon. . . . But you're young, you don't need that much rest. Come on. You're doing something that you love, you've got this beautiful daughter and this wonderful husband and life is good, you know. . . .

Kravenko's first job in Las Vegas was with Madame Bluebell's troupe in the "Lido de Paris." Bluebell had a strict policy of *not* mixing and she made sure that her contracts prohibited the practice that existed at other properties including the Sahara, where Gail McQuary danced. Later on in her dance career Kravenko worked at the Dunes for Ron Lewis, and that property encouraged mixing. Kravenko explained the availability of so-called house girls for the customers and how sometimes dancers and house girls were one and the same.

So we did an opening number and then there would be an act and then we would do a second production number and then the big act would come on. Well, we were free most of the time after that second show. . . . And in those days, of course, they had . . . girls, if they wished, [who] worked for the hotel. They would go out between shows and entertain. Some of them used it for prostitution, I must admit, and that was their business. Nobody forced them to do that. That was their choice. So, when we started the second lot of shows [around 1961 and 1962] with Ronnie Lewis, who was a prodigy of Donn Arden, some of the showgirls, I should say—still chose to be house girls, and I want to emphasize this was not forced. This was totally their choice. And he said to us, "I welcome you in the hotel. If you wish to sit in the bar in between shows, please do. The drinks are on the house. If you wish to invite your husband to come and sit with you, please do." And he was wonderful. My husband and I had a drink between shows. You didn't really do that because I can't drink anyway, so probably a Coke I had and he had a beer or something.

But some of the girls did work for the house and they were very good for the house. Sometimes by the third show on a Saturday we'd count heads and there wouldn't be enough showgirls available. . . . And we'd go out to the security guard—his name was Woody—and we'd say, "Woody, we haven't got enough girls," and he'd say, "Okay," and so he'd go out to certain rooms and bash on doors and say, "You've got a show to do. Come on down." And of course some of them were women who had done this a long time and really nice girls, you know, and they'd go, "[I] just got up there. I'll never find him again if I have to come down and do a show." And we all thought that was very funny. And again that was a shock for us because we were from the Bluebells where we weren't even allowed to speak to anybody. It was a different kind of show business for us. . . . These were just working girls that were providing for their families too. . . .

Hey, let me tell you, I know that when the so-called mob were in this town—at least visibly, . . . there's a lot went on but people knew people, and you needed something, you needed a job, you needed help, you could go—I'm not saying you went to the mob but I'm saying like when my husband came for a job, we walked into the Riviera: "Hi, Billy, what do you need?" "Hi, how you doin'?" "Oh, you got married. Great! What do you need? You need a job? Hold on a minute." Phone call. "Okay, tomorrow morning. Go see so-and-so over at . . . "

Yeah, and you can't do that now. It's too many people, too many people. And [by] the same token, people would say [or] you'll get a phone call now, "Look, you watch out for so-and-so." You never asked why, you just said, "Okay, thanks." But that was when we were a small town, and now we're a city.

▪ Kravenko stopped dancing when her children went into school full time. She said she always knew she would have a dance studio, though: "That's what you do in my family." She also believed it was important to have an independent means of income. When her daughters both reached high school, she started teaching dance in the city recreation department. After about a decade she opened her own school, the Kravenko School of Dance, currently the Kravenko Dance Academy.

It's very hard to raise a family and have a dancing school, because at four o'clock you need to be in the studio and your children are coming home. Unless you've got someone [who] you can trust to take care of your children. I mean I'm teaching from four until nine thirty at night, so that's the evening with your children. By this time, I think Jane would've been in her junior year and Alison was in her senior year. . . . I figured they were both stable so I could do that. So that's what I always did.

▪ At the time of the interview, both daughters had joined Kravenko as instructors at the studio. Janet Kravenko, a certified ballet and tap teacher, continued to teach.

McQuary and Kravenko did not comment on the racial divide in the entertainment world until asked about it directly. Their ease of employment contrasts starkly with that of dancers of color. D. D. Cotton's narrative offers a perspective from an African American dancer on the costs and benefits of working in Las Vegas.

> *I also found out, when I came back, that the magic was gone,*
> *because now I'm in a segregated town.*
> —D. D. Cotton

D. D. Cotton grew up in a section of Manhattan known as Sugar Hill during the 1940s and 1950s. It was, she said, an "upward-motivated neighborhood where everybody either worked the railroad or they had good post office jobs." The *New York Times* called it a cross-class African American neighborhood in which leaders of the NAACP, entertainers, and professional African Americans lived among "civil servants and postal workers" up to the 1970s.[14] Cotton remembered that people who would become American legends lived near her family. Willie Mays lived across the street, Joe Louis around the corner, and Leslie Uggams lived up the street. She went to school with Diahann Carroll. The singer Frankie Lymon lived nearby. Despite the fact that her parents divorced when she was an infant and Cotton's mother remarried, she remembered her childhood as a stable life.

Around age four or five, Cotton started ballet lessons. "If you don't take ballet, you'll never really learn to dance. . . . You just can't go further," she recalled. She danced through high school and earned extra money performing with a team for clubs like the Links.[15] Along the way she trained with modern dance legend Katherine Dunham.[16] Her narrative begins with her entrance into professional dance at age fifteen. It continues as she moves into other lines of work in Las Vegas hotel-casinos.

I started dancing in the nightclubs.[17] Then that led to a thing where I started dancing by myself, and then that led to auditioning for something for this outdoor chorus line, and then I did another couple of shows inside at the Apollo. . . . That's what happened. That was before I got into the chorus thing. We sort of had this little act together and we would do things. Then after we couldn't get any jobs, you know that's what I wanted to do, then I started looking and I said, "Well, I gotta do something." And that's when I started going in the chorus lines.

Cotton spent a few years working what she called the chittlin' circuit.[18] Shows would rotate their performances among different clubs that catered to African American customers. Her circuit included the Apollo Theater in New York City and the Howard Theater in Washington, DC. Other clubs in Baltimore and Chicago completed the circuit, but she didn't work those cities. In the passage below, she discusses her audition for the "Cotton Club Revue," a Murray Weinger production. Weinger produced shows and owned clubs in Miami Beach after World War II; this particular show was not linked to the various Cotton Club nightclubs around the country, however. Cab Calloway was the star and Cotton danced in the line behind him onstage. She had been in shows before, but this was the biggest production in which she danced.

This was my biggest, but not my first. I had been in other productions before this. But this was my big one. It had Lonnie Sattin in it. . . . Norma Miller, and two sisters, Teddy and Delores Boyd. Teddy was married to Johnny Hartman, the singer. And you got Norma Miller, who was one of the great jazz dancers—the Lindy Hop. You have Michael Silver, [he] was a drummer for this thing and also, after all this was over, [he was] Sammy Davis's drummer. You have Frank Orange, who was a piano player, who up until recently was doing "Showtime at the Apollo." He was the conductor for that.[19] . . .

What happened was, you did the audition in New York and then after they got their thing and all their rehearsals, then we took a bus to the show [that] opened in Miami, Florida. Now, after all this was over and Murray Weinger died, he had to have had this show booked here in Las Vegas, Nevada.[20] . . . We were on a prop plane . . . a cast of at least fifty people or more. . . . The plane came from Miami, it stopped in Texas, and then I guess it had to fuel up again. I mean, it's like drivin' a car. I guess it had to fuel up again or whatever it did. Then we eventually came to Las Vegas, Nevada. Now that, I guess, would be where my life really, really begins. I did all this other stuff, but it really begins there, getting off that plane that night [circa April 1957] in Las Vegas, Nevada.

The Cotton Club's all-black cast performed at the Royal Nevada Hotel, the eighth property built on the Las Vegas Strip. It was located near the future Stardust Hotel and Casino, which eventually bought it out.

Cab Calloway, Norma [Miller], and the Savoy Dancers did the opening. We wore white [tuxedos] in the opening and then you had the chorus girls out there. I think we wore a pink costume [in] that opening number. Then I think Joe Chisholm, [who] was a song-and-dance man or someone that I can't remember, did something there. And then Norma and Cab did a thing called "Rock 'n' Roll" and they came out [dressed] in what would be like in Shakespeare, with the little balloon-y pants and then the veil. Then we did a great jungle African number and it was called "Call of the Wild." This is where Lonnie Sattin was in there. . . . We had the Watusi and it was just beautiful. Then they did this thing with this guy, Joel, who put the flame down his throat. Yeah. He was a fire eater. And then we had George Kirby and George was a comedian. . . .

I was in the line. There were two girls. When you're little, I'm not very tall, somewhere like four-eleven, so you're called ponies. There was another girl, her name was Roxie, Roxie Young; [she] lives in California now. She was on one end of the line and I was on the other end of the line. So it comes up from the littlest girls to the tall girls right in the middle. You don't see too many pony girls anymore. I've seen a lot of shows now and you don't really have that type of line anymore.

It was really, really kind of neat and I'll tell you why. We were in [Las Vegas] and then another black show came in and they worked the Dunes. But you were segregated. You couldn't live on the Strip. You had to live on the West-side. In fact, this is how I met my husband. You didn't really see that because we were not allowed in the casino, in the hotel that I worked in. The stars all had trailers. George Kirby and them, they dressed in a trailer outside. The girls, the chorus girls, they had dressing rooms inside and they had really nice dressing rooms. Now all you could do is come on the property, do your show, then you had to leave the property. But they fed us. So in between shows you could go in the showroom where we were working at and you could eat. They would see that the waiters and staff brought us food. In the showroom. We were not allowed to go into the casino at all. . . . So we were packed every night. Everybody wanted to come see these beautiful black girls dance and it was really exciting. . . .

I personally have never danced in an integrated line. The only lines that I ever danced were all-black shows. I've never danced in an integrated line. Never, never . . . You have lines that are integrated. You have 'em now, if I'm not mistaken, in this town.[21]

When asked by the interviewer if Cotton thought her career had been stymied by racism, she responded that she would never have been hired as a dancer in an integrated line on the Strip. There would not have been an opportunity to audition. To continue her career in dance at the time (1957), she would have had to move to New York City.[22]

My in-laws, my husband's stepfather [James Calvert] had owned the Cotton Club [in Las Vegas] and when I came here, it wasn't [open]. So they had what you call a bankroll, in a place called the Town Tavern, and they ran the gambling part. Another guy named Earl Turman really had the club. It was like a gambling part and then there was a nightclub, a bar. This was really great because all the dancers would go after work and they would sing and they would dance and everybody would perform.[23] Then all the white entertainers would come to the Westside of town and they would gamble out there. They would get up and they would sing and they would dance. It was like it was just so much partying going on. I'm still young and it's just so much partying. I mean, we were up all night. You would do that last show and then it would be daylight before you would ever get to bed. It would be twelve or one o'clock in the afternoon and people were still singing and dancing. It was just great. . . . Then the show closed here in Nevada and I went to finish it [in] Washington, DC. Then it finished in New York City. Then I auditioned for Broadway. I wasn't thinking about getting married, but I guess I [must have] thought about it. . . . I guess maybe I failed my audition and then I thought, "Well, maybe I'll get married." So I came back and I got married. . . . I came back independent, no show business, no nothing, no friends, nothing.

I also found out, when I came back, that the magic was gone, because now I'm in a segregated town. Now I'm confined to the Westside area. I can't go anywhere. I can't go on the Strip again. There's nobody that I can get in with. One of my first experiences, I got dressed one afternoon and I went to the Golden Nugget, and they had keno on the Westside, so I knew how to play that. So I went and sat down and I thought at the time that I looked very nice. I went and sat down and I put a couple of tickets in and nobody said anything. They just kind of looked at me. So I said, "Well, if I got this far, I can venture out." So I ventured to the crap table and made a bet on the crap table, and a security guard walked up to me and he says, "I'm very sorry, you'll have to leave." . . . That was my first encounter with being back in town with the racism. Not too long after that they integrated the town and it got to be all right. But I'm saying, that magic was gone with all your show business friends and stayin' up all night. You had to get in the real world and I got in the real world. . . .

When I came back and got married, I had to get a job. So my in-laws were still with the Town Tavern. You're supposed to be twenty-one to do these [gambling] things. They had gambling like the craps and twenty-one, but some Orientals had the keno games and they showed me how to write keno, and I learned to write keno. That's one of my first jobs that I did in this town. I learned how to write keno. Eventually they opened up another place called the El Morocco and I was a change girl, and I learned how to work with the cage. They had a small cage in there and I learned how to do that. Then they opened up another place called the Carver House. That was the first sort of major hotel that they opened on the Westside. What I did at first, I went to work in the show. Then I went to dance again. So then I worked in the show and the Treniers were in the show. . . . In the Carver House.[24] That's what I did. I hadn't danced during that time, and when they built this place then they wanted to put a show in there. I auditioned for the show and got the audition. The Treniers were in that show, Billy Ward and the Dominoes were in that revue. . . . I forget how many girls were in it, but there were a few girls in it. I met a guy named Ash Resnick and his brother. . . . Ash Resnick, who everybody knows was a big boss in Caesars [Palace] and all that. I didn't know it at the time, but I will meet him again later. So anyway, they had the show in there, and we did the show in there, and then it folded. They had claimed that there was money in there, and they were stealing the money. I don't know because I wasn't into the gaming end of it. But it had all-black croupiers, or dealers. They had all the games and they had the show. It was just a small-town version of a Strip hotel. Everybody really came over there, so white people startin' to come back across over here again and again. It got to be where I guess white people just don't want to see you mix. If they see other white people having a good time and they [are] not having it, it's wrong. So that happens. . . . I worked the show and then they closed. When the El Morocco opened, I went across the street and I became a change girl over there. Then I started to get into cocktails, and they opened the Carver House back up again with a lounge and some acts. But they didn't open the showroom. It was just small and people would still come. They liked jazz and a couple of things like that. And that went for a while. . . . I went back as a cocktail waitress. So this was a good thing. Cocktail waitress is a good job. Then, after that, Bob Bailey had a place, and I went to work for him.[25]

In fact, all this stuff really kind of happened in the 1960s because my son was born in 1960, and I know that he was already born, and that's when I went back to dancing. So all this happened in the 1960s. That's when that Carver House opened, and all these things opened. [My husband] said the Carver House was open from 1959 to 1963. I'm not sure of that, but I do know that I had been pregnant. I know that I had my son and then I went to dance in that show. . . . It was a cute show. It wasn't really lavish or anything like that. [It was a] small production and a small lounge. It had a nice little stage and they had dressing rooms.

The Moulin Rouge dancers backstage with Lionel Hampton, 1955. Open
only six months, the Moulin Rouge was the first interracial resort. *Clock-
wise from left:* Lionel Hampton, Anna Bailey, Valerie Follins, Clyde Webb,
Jimmy Fields, Dee Dee Jasmin, Jean Thomas, Sterling Bough, Barbara
McCarey, Norma de la Cerna Talbut, and Martha Washington. Courtesy
of Special Collections, University Libraries, UNLV.

After working at several of the West Las Vegas clubs, Cotton became involved in efforts
to end discrimination in casino employment. Public accommodations had been opened in
1960 with the Moulin Rouge Agreement (see chapter 2), but job segregation by race and
gender continued. With passage of the 1964 federal Civil Rights Act, groups on the local level
began testing the law. Cotton became the first black cocktail waitress on a casino floor when
she worked downtown at Diamond Jim's Nevada Club. She did that again on the Strip when
she worked at Caesars Palace in 1966. She took the title of first again when she became a

floor supervisor at the Tropicana. From her perspective, the Culinary Union and the NAACP led the charge.

The town was integrated, but now they're going to put everybody to work. I had joined the [Culinary] Union, and the man that was the head of the union was a guy named Al Bramlet. And they were considering sending black people out to get jobs in white hotels. I went to them and they were going to use me like a little puppet there. I went to every place in town. One of the first places I went to was the Castaways. There was a guy named Pappas that was a bar manager up in there. They looked you over and they talked to you, and then they would finally tell you, "I'm sorry. We just can't hire you." So I would just [say], "Okay. That's fine," and I'd go again.

There was a lady here named Sarah Hughes and she was a business agent for the union. She knew me and I knew her, and she had seen me work before and they sort of just pushed me. I guess she thought maybe because I could deal with most people. I could pass an interview. An interview was not that hard to do if you're going to talk to somebody and just sell yourself. I think I could sell myself. So that's what I did. That's why she just kept pushing me in

D. D. Cotton integrated Diamond Jim's, a downtown casino, as the first black cocktail waitress working on the floor. She did the same thing at Caesars Palace when it opened in 1966. Courtesy of D. D. Cotton and the Las Vegas Women Oral History Project, UNLV.

and Al Bramlet went along with it. I went every time they [wanted] somebody to go out there again. A lot to no avail. I had met the bar manager that was at the El Cortez, Harry Brown, and I went back to the El Cortez, and I still couldn't do anything. He always told me, "Well, D. D., don't worry. If I get something, I'll take you with me." Bramlet and Sarah sent me down one afternoon, and they were very confident about this particular thing. So I went and I met a man named Van Satten, and he says, "Are you going to be all right?" And I said, "Yes, I am." And he says, "Well, I'm going to give you a job."

▨ D. D. Cotton moved downtown as the first black cocktail waitress at Diamond Jim's Nevada Club. She and Richard Walker, who was hired as a craps dealer, became the first blacks hired on the casino floor downtown.[26] They endured name calling and abuse from customers, but Cotton recalled, "You know you want to cry, but you know that you're doing it for a cause. Because if you do this then there are going to be more after you. There's always got to be a first." Her next big change came with the hiring for the Caesars Palace grand opening.

I passed audition. It was like you were really going to do an audition for a theater or something like that, because you had some girls there to try to get *this* job. They were coming from every nook and cranny to try and get *these* jobs. I mean, it was like as they say in show business, it was a cattle call. . . . You'd go up and say your name. You wore high heels and you wore stockings, and I'm trying to think if you wore shorts, but I don't think you did. Not at that one. But you had to look nice. You had to have your hair fixed, you had to have your makeup on. Then after they picked you from that, they called you back, and they had rented a suite or something in the Dunes Hotel. They had that costume that they have right now, and every girl that came that far had to try that costume on. . . . They picked you from how you looked in that costume, and how you spoke to them, and how you answered their questions. Even though I knew Harry Brown, his was not the last say, because these other gentlemen were involved in it. Knowing him got me that far but then you had to sell yourself to these guys to get the job. Peggy Walker and I were the first two blacks, and we had that job.

When I went to Caesars, Walker and I went there together. . . . We got hired for the opening of the hotel [1966]. The cocktail waitresses and the dealers at that time used to eat upstairs in the coffee shop. Nobody wanted to sit with us and we were the only two black people in the whole place. Nobody wanted to sit with us. We would sit together when we went on our break together, but if we were not on our break together, they didn't sit with us. I guess they thought we were lepers or something. But we had the job, and we were doing what they wanted us to do, and we were looking good. There were two dealers, two white guys because there weren't any black dealers in there, and they came and they sat with us. They said, "Damn the rest of 'em, we're gonna sit with you guys." They sat with us, and eventually everybody sat with us or we sat with them. It took 'em about maybe a month, two months, or something like that, until they got used to seeing us around there. Then that was it. . . . It just goes to show you that some people just don't really care. You're just another human being. It's a shame, but racism runs rampant in this town as of today. So it's the same thing. You get one or two people that want to be with you and that's it.

Cotton worked at Caesars Palace for four years as a cocktail server in Nero's Nook, then reassessed her future and decided to learn to deal cards. Between leaving Caesars in 1970 and moving to the Tropicana in 1973, jobs for women dealers began to reopen downtown and for the first time, at Las Vegas Strip hotels.[27] Her best friend's husband had a friend at the Tropicana, Sammy Sands, and she said he helped her to get an audition. Once hired she became one of the first women dealers on the Strip and the first black woman hired. After dealing for several years, she continued to move into previously male-only jobs as she became a floor supervisor at the Tropicana. She knew her own success was part of a larger movement to open up jobs for African Americans and women.

They wanted to integrate the town. They wanted to have 10 percent and everybody was fighting for the 10 percent. Everybody was trying to do the right thing. It doesn't seem like they want to do the right thing anymore. It's just a mystery to me, because it seems like you would have much more, even men, in bigger positions. . . . You know, I've lived here a long time and I know of one lady that's at the Nugget, she is a shift boss, which is a very good job. I've known a few other floor ladies. They've got floor ladies at Caesars. I don't know who they are. . . . They have them in the MGM Grand because there is a girl over there that's a pit boss now that I know of. You've got 'em but when you have 'em, you only have maybe one or two. It's to say that, "We have color here. We're not prejudiced." But it's not like it was.

I tell you what, when I went to Caesars at one time, in fact even when I was working in the Nugget, they were getting everybody to have blacks in place. I may have been the only woman that was there, but in the dice pit, where men [were] dealing, there had to be ten or twelve [black] men dealers they hired. You know they were there. Some of these went on to Caesars. . . . Every hotel downtown had a lot of blacks working. Then, they went out and got jobs in other places.

When asked specifically about her knowledge of the work of the NAACP to open jobs up to African Americans, she said she knew that Dr. James B. McMillan, head of the NAACP at the time, had been working with hotel-casinos and unions to open up employment opportunity.[28] He threatened an NAACP march on the Las Vegas Strip in 1960 if hiring discrimination continued. Cotton credited McMillan with helping her to get and keep her Tropicana position when he was president of the NAACP.

I was having a very difficult time getting a floor job. There was someone that said that I couldn't learn it, or I didn't know enough, and they gave me a temporary [position] for [a] couple of weeks. And then they said, "No, she can't do that." This was the Tropicana. They said I couldn't do it and I had to go to a meeting with the Equal Rights Commission and go through all this. Because they had given some white lady a job and it was a long, drawn-out thing. Anyway, I got Dr. McMillan to come out there and he spoke to them, and they found that I could. They had never given me an opportunity to do it, see. After they got pressed into the thing, where they had to, then they gave me the job. And I've had the job ever since.[29]

At the time of the interview in 1997, Cotton believed she was the first and still the only black woman in a floor management position at her property. While positions may have opened on the hotel side, the casino side still had a poor representation of African Americans.

For several decades after the war, Las Vegas had a boomtown economy. Dancers were among those who migrated in and out of the area for work. As this chapter demonstrated, some stayed and helped to build the town into a city. These entertainers came with their companies to the showrooms of the Strip hotel-casinos. Some came from nearby states, some from across the country, and others came from Europe. Dancers auditioned in major cities like Los Angeles, New York, or Paris, but the work took them on tour to venues strategically placed on a circuit. For Bluebell Girls like Janet Kravenko, the venues were global. African American dancers like D. D. Cotton, though, performed for predominantly black audiences in select cities. And for the all-white troupes such as Moro Landis (and dozens more), there were regional circuits of supper clubs across the country. As one narrator noted, all the auditions took place in Los Angeles, but the work was in Las Vegas, so the dancers eventually moved here.

All of the dancers mentioned, in passing, the tough work schedules. The full transcripts share much more about the physical demands of the job, as does the previous chapter on Fluff LeCoque. Many reported working weeks on end without a day off. They danced with high fevers or injured feet. They reported a work ethic that demanded the production go on. They knew their absence from the performance put a hardship on their coworkers because some troupes didn't have swing girls in the early decades. Although not noted, they may have also thought that their absence from the show would leave them vulnerable to replacement. Other narrators discussed at length the dangers of the early showrooms, such as climbing onto backstage ladders with full headdress and heels, and descending from high platforms on narrow steps without the ability to look down. They worked in the years before the implementation of the Occupational Safety and Health Administration (OSHA) standards of workplace protections in 1970.

Although dancers initially came here for a job, the reasons to stay in Las Vegas focused on continuing job opportunities and forming their families. Abundant jobs for dancers meant that McQuary and Kravenko could find jobs quickly through personal relationships. The small town network and their reputations made that easy. Cotton could find work through a network as well, but not in her profession of dance. The hiring practices of showrooms excluded African American dancers until the 1970s. Cotton chose to step away from her dance career and move into casino work. These experiences undoubtedly influenced her later commitment to desegregate jobs.

The three dancers highlighted here, like many other dancers in the oral history project, formed families and adjusted their careers as their families developed. They adjusted work schedules and jobs around births and the demands of childrearing. They found child care through family members or through home child-care providers. The solutions varied by individual, but the majority combined jobs with family.

Iconic showgirl Sue Johansson, 1978. The showgirl image continued to develop and reached its peak in the late 1970s and 1980s. Courtesy of Las Vegas News Bureau.

More than other workers in the early casino industry, the performance of dancers and showgirls carried gender-specific meaning far beyond the work they performed. Casino publicists exploited the changes in sexual behavior in the United States during the 1960s and 1970s in their representation of the dancer and showgirl. In publicity photos we can see the transition from the innocent starlet in a bathing suit to the statuesque nude showgirl. The interviews in this chapter cover that transition and offer contesting views that contrast with the publicity campaign. Gail McQuary refuted the assumptions that dancers were also prostitutes and emphasized the respect afforded her and the protection offered to the dancers by management. She articulated a sense of power and prestige based on her beauty and her position as a Saharem Dancer. Janet Kravenko discussed the range of sexual behavior among dancers that she observed as a young married woman. She offered some information on the role of the so-called house girls who worked as prostitutes for customers. D. D. Cotton's narrative does not discuss the sexuality of dancers with whom she worked in the African American revues. The history of African American women and the use and abuse of the black female body may be part of the reason for her silence. She discussed her years with revues as being a lot of fun. Despite the variations in their portrayal of sexual behavior, and because of their own perspectives, a greater distinction must be drawn between the way in which promoters used women's bodies and the way in which some of those women interpreted their own lives.

Chapter 6

LUCILLE BRYANT

Housekeeper and Uniform Room Supervisor

They were leaving Tallulah as fast as they got some money to travel on. They were leaving as fast as they could. And then they wrote back to tell people to come out there.

—Lucille Bryant

If dancers gave structure to the showroom entertainment, housekeepers provided an essential service of the hotel. Among the service jobs, housekeeping and food service offered entry-level work for those without advanced education or those who were recent immigrants. The first generation of housekeepers included many African Americans from the South. By the 1960s and 1970s, immigration from Latin America and Asia had opened, and immigrants from both areas became an increasingly large part of the Las Vegas population as well as of hotel housekeeping departments.

Lucille Bryant spent her earliest years in rural Louisiana where her father grew cotton. When she reached school age, they moved into the town of Tallulah, Louisiana, so she could attend school. The town was small then and remains small today. Located in northern Louisiana just off Interstate 20, it is approximately ten miles west of the Mississippi River and twenty-four miles west of Vicksburg, Mississippi. Lucille's mother stayed home and kept house, but she died when Lucille was eleven years old. Her father raised the children until he joined the Army during World War II. After he left, her grandmother raised Lucille and her siblings until they were grown. Bryant describes growing up in the racially segregated South, but among a loving family and community.

Like the other narrators in this book, Bryant moved to Las Vegas with many family members in what historians have identified as the second great migration. That term refers to the movement of several million African Americans from the states of the Deep South to the urban and predominantly industrial areas in the West, upper Midwest, and Northeast, where they hoped to gain greater access to jobs and civil rights. It began shortly before the United States entered World War II and continued through the 1960s. Bryant's narrative indicates that she went first to Chicago, but returned to Tallulah before moving to Las Vegas. Some African Americans came to southern Nevada for wartime jobs, but the attraction for many more came a few years later during the 1950s when several new hotel-casinos opened on the Las Vegas Strip. The hotel jobs offered African American men and women numerous opportunities in the service sector. As Bryant's narrative makes clear, the jobs offered better wages than they could find in the South, but the work remained segregated in practice if not

115

in law. She spent the next thirty years working in housekeeping and moving up through the ranks to the position of supervisor, the position she held when she retired.

Central to the positive work environment for Bryant and thousands of other service workers in Las Vegas was the strength and organization of what workers called the Culinary, which is Local 226 of UNITE HERE, the Hotel Employees and Restaurant Employees union. According to James P. Kraft, this local formed in 1938 and secured initial labor agreements with hotel-casinos and union workers under the leadership of Al Bramlet from 1954 to 1977.[1] After difficulties during the 1980s, the union reenergized its recruitment campaigns under new leadership and won strong contracts for its workers. Bryant started work as a housekeeper in 1953 and had little recollection of union activities in her early years. However, as she moved from housekeeping to the uniform room and then to the position of supervisor, the union played a major role in reducing conflicts and providing job security.

I decided to come to Las Vegas in 1953 to get work for myself.[2] There were no jobs in Tallulah—just domestic work, or during the summer, working in the cotton fields. And you worked, backbone work, and you didn't get paid anything for it: $2.50 a day for chopping cotton or picking cotton. I started in the cotton fields when I was eleven or twelve years old and I did it every summer until I left and came to Las Vegas. You got paid more in the fields because you got paid by the day. I could make $2.00 a day or $2.50 a day. And then, when we get to picking cotton, if the cotton was $2.00 a hundred, I could pick over 200 pounds, so I could get $4.00 or $5.00 a day in the fields. But it was backbreaking work. Your neck would be so tired and hurt so bad when you got home. Especially from the chopping cotton because you're like this [the narrator indicated a standing position slightly bent at the waist] all day with your head laying down, chopping, you know. When you got home in the evening, you'd have to rub down with liniment and everything. In the winter I would do domestic work. And I worked in the kitchen of the white lady's house. I did everything in her house except slept with her husband. I mean, you did all the work. You washed, you ironed, you cooked, you took care of the baby, and the highest I ever got was $5.00 a week for that.[3] . . .

You know, we were poor but we really didn't realize we were poor because we were happy. With all our cousins, and then the neighbors, everybody got along. Everybody helped you with your children, and you helped with their children, and it was like one big happy family. Everybody tried to raise a little hog with chickens or something like that. And when you killed a hog, Miss So-and-So down the street got some, and somebody else got some, and when you got through, you hardly have anything for yourself. But it's the same thing when, next week, if they killed a hog, you got some of that. So, it kept us eating, you know, especially in the winter time. It kept us eating that meat in the wintertime.

In the summer time, everybody raised their gardens. Oh, my goodness, I can taste the butter beans and okra right now. They were so good and fresh. Another thing I remember about my childhood is early in the morning the fresh air. . . . And most of the people had peach trees or plum trees or something in their yard. You canned apples and you canned peaches. The foods you grew during the summer, you canned and had it ready for the winter. We made it.

I was twelve years old, I believe, before I ever went to a doctor because they had all these home remedies. You know, they greased you and rubbed you. They would go out and get some kind of leaves. I had malaria fever one time. And they would go out and get these leaves, boil these leaves, wrap you in these leaves and things, and give you a bath in the water that they had boiled these leaves in, and so many home remedies—medication that they gave you. This got us over the colds, and the chicken pox, and the measles, and whatever we had.

I was sixteen years old when I got married—very young. I was still in Tallulah. His name was George Bryant and he was nineteen years old. You know, Tallulah has so many little rural areas around about, but Tallulah is kind of like what you'd call the big place where you come and do your shopping. His parents lived on a little place called Mrs. Scott's Plantation. Every plantation had its name. He came to Tallulah when he was about fourteen or fifteen years old, or something like that. But I met him when I was fifteen and I married him when I was sixteen. We had five children together. I had two children to be born in Tallulah, one to be born in Chicago, Illinois, and two in Las Vegas. I'm the mother of six. I had one stillborn, also, in Tallulah.

George worked at the mill or he did what we called catch the truck. A truck would come and people would load up on the truck and they would take you to the plantation so you could pick cotton, like you're doing day work or something. He did that and worked at Chicago Saw Mill, when he worked.

I worked in the house. We had wooden stoves that you had to use wood in and heaters that you had to use wood in and he'd cut the wood for the fireplace. I washed, I ironed, I cooked. Oh, he would help with the baby. He loved the baby and he would help with the baby. But, you know, in those days, it was considered a woman's work, in those days. So, we did the work. You bought material, you made clothes, you made everything you wore. You could not afford to buy store-bought clothes. So you made everything you wore. Your shoes, one pair of shoes, you wore those, at first, for weekdays, for Sundays too. Then finally, you might get a pair for weekend on Sunday to wear to church and you had some old pair to wear during the week.

Between blacks and whites, it was like, you didn't go into their places, their little clubs, their churches, their schools, you didn't go there. You had your own church, your own clubs, your own school. You didn't vote, you could not vote. I can remember walking down the sidewalk in Tallulah, these little narrow sidewalks where only a couple of people could walk, and if you saw the white people walking toward you, you had to get on the edge or get kind of down in the ditch almost, so they would pass by. It was like it was their town, they owned everything. You were considered nothing. But we were always told by our elders that you are somebody, regardless of how they feel about you, you are somebody and things are going to get better one of these days. But now, it was whites that had the upper hand. They had the better jobs. Black people did not work as cashiers in their stores, they had white cashiers, and you could not get a job at the post office. Any other place of business—the power company, the gas company—you couldn't work at those places. Your work was doing domestic work or maybe some black peoples wrote insurance, or something like that, or had their own business, their own little club, restaurant, you got jobs there. But, other than that, it was really divided. It was segregated. Tallulah High was the white school. Our school, the black school, was then called Madison Parish Training School. When I left, it was still segregated. Blacks were not going to school with whites, they were not voting. It has happened since I left there.

I heard that in Las Vegas it was dusty and it never rained and that you made good money. My relatives started moving to Las Vegas in '41. My uncle was already out here and some cousins were already out here. My dad had been out here. My aunt had been out here. They were leaving Tallulah as fast as they got some money to travel on. They were leaving as fast as they could. And then they wrote back to tell people to come out there.[4]

Some people took the bus, but it was cheaper to go in a car. Quite a few took the bus. In fact, so many was taking the bus at one time that the people at the bus depot stopped selling blacks tickets to go to Las Vegas because all their help was leaving. That's why. People didn't want them to leave. And then they would have to go to Delhi or Monroe or somewhere, go over there to catch a bus. Also, the blacks started leaving after midnight, late in the wee hours of the morning. The saw mill, it finally closed down. I don't remember the year, but [it closed] after I left. Then there really was no work in Tallulah. People would go into Vicksburg, Mississippi, to get jobs, and to Monroe to get jobs.

I came in a car. We left there about two or three o'clock in the morning. This man, Mr. Harvey, I believe his name was George Harvey, that's just about all he did was bring people to Las Vegas, pick up a load of people who wanted to go back home and visit, and then bring another load out to Las Vegas. He would do that, oh, I don't know how many times a year, but he did it quite often. So, I came out here with him. I think it was $25 that he charged to bring us out here. I had my son Joey with me. He was the baby, so, I brought him with me.[5]

It took three days and four nights or four nights and three days or something like that, because we came on—do you remember the song "Route 66?" Well, then that was just a two-lane highway. The freeways were not there. We slept in the car. Yeah, we would pull up on a service station or something where some lights were and you'd pull up there and you'd sleep. Well, we slept in the car because you didn't have the money, but I'm sure you probably wouldn't have been able to stay in a motel because you were not allowed to go in. If you stopped at the service station, you could not go into the bathroom that the white people went into or you could not drink water from the fountain that the white people drank from. It would have signs that said, men, women, and colored. White men and women go over here, and there's a little dingy place in the back where colored could go. They would call you *colored* and you would have to go out there to use the bathroom. If you stopped at a restaurant, usually it said colored. There was a sign in the back, you had to eat with the colored. But, what we usually did, we brought our food with us. You had your peanut butter and jelly sandwich or bologna sandwich.

I came in '53, so I must have been twenty-three years old. My husband was here, maybe six or seven months before I came. He was working at the hotels; I believe it was the Last Frontier. There was only about eight hotels here then. I must have had fifty or sixty relatives out here or more. I might have had a hundred, I don't know. It was such a big family. The majority of my relatives had come to Las Vegas. There were some up North, but not as many as in Las Vegas.

I didn't like Las Vegas at first because it was so dusty here. The wind blew, it seemed, every day, and it was blowing sand. There were very few trees, very little grass, and there was nothing to keep the sand back, and it blew every day. We lived in little trailers and things, little huts, and you would clean your house up at night when you got off of work and dust everything up and come back and go to bed. Sometimes when you woke up dust was laying in the windows and the doors and things and it was so thick you could write your name in it. When you came home the next day, oh, the dust was so thick in your windows. Sometimes you'd have to shake your covers to get that dust off your bed. And, it was the hottest place. We didn't have air-conditioning, we didn't have hand fans. You just opened the window and that helped the dust to come on in, too. This was the hottest place. I did not like Las Vegas then, because of, you know, the weather.

We had a little trailer. It had a little living room area in it for a couch, a table, a lamp. The next little area was the kitchen area—stove, sink, and little cabinets. And, the next area was the bedroom area. All of these little areas were small, because it was really a small trailer. Later on, we got a trailer that was larger. This was a small trailer. Then there was a bed and closet in the bedroom.

We were on the Westside, on B and Monroe. We were right up on this great, big, beautiful tree, and the people that we rented from, the Shaws, they had a house and they would rent trailer space out to people there. There were not many homes, but they had a two- or three-bedroom home there, where they lived. It was a neighborhood. It was okay; it was small enough for you to know your neighbors, everyone knew everyone. When I went to Chicago, you didn't know the people next door to you. I went to Chicago before I came here and you didn't know the people next door to you. It was too big. But when I got here, this has the feeling of Tallulah and there were so many people here from Tallulah, until it was almost like walking down the street in Tallulah. When you went out, you saw somebody, "Hey, so-'n-so, hey, how are you," and blah, blah, blah. So, it was nice being with your family, your extended family, you know, people that you knew. The weather was the only thing that I didn't like, so, I said, I'll just make me some money and go back home. But, I grew to love Las Vegas, Lake Mead, Mount Charleston, and everything. You go up to Mount Charleston if you wanted to get some snow or something. You go out to Lake Mead if you wanted to get in the water. It was nice and I finally grew to love Las Vegas.

I wasn't acquainted with any whites and I wasn't living near the whites.[6] It was predominately black over here [in the Westside] at B and Monroe. There were some whites down there at Vegas Heights, but they began to move out so fast as blacks began to come in. You know, it seems like the only time I saw whites is when you went on a job on the Strip or somewhere where you were working at.

Most of the men worked in the hotels—in the kitchen department or in the housekeeping department. That's where most of them worked as a houseman. A houseman kind of gets the linens and brings it to the maids, or they do the floors, something like that. That was a houseman's job—to do the heavier work. Where the maids could do the beds and dusting and things like that, the houseman does the heavier work. And then in the kitchen, they were washing dishes, they were cooks' helpers, they were runners for the cooks, and thing like that. I don't remember seeing black cooks in the beginning when I first got here. Later on, I remember seeing some. Because I remember saying, this place is more segregated than Tallulah is. That's what I was saying about Las Vegas, this place is more segregated. But, after Martin Luther King and the civil rights movement, things began to get better.

I got here on the 4th of October of '53 and I got a job the very first day, you know, at the Algiers Hotel. When I got here that morning, my cousin Gladys was getting ready to go out to the Algiers Hotel where she had been working and she was going out there to quit her job because she had found another job. So she said, "You want to go with me?" I said, "Okay." We got out there and, I can't remember the housekeeper's name, but I asked her, "Do you need some-one to work today?" And she said, "Yes." So, she took me upstairs to show me the rooms and what I was supposed to do, clean the rooms and do the bathroom. I think it was only about seven or eight rooms a day and something like that and she said it paid $8.00 a day. What? Eight dollars day! Lord I was so grateful, I was so thankful. Eight dollars a day. "Yes, I'll take the job!" And I said, "Gladys, you go on back, I'm going to work today, come by and pick me up this evening." When the lady left out of that room and came on back downstairs, you know, I got on my knees, I got on my knees right there in the Algiers Hotel and I gave God thanks. Eight dollars a day and working in the shade. You know, not backbreaking in the sun. Eight dollars a day—all this money. I wrote back and I said, "Everybody come on out here. White folks gone crazy. They're giving us $8.00 a day for making a bed and cleaning a bathroom."

I worked about nine months at the Algiers Hotel. You had eight hours to do your work and, I think, it was one hour off for lunch. You would go into

Right: Waitresses at the Dunes, 1958. In the 1950s and 1960s floor jobs were generally held by whites. Cocktail servers delivered drinks in modest uniforms relative to those of the 1990s. Courtesy of Special Collections, University Libraries, UNLV.

Below: Housekeepers and porters in front of the Thunderbird Hotel and Casino, 1950. This rare photo of African American service workers illustrates the race and sex segregation of jobs at the time. Courtesy of Special Collections, University Libraries, UNLV.

a room, you had to make the beds up. You had to change the beds every day. You changed the beds, you would dust the room, you did the mirror if the mirror needed cleaning, you were told if there was something personal, their things laying around, you didn't touch them, you just dusted around them. You didn't touch their clothes. You vacuumed the room. You had a little small vacuum, a hand vacuum, or something we had to do the floor. Then, you go in and clean the bathtub, the sink, and the commode. . . . Make sure the room was looking nice and clean, just like you were cleaning your bedroom or your bathroom. I think we had about, I don't know, it looked to me like we had about eight rooms to do. I'm not sure because it wasn't a lot to do to me considering where I had come from. It wasn't a lot to do. Nowadays, I hear that sometimes, at some of these hotels, the maids have twenty rooms to do, they have eighteen rooms to do, fifteen rooms to do. How do you do all those rooms? But in those days we only had to do eight rooms. Maids' work wasn't strenuous to me. You'd have to get on your knees sometimes to get in the corners, you know, make sure you get the floor clean in the bathroom, to look up under the bed to know if everything was clean up under the bed. That wasn't strenuous to me. . . . Sometimes you'd have a tip in your room. When the guest would leave, they might leave you a silver dollar or something like that. . . . We were having fun. We'd catch the woman downstairs and we'd get in one room and laugh and talk. We always found a way to be happy. That's where I met some of my friends.

All the maids were black and, in the beginning, the supervisors were always white. Mrs. Effie Conway was the first black executive housekeeper at the Stardust, when the Stardust was built. The Stardust was built in 1958. She was the first black executive housekeeper. . . . There were no advancements there at the Algiers, that's a little small hotel. I think the highest position for blacks was kind of like a little assistant to the housekeeper, an inspector, or something; she'd inspect the rooms after you got through with them.

I believe my next job was at the Silver Slipper. I worked at the Silver Slipper in the powder room. In the powder room you keep the bathroom clean. You keep the countertop clean, you know, and Kleenex out and everything like that. It was so much easier than doing maid's work. This is when the ladies come in to powder their nose; you had combs, sometimes you had a little lipstick tray or something there if they wanted to put on makeup and didn't have theirs with them. So, I worked in the powder room at the Silver Slipper.

[Next,] I went to the Sands for about three years. I worked the graveyard shift there . . . midnight to eight [in the morning]. I asked for that shift because I wanted to be with my children during the day and I could be working while they were sleeping during the night. So, I asked for the graveyard shift and I loved it. I always loved graveyard due to the fact that I could be with my children during the daytime. . . .

There were black inspectors at the Sands and you could have applied for the inspector. They were higher than the maids and they came around and inspected the rooms, but after I got on the graveyard shift, that was where I wanted to be; and on the graveyard shift, it was more like, you just took care of what had to be done on graveyard. If someone's checking in after midnight, calls and says, "We need a cot in room such and so," the porter and I would go and put this cot in. If they called and said, "We need some towels," we would go over and take the towels. It was like whatever they needed, you did it. Sometimes they didn't need anything. You were just there all night. . . .

Then my cousin Willie Graves was at the Stardust and at this time the Stardust had been opened about a year.[7] . . . Miss Effie Conway was the first black housekeeper at the Stardust. Miss Effie Conway was also my fourth grade teacher in Tallulah. I had been to her, maybe, three or four, six months ago, stopped in and asked about a job and she didn't have anything. . . . At the Stardust, the kitchen uniform room was separate from the housekeeping uniform room [and] it had never been opened. And they wanted to open the uniform room. [Miss Conway] sent word to me by my cousin, "Ask Lucille, does she want a job? I have a job for her." . . . So, I went out to see her and she said, "Lucille, do you still write pretty like you used to write?" I said, "Yes." . . . She said, "I have this job, I want to open up the uniform room over in the kitchen department at the Stardust," and she said, "you're going to have to be doing a lot of writing because you're going to have to do inventory. You'll have to keep up with everybody who's coming in, those who are going out, which uniforms you'll need," and blah, blah, blah. So, she said, "and my sister Bessie wants to work the evening shift. Would you be interested in the morning shift, early morning shift?," and I said, "Yes." And, she said, "Be ready to start tomorrow." . . . I went to work at the Stardust, I think I went, like six in the morning until two [in the afternoon]. . . . I came to the Stardust, July the 4th, 1959. . . .

The abundance of jobs made it easy for Bryant to find work, albeit in a segregated market. An informal network advertised openings by word of mouth among neighbors and friends. Moving up in that limited job sector was far more difficult, however, as the ambitious competed for a few spaces. Her timing was good because there was a building boom on the Strip during the 1950s.

At the time that Bryant entered the Las Vegas workforce, a number of the hotel-casinos were financed and operated by representatives of various mob families. Tony Cornero had begun construction on the Stardust, but died before it was completed. Moe Dalitz picked the property up and started its operations. Howard Hughes, who received credit for cleaning up the casino business by buying out mob-owned properties, could not add the Stardust to his long list because he already owned too many and regulators thought his company could monopolize the business. In 1984 the state's Gaming Commission fined the Stardust for skimming profits. It was sold the following year to the Boyd Corporation.[8]

Many workers expressed their appreciation for the bosses' paternalism—their generosity when a family member died or a child needed an operation. Bryant had a very pragmatic response. "We kind of thought, well, if they are mobsters, well, they are good to us, you know. We didn't know if they were or they were not, but we know that they were good people to us. You could go to them and talk to them, and try to straighten things out if something had gone wrong. They always tell me, 'Lucille, if you do what I say do, if you run the place like I say run it, you will have me on your side.' . . . They were always on my side. I got along with them."

When you got through working, you headed right on back over here [to the Westside]. You were only allowed in the hotels and casinos for washing dishes and making beds, whatever your job was, and then you came on back over here where you belonged, they thought. . . . It was like an understood thing. You knew what you were supposed to do. During your shift, you were not allowed in the casino. I've heard you couldn't even go in there to cash your checks. You had to go to the bank or come over here somewhere and cash your check. You know, in the casino with all that money you should be able to go in there and cash your check, but you couldn't do it during those times. I'm not a gambler, so it never bothered me, seeing them out there, the gambling going on. It never bothered me. It was beautiful; it was a beautiful sight, the hotels and things. . . . If I did [see performers], it was from looking from backstage. I think I saw Sammy Davis Jr. once, you know, working graveyard shift. . . . I was peeking behind the drapes, on the outside looking in. . . . You could peek and look, but you couldn't go out there.

It was the talk of the town when Sammy Davis came and the others came and they could not stay out there [in the hotels where they performed]. They had to come over here [West Las Vegas]. . . . They did their gambling at the Cotton Club here on Jackson Street. That was hot. Jackson Street was hot when I first came—Jackson Street and the Town Tavern and those places. This is where they had to come and do their gambling and they got rooms in places.

I think somebody had a boarding house on F Street. . . . I was not a nightlife person because I had children and my number one thing was to take care of my children. But I heard about those times and I knew it to be true because too many people said it, you know. . . . Once they finished entertaining for them, they had to come over here where we were.[9]

▪ Child care was a big issue for working mothers and they dealt with it in a variety of ways. With such a large extended family in town, Bryant was able to rely on relatives most of the time. When she first came to town, one cousin watched her baby. Later, her sister moved out to Las Vegas and lived with her family and helped with the children. She recalled, "When my sister came out here, my sister worked days and I worked nights and I kept my kids like that. And then I got on graveyard and my husband was at home." Recreation for local families included trips to Lake Mead and Mount Charleston. "Other than that," Bryant said, "it was church functions, getting with the neighbors, other kin folks, and having a good time like we did back home." She also became active in community groups that revolved around her children, such as the Parent-Teacher Association and the Cub Scouts.

In addition to church and family, Bryant credited the Culinary Union for her ability to provide for her family.

We did not have a union at first and I remember when it came in because during those times, if you wanted to work seven days a week, you could work seven days a week and they only paid you straight time.[10] Whatever you wanted to do, they didn't care, and they only paid you straight time. When Culinary came in and organized the union, everything over five days, time and a half, double time, you started getting paid for it. They are the ones that started giving us meals. . . .

Yes, to work at the hotels you had to join the union . . . and the benefits were so good because your children could go to the doctor and you could go to the doctor, dentist, eyes, anything, and they took care of it. I still say they got the best insurance. I was so glad to get into the Culinary Union because it really did help me. . . . I had a little problem on my job once. I called Al Bramlet, because he was the organizer of the union at the beginning. I called him the Great White Father. . . . He stood up for us, he fought for us, and I guess that's why they killed him, too. Because, you know, he was killed, taken out in the desert and killed.[11] He was never too busy to talk to you. You could go there and he would say, "Come on in." You looked like somebody that he didn't even know and he would listen to your problems and he said, you know, he would try to solve them for you. Well, I had a little incident at the Stardust once and he sent Joe Hayes out there. They straightened it out right away.

As far as people that I know, we all were for it because it helped us. It helped us. We were for it. They loved the union. You know, the benefits, the health benefits, most of us were not making enough money to take our children to the doctor, to see a dentist, or to get glasses. We were not making that kind of money and I don't know if we paid a copayment? If [there] was [a copayment], it wasn't very much, and with my husband's insurance and with my Culinary insurance, I never had to pay anything. Uh-uh, I never had to pay anything, so we black people loved the union because it fought for us.

[Today] I can go to any show that I would like to go to. I can get a job any place I'm qualified for, you know, if I'm qualified. I see jobs, but at that time black people didn't get in the higher jobs. As I said, they were maids and porters and teachers of the black kids, and the higher jobs, they didn't let the blacks into them. No one work[ed] at the power company and the water district. You didn't see them in the department stores. You just saw blacks clerking around the stores here in West Las Vegas, but other than that you didn't see blacks driving trucks, like you do now. Job-wise it has bettered itself.

▮ Bryant's narrative encompasses the gaming industry from the mob-controlled days to corporate ownership, from the poorly organized union to the days in which Culinary workers could send their kids to college and buy houses. The paternal concern she received from the mob bosses evaporated with the new efficiencies of the corporation. A reorganization of duties gave her more work to do with the same staff. The flexibility she previously experienced was replaced by greater regulation. Through the changes, the union negotiated on wages and benefits.

Bryant took pride in her ability to prosper at work while she took care of her children. Yet for her, like for many who worked in the low-paying service sector, the job did not define her. As Gretchen Lemke-Santangelo wrote of women who migrated to the East Bay communities during World War II, they "created an alternate source of status and identity as homemakers, church women, and community workers."[12] Within a few years of the interview, Bryant had retired from the industry. The next chapter continues to discuss the experiences of back-of-the-house workers, with the narrative of Hattie Canty.

Chapter 7

HATTIE CANTY

Culinary Workers Union Organizer

*In this town I am living proof that a maid can own a home, she can buy her cars, she can
pay taxes on that home, she can send her kids to college. These jobs represented
stability to me and every other maid out there in this town.*

—Hattie Canty

Hattie Canty didn't expect to be a labor organizer.[1] In fact, she thought she would follow her mother's example by taking care of her family and going out to work only when absolutely necessary. But life turned out differently when her husband died and left her the sole support for eight of her ten children. The only thing she knew to do, she tells us, was housework. So Canty worked as a maid and janitor during the 1970s. She knew little about the UNITE HERE union, except that she needed a referral to get a job and to pay dues. These things she did gladly in order to have a job with benefits.

Canty took a more active role in union activities when she realized how vital the union had been in sustaining her economic independence as she raised her kids. In her mind, the civil rights movement and unions were intertwined and the Culinary Union, as Local 226 of UNITE HERE is known, became her vehicle for maintaining those rights. The 1980s were difficult years for the Culinary workers as corporatization of the hotel-casinos and fragmentation in the union led to loss of contracts and a new labor-management regime. New leadership revitalized the Culinary and started a membership drive; Canty started to volunteer as well as serve as a committee person. She learned how to negotiate contracts and build support with other workers. She participated in and learned from significant contract efforts at major hotel-casinos in downtown Las Vegas. In 1990 the Culinary membership elected Canty president and continued to reelect her until 2002. Within a short time after becoming president, the union embarked on a long strike at the Frontier Hotel and Casino, which was owned by the Elardi family.[2]

Hattie Canty's personal journey corresponded with a transformation in the size of Las Vegas casinos and correspondingly the number of back-of-the-house service workers. During the 1990s nine of the ten largest hotels in the world were located in Las Vegas. Those hotels depended on thousands of housekeepers and food service workers, employees who were the constituency of the Culinary Union. During the postwar years, job segregation reserved these jobs for African Americans. By the 1980s Latinas/os had become the area's largest ethnic group and a significant labor pool for the hotel-casino industry. Canty's administration took care to avoid race and ethnic divisions between workers, and to focus instead on unified strength. With increasing numbers of unskilled workers coming in to the industry, she recognized the need for the union to provide something extra to distinguish union workers from nonunion workers. She pointed to the development of the Culinary Training Center as one example of what the union provided. The Center taught new industry workers the required work standards, while retaining union control.[3]

Canty's narrative reminds us of the many paths taken by American women to gain equality during the 1960s and 1970s. Laws needed to be changed, but legislation alone was insufficient. For Hattie Canty and millions of other service workers, unions played an essential part in achieving workers' rights.[4]

I'm just a Southern country girl and one who will not take no for an answer. If you said it can't be done, why it can't be done. Let me try. If it can be fixed, I can fix it or I'll get somebody to fix it. I am not gonna be beat down by the system or not gonna be beat down by the community. I guess that's what makes me a little different. I got what it takes to overcome—what Reverend King was talkin' about. I got that. . . .

I'm originally from Alabama, sixty-four miles from Mobile, Alabama. St. Stephens. Many, many years ago, St. Stephens was the capital of Alabama, not Montgomery. . . . Today it has maybe three to five hundred people. And that's a maybe. . . . My dad died when I was maybe seventeen months old. He was in an accident. My mom remarried. . . . She was a homemaker. She didn't do any kind of work. But mostly what black women did, they cleaned homes for people. That was the only work back there for black women who were not educators. I only remember black women as being schoolteachers or working in somebody's home. . . . I didn't work in high school, because I lived out in the country. You had to catch a bus to go to school and you caught a bus to come back home at night. You got home, you did your homework and whatever chores that you had to do. There wasn't time. . . .

I was eighteen years old when I left. I had finished high school [around 1957] and I went out there [to California] to live with my brother because there were no opportunities in Alabama for me to get a job. All four of us kids had left home. . . . Well, you know what your mom do, as a rule, the daughter does it. When I got to California, I got me a job as a housekeeper and I was cleaning somebody's house. . . . I worked out in La Jolla, California. I worked out there until I discovered that I had some ability to be a cook. Then I got me a job at the Pancake House in La Jolla, California. . . .

When I first got out there, I met my husband, maybe like the second week I was there. We got married and we had all these babies. Then we moved here to Las Vegas because by trade he was a carpenter and there was no work in San Diego at that particular time. So he was looking for work. He first went to Arizona and there was plenty of work in Arizona, but it was minimum wage. . . . Then he wrote me and he told me, "Hattie, there's a place called Las Vegas. I can get a job there." . . . So my husband came [to Las Vegas] and he got this job and after he got his first pay, he came back to San Diego. Everything we had, we put in a car and got a little trailer and we came to Las Vegas on Sunday [in either 1969 or 1970]. By that time I had six kids, two from a previous marriage.[5] . . .

I was a homemaker. I took care of my family. I took care of my husband. By the time I did decide to go to work, I was taking care of so many people that I was trying to get out from under all of that. I really didn't know how. The only way I could get out from under it, I thought, was if I got myself a job as a maid. I did not know of anything else to do. I had not gone to college for anything. I wasn't trained, had not taken any kind of course to do anything else. But cleaning a house, I knew I could do that. . . . With the family, I needed something that didn't require a lot of thinking to do. I wanted to relax a little bit because when I get home at night, I didn't want to be so uptight that I couldn't be mom. I had to be mom once I walked into that house. Then for the next four to six hours, I was really *mom* because I was cleaning and cooking. Maybe by twelve o'clock, I got to bed.

I went to work in the latter part of 1972 at the old Thunderbird. In the beginning, I didn't join the union. I was one of those people who had never worked in a union house. I didn't know anything about a union, and when I first got to work, I just went up there and they hired me. I never shall forget. I believe it was Rachel Coleman, she came out and she wanted to see my [union] referral and there was no referral for me. So she told me, "You have to go to the union hall and get a referral if you're goin' to work this job, so you get so many hours." So I came down here and I got the referral and I went back out there and I was legal. That referral made me legal.[6]

Sarah Hughes was the union rep at this particular hotel. The first time I saw her, I knew she was a very powerful woman. . . . Whenever she spoke, people moved. She was a shaker. They moved. I don't care if it was management or the maids. . . . I didn't know a lot about her but she was a black woman that represented strength. That's what I saw in her. I saw strength. I saw courage. I saw a woman who was willin' to do the job. . . .

At this particular time, my husband did not want me to work. I'm working because I'm tired of all these people that are running me crazy at home. So I'm focusing a lot on me and what's happening to me. I was real selfish at this particular time. I didn't get too involved in the union, except paying my union dues. I believed I should pay my fair share and my union dues was my fair share. I wasn't a person who caused the union any problems or caused my job any problems. I did what I was told to do and I expected a fair day pay for a fair day of work. I was making something like $32 or something a day. . . . It wasn't very much.[7]

I probably stayed at the Thunderbird, totally, about three years. My husband got sick in 1975 and when he got sick, eight of those ten kids—I had ten kids total by this time—and eight of those ten kids was at home. So I had to take a leave of absence and stay home to take care of the kids and take care of him. I did that and that was a challenge. I didn't think that I would ever be able to do that because my husband was the type of husband who had always taken care of me and the kids. While he was well, I didn't have anything to worry about. But now the table turns, where I'm taking care of him and I got everything to worry about. I stayed home and I took care of him and then when he died, that's when reality set in. I had to live off like a fourth of the amount of money he was bringing home. My money dropped like that. So everything had to be readjusted. That was in 1975.[8]

So then I didn't go back to the Thunderbird, I went to the school district because I needed to work a shift that I thought would let me take care of my kids even better. That was a straight swing shift.[9] At the hotel I couldn't get a straight swing shift. I worked for the school district for one year as custodian. After that year, I worked out here at Red Rock School, and then the next year they wanted to send me to Henderson at Voc Tech [Vocational Technology school].[10] I just couldn't work swing and drive all the way from Voc Tech at eleven or twelve o'clock at night because I'm one of those people who go to sleep real early. I went out and I talked to the guy and he wouldn't make concessions for me. He didn't take into consideration me being a single adult with all these kids. It was either, "You take it or you don't have a job." So I just didn't have a job anymore because I couldn't take it.

The Maxim Hotel was opening up [circa 1977] and I went out to put an application in and I got the job out there as a maid. You know when you don't prepare yourself for anything, you don't know of anything to do, but I knew I could take care of myself and those kids. So I went to the Maxim Hotel and I got that job as a maid. . . . I hope I was a real good maid, because I worked there for like three or four years. Then the Maxim added on. They added like four hundred more rooms onto the hotel. . . . When they built these other rooms onto the hotel, my friend said, "Hattie, go out there and apply for uniform attendant. It pays $10 a day more and so you should be able to do a little bit more for your family." I go out and I apply for a job and when they finished building these rooms, I'd gotten the job as a uniform attendant. . . .

The duties in the uniform room are similar to the duties in a cleaners. If you was a cocktail server, when you came in the morning I had to give you your personal uniform. I couldn't give you just any uniform. There's a uniform for every cocktail server there. As a rule, that uniform has that person's name in it or her number. You send those clothes out by that person's name and you check them in by that person's name. So if I lost a cocktail server's uniform, I would be held responsible: not pay for it, but I could get in trouble over that. So I never lost a cocktail server uniform. I never lost a uniform, period. . . .

Uniform work is a hard job because most of the time you stand on cement. You got to go through every uniform to make sure the buttons are there, to make sure the hems are not out, to make sure the pockets are not torn off, to make sure that uniform came back clean. You got to look at the collars because some uniforms got white collars and they could come back and they're not clean. Most girls will not wear a real dirty-looking uniform, even if you say it's clean. Even the pants, you got to go through and make sure that zippers are always together, make sure buttons are on those, hems are not out of those uniforms. You got your cook jackets. You got to make sure those executive chefs, those sous chefs—they don't just wear any jacket in the uniform room. You got to make sure that James's jacket is hanging in James's spot, all of John's jackets are together. . . . Over at the Maxim we had to make sure everything came back like it should come back.

We tagged repairs. If a button was broken off of a dress, we would tag it. They had a little tag that said "button needed"; we put that in there and we threw it in a special place and Western Linen would put those buttons on. Western Linen would hem. Western Linen would sew up a pocket that was off of there. We didn't have to do that. Now special clothes, like the cocktail server dresses, we had a special girl who sewed for those people that worked right there in the linen room. She would sew up or she might readjust or she might hem or put lace back on. Because you know, those dresses are very delicate and you had to keep them up. . . .

This job didn't make me whole. Hattie made this job what it is because of what I have down in me. My kids have always seen that. When my husband died and I was a maid, they saw how I could keep that family together. I had to show strength then and I show even more strength now. They saw that when I didn't have but a little money I could yet put a decent meal on the table. They don't remember the lights bein' ever out or the water bein' cut off, because I always was the type of person who took care of business. I had to take care of my business. I never really liked responsibility, but I could accept it much easier than most people that you know. I accepted my responsibility and I took care of it. . . .

I worked there for a long, long time, but in working there and working for the Maxim Hotel I began to learn what kind of union organization with all of these great benefits that I had gotten. Some of my childrens had gotten sick with some serious illness. One of my boys had a cancerous growth removed from the nerve right by the ear. If I had not belonged to the union and if I had not had that Culinary insurance, I wouldn't have been able to get that operation. I learned how beneficial it was for me, as a poor, black female, to belong to a union. My childrens, by this time, began to get bigger. They was graduating from high school. Some of them was goin' off to college. If it had not been for the union in this town—if I had been in Los Angeles—I would have been totally on welfare. But by being here in this town, every time somebody wanted to do something, he had to go get a job so he could help me so we could do these things. My daughter, who's a registered nurse at Valley Hospital, she'll tell you quick, "If it had not been for union money, I would not have the job that I have now." That's the way we put it.

In this town I am living proof that a maid can own a home, she can buy her cars, she can pay taxes on that home, she can send her kids to college. These jobs represented stability to me and every other maid out there in this town. And we are appreciative to work here in this town. What we try to do— the reason I say *we*, I'm not the only one who is tryin' to do this—is show younger women and men how beneficial it is to be in a union town. Because the union stands for so many things in my life. If it hadn't been for the union, there wouldn't be no minimum wages. . . . If it were not for the union, there wouldn't be no breaks. And we don't negotiate for that. The government says you get that lunch break. But we enforce that and try to make sure that the maids, the porters, and the dishwashers continue to have that. It has been a struggle to pull things together. . . . I thought at some point, "You've got to separate the civil rights movement from the labor movement." But you can't do it. There's no way you can do it. Anytime I fight for anything in this labor movement, it benefits me and the civil rights movement. That's what a lot of peoples don't understand.

I started getting involved with the union in 1984. That's when we lost so many hotels.[11] I think it was about six hotels we lost. On my days off I would always go up to the Marina. I would picket every off-day. That's where I would go and my baby would go with me because he was five years old. We would go up there and we would spend all of our time there. . . . Things began to happen in my mind. I begin to see that we had lost all these hotels and if I got active, if I did what I could, maybe this wouldn't happen. I was thinking about what I could do. But it had to take all of us to stop what was goin' on in this town. We didn't stop it in 1984, 1985, 1986, or 1987, but we began to work on it. And some of those places that we lost in 1984, we have gotten them back today. But it's because of the hard work that I did, and many other union members. At this particular time, I had no idea that I would be the president of the Culinary Union. . . . I did it because, by this time, I'm a single mother with all those babies. I needed that union salary and I needed the health and welfare. The pension, I didn't think too much about that, but health and welfare I did. . . .

I remember one time in 1984 the Desert Inn was out on strike. . . . I was takin' my son to work. I was goin' to the Maxim and he was goin' to his job. He said, "Oh Mom, I know this guy. Pick him up." So I picked his friend up back down on Martin Luther King Boulevard and probably Vegas Drive. And by the time we got to Bonanza, this guy's tellin' me that he was on his way to work at the Desert Inn. And I say, "What you do at the DI [Desert Inn]?" He told me what job he was in and I say, "The DI is out on strike." He say, "Yeah, Miss Canty, but I got to work." I stopped my car. I says, "Scab, get out of my car. I am not takin' no scabs to work." And my son said to me, "Mom, don't." I said, "Get outta' my car." I put him outta' that car. I could not support him and support the strikers. If I'm gonna walk the picket line for the strikers, I am not gonna take a scab to work. You can only do one or the other. So I explained that to my son and now my son laughs about it. He said, "Boy, you are really into the union." . . . After the Marina and after all of that, I never went home and sat down on the union. I have always been involved from that day forward. . . . We will forever be in a struggle here in this town and sometime I wonder if these younger peoples are gonna pull it off, because it's a certain group of people that's really, really makin' sure this union continues to stay together. . . .

[Sometime around 1988 or the early part of 1989] I got involved to see what I could do. And what I could do was right there at my hotel—to talk to the girls about the union and to get them feeling, hopefully, like I was feeling. I was a committee person for the union. I would talk to all of the workers, at least ten or fifteen workers, about what's goin' on between the company and the union, especially when you're in negotiation. You have to inform your coworkers about what's goin' on. . . . A committee person is a worker who wants to do it, who got it down in them to work for the betterment of the workers and the community, because they have realized, we're not dealing with mom-and-pop operations anymore. These corporations are coming here and they will blow a worker out of the waters. The workers got to get involved in their jobs and in the unions.

By this time, it was contract time for the Maxim. So I told the girls, "Look, we've really got to get this thing together because if we don't, we are not goin' to get no contract." They said, "Oh, we'll get a contract," because the Maxim had always done what they thought was the right thing. I would tell them, "This company is like any other company. The right thing to them is the dollar. They are not thinking about the workers." That's just how I felt. So I said, "We gotta get ourselves together. If we don't, we gonna lose." . . .

When we really got negotiating with the Maxim Hotel, one of the head guys, he was the comptroller and he would always tell me that I was a leader. I didn't feel like I was a leader. I felt like I was just doing the right thing. So this guy would always tell me that we'd have a contract by a certain date. When that date came and we didn't have the contract, I'd go back to him. He said, "Well we'll have it by this date." So when we got into negotiations and he said, "Well, I tell you what, I want to hear from my workers." He says this to the negotiator. He called on different ones to speak. He said, "I want to see what Hattie got to say." And you know, out the clear blue Hattie said too much. I said, "Look, you lied to me four times." And I told him what times that he had lied. After I said that, a little fear come in. Here I am telling this man—he is my boss and he signs my check—that he's lyin'. And I say, "We need a contract. We have to have a contract." So everybody got so quiet. They got real quiet around that table. I went to my friend and I said, "Dorothy, I'm in big trouble, huh?" She said, "No. Just go on. You just told the truth. You told what he said and he hadn't did what he said. So *he* lied, not you." I finally got over that but it took me a couple of weeks to get over that. . . .

Now by that time, I was fifty-five years old, the only thing I wanted to do is to retire. I said, "When I'm sixty-two years old, I'm gonna retire. I'm gonna get out of all this." Because you know, it is tiring. . . . Peoples beat you down. Every day you take a beating. . . . This town cannot come in here and afford to let the union be blown out of here, because too many peoples depend on these salaries. . . . It's getting to the place now that a maid cannot buy a home because the salary is not where it should be and homes are more expensive than what they used to be. We gonna always have to focus on things that maids, porters, or dishwashers are gonna be able to do. . . . So it was good that I was talkin' about the union because if I didn't stay focused on keepin' the union in that hotel, the management could have took us on. I didn't want them to take the union on. They'd start a campaign and would blow the union out. I had to keep my campaign alive to where the union would always be in that hotel. . . . The type of work that I was doin' in that hotel, these hotels can't pick it up and take it to Mexico. It's here in this town, it is a part of our community, and it's here to stay, so why not make us a part of it. We gotta get our fair share of that pie. We don't want a sliver no more. We want a slice of pie. . . .

My next step in the union was the downtown four. We called it downtown four because there was the Golden Gate, the Las Vegas Club, the Union Plaza, and the Showboat. They had reneged on a contract and we had a picket line at this particular time on Friday and Saturday. I would go down there every Friday evening and go back home Saturday morning. I'd take me a rest, then Saturday night I'd go back down there again. So I really got involved. . . . After the [downtown] four settled, we felt like we could take a break for a while, you know. Then in 1989 or 1990 there was a nine-and-a-half months strike at the Horseshoe that went on. Right after that, the Frontier took us on.

▮ In 1990 Jim Arnold, the secretary-treasurer of the Culinary Union at the time, asked Canty to run for president of the union on his ticket. She recounted her first thoughts about the proposal.

So I went back to work and I told Dorothy Hardin, "You know, Dorothy, I can't take that position. People will think I'm crazy. I don't have no education." She say, "Very few labor leaders went to college to be a labor leader. And members elect you and if the members elect you, then you got that position." She say, "I'll tell you what. You think you crazy now; if you don't take that job I'm gonna think you're crazy." Well I wasn't getting no help from her so I decided that weekend I'd better talk to my daughters. So all the family comes over and we talk. I told 'em, "I just can't do that." And my daughter, she said, "Mom, don't worry, I'll help you with anything. I'll help you. You don't gotta worry about nothin.'" I said, "Well what you gonna help me with. You gonna be somewhere when they gonna be wantin' a report from me. I'm gonna be down there and I'm not gonna be able to give 'em a report." She said, "Mama, I'll get the report ready for you the day before." I said, "Okay, Dell." I've never had to call on her to help me. I don't know what kind of report she would have done, but everybody was willing to help me. . . .

I won the election like three to one. That was May of 1990. Then in 1993 I ran and was elected again. That was the same way, three to one. It might have been higher than that because by this time, [I was running against] somebody that wasn't known. Then in 1996 I ran again and I won and it was a landslide. I mean, the person might have gotten four hundred and I got like fourteen hundred votes. Next year is the next election. So I'm playing this by ear. I don't know how the health is goin' to be doin' because I'm sixty-four years old. I be sixty-five in June. Everybody say, "You gotta run," and I say, "I gotta see if I want to get up." I feel good. And I feel like I've given a lot to the union and I feel like there's a lots more I can give. I'll do it as long as I can. My mind is good. I look at some of these young peoples today, they don't have no mind. I wonder what happened to [them]. . . .

The longest strike to date in Nevada's history began on September 19, 1991, when workers at the Frontier Hotel and Casino, who had been working without a contract, voted to strike. The owners, Margaret Elardi and her sons Tom and John, were committed to resist union demands and to replace the striking workers. The strike lasted six and a half years, and included mass marches, pickets, and a gruesome fight on the picket line. The length of the strike and its bad publicity raised concerns among business and political elites. Casino owner Bill Bennett of Circus Circus provided meals to the strikers in a show of support. Governor Bob Miller of Nevada and US Senators Harry Reid and Richard Bryan asked the State Gaming Control Board to review the Frontier's actions for possible violations. The strike ended with the sale of the Frontier and the union claimed victory in early 1998.[12]

Well, you know, we had a bunch of people who felt like if this woman [owner Margaret Elardi] did not want those five-hundred-and-some workers in there; why didn't those five-hundred-and-some workers go get a job some other place. Then you got a great big group of people who said, "Stay there. Don't walk away from there because if you walk away from there, this thing's gonna

Hattie Canty, (*left*) president of the UNITE-HERE Culinary Workers Union, Local 226, celebrates the conclusion of the Frontier Hotel and Casino strike that ran from 1991 to 1998. Courtesy of Culinary Workers Union, Local 226.

spread throughout the city." They felt like, "We'd better stay here and fight for our rights." When there's a strike like that, you not just strikin' for the benefits from that hotel, but you're learnin' to take up for yourself. You're learnin' to defend your rights. You're not lettin' people just run over you, or you takin' anything they give you. You're sayin' to that company, "No, I'm not gonna take that. I want this from you. You not gonna gut my contract. You gonna leave my contract intact and you just not gonna do me like that." . . . All these people you see walkin' the picket line, they walkin' the picket line to continue to save jobs in this city, to continue the cost of livin' that we have in this city, to continue what we are used to. Because if there were not picket lines, we wouldn't be getting the salaries that we are getting. . . .

Our responsibility is support for strikers. We have to go out on the line.

We walk just like the strikers do. I walked many a day out there on that line, myself. We yet have to keep the business of the union goin'. We yet have to take care of the members in the rest of these hotels. . . . There are so many things you have to do to keep that strike goin' and everybody work together. If you see where one is getting burned out, you have to put him some other place. Or maybe they're leafleting out there at the airport. We did many things durin' that strike. We were leafleting at the airport, lettin' peoples know that there was a strike at the Frontier. So there were many things that peoples could do and was doing. . . .

When you cease to grow, you dead. And this labor movement is alive, very much alive. We have to grow right along with the hotels in this industry. Also, we would love to work as partnerships with these companies here. We don't want to always be their enemies, or fightin' across the table. Things are much better when we sit down and work things out, talk things out. That's what this union is about. . . .

We organized the MGM. That was a struggle. That particular time, there was over five hundred peoples that got arrested [and put in] jail and I was one of those people. I've been in jail a-many time. Never thought that I would go to jail for anything because I've always been a good person. But for the labor movement, I've gone to jail quite a few times. . . . I'm sure if Dr. Martin Luther King was here today—these were some of the same things he did back then in the 1950s and 1960s. So we are really takin' charge from what he did. . . . We listen to King. We read books so that we'll do this the right way. . . .

To be honest with you, when I first started getting involved, the participation [in unions] wasn't very great in the black community. It wasn't great at all. See, blacks has been treated so bad. Not just by the Culinary Union, but in other unions they was iced out of good jobs. Young black mens, even in construction, couldn't go get jobs that paid good and that other people were getting. As a rule, when people talk about the unions, if they was talkin' about somebody diggin' a ditch or drivin' a truck, . . . they said, "The unions ain't no good." That don't necessarily have to be true because what this union have done, . . . we tend to work on our problems. That's one thing I like about the Culinary Union. We are tryin' to work on problems that we have had. We don't have anything to do with who the hotel hire. We do send peoples to jobs; we send out three peoples for every one job that a hotel might want. There are blacks, Latinos, and whites that we send out. Now, when that person gets to that hotel, whoever the hotel hire, that's the hotel's business. But there are certain things that go on in the industry that we do make our business to change.[13] . . .

I don't see a lot of blacks in certain positions and I do want to see more blacks there. You don't see a lot of black cocktail servers out there on the floor. You don't see a lot of black slot foremen out there on the floor. And there are different jobs that you just don't see a lot of blacks in. High-payin' jobs at the hotels, you don't see a lot of blacks there. But what we try to do, we try to go to these companies and talk to them and let them know how we feel. There are gonna be some issues that we're gonna take as top priority and things are goin' to be happening. I don't try to hide it. With all the blacks in this town, we don't have a lot of blacks workin' in the hotel industry at all. . . . This is why I'm constantly talkin' to black young women, "Get involved." Because if I had never gotten involved, I would not be sittin' here at this desk today. It's the involvement. It's the leadership. It's the honesty that I had. . . . If I had been a flim-flam person, they wouldn't have seen anything in me.[14] . . .

You need to have somebody to work with you on that civil rights part because you can't do it by yourself. That's what I love about this union. If there are things that bother me, there are higher-up people I can go to and I tell 'em what's bothering me. I tell 'em my concerns and I have done that. Some of my concerns is about the low percentage of blacks in high-payin' jobs. When I first started the maid work, most of the maids was black. Now that maids are bein' paid a decent salary, they are not there anymore. That bothers me. And only we as a black community gotta do something about it. We got the right vehicles to do something about it. . . . But it's gonna take the community to help me to get some of these people into these programs. It would be wonderful if blacks never had to be a maid, but when I tell you that is a vehicle to you gettin' to be in the White House or whatever house you want to be in, that's sometimes what it take. You take those entrance positions and you get into the corporation and you look around and see what you want. Then you say, "That's mine," and go working for it. . . .

We gotta get our blacks into these hotels and into jobs that's payin' decent money. I'd much rather see a black woman in a union job than to see her in a nonunion job, if she got six or seven childrens, because in that union job she's makin' a decent salary, she gettin' $0.45 an hour goin' into her pension, she gettin' $1.82 goin' into her health and welfare. The benefits are out there for her. We have great benefits. I go get my glasses. I don't pay nothin' for my glasses. I go get whatever I need. I don't have to pay a lot for it. I would much rather see a poor woman, black, or white, or Latina, go into a position where you gonna have some benefits. That's the one thing that drew me to it was the benefits. I learned how to appreciate it and how to work to help to keep it. . . .

An example of cooperation between labor and management that Canty appreciated was the development of the Culinary Training Center, presently called the Culinary Academy of Las Vegas. This partnership of the Culinary Union 226, the Bartenders Union 165, and twenty-six major Las Vegas Strip properties operates to train workers for the hospitality industry.

It's just for certain jobs, but it's the majority of our entry-level jobs. . . . One reason I'm so proud of it, we trained many people, but over two hundred on the welfare rolls. And 70 percent of those people are workin' at a hotel right [now]. That's one of the reasons that I'm so proud of the Culinary Training Center. . . . We have a lady who teaches women how to do maid work. You would think all of us know how to do maid work but we really don't. . . . Ninety percent of our girls or ladies that go through that Culinary Training Center get jobs. They know they gonna get a job if they go through the Culinary Training Center. We have a restaurant. We teach people just how to prepare food, how to serve it, how to cook it. . . . I would love to say that I came up with the idea but I did not. It was born before I got to be the president. I just happened to be one of the people that got involved from the beginnin' of the school.[15] . . .

We have the GED [General Education Development] program at the Culinary Training Center. If a person come here and wants to take a GED test or get that GED, we have that at the Culinary Training Center. We also have ESL [English as a Second Language] classes. If a person wants to learn English, we got that class. . . . The Clark County School District provides instructors for those classes at the Culinary Training Center.

That is one true partnership that Culinary has with management in this town. Management pays $0.03 an hour for every hour that a worker works. That's how the trainin' center's run, $0.03 an hour for every worker. Management pays for that. So all of these students that you see down there, they don't pay nothin' to go through that trainin' center. It is paid for already. That course is about twelve weeks long. . . . We don't graduate nobody who gonna be a problem to the business when they get out there. That's not what management is payin' for with this course. You learn how to work in that environment when you get into the hotel. So, as a rule, when they go through there, they are ready. . . .

You know, women are over one-half of the people in this union. Women are just goin' forth. They are just doin'. We know what to do and that's to take care of the responsibility. Take care of the membership out there. . . . Women are very aggressive in this union. It's much easier to organize women than it is to organize mens and you're not goin' to believe it. Mens are so fearful of the boss, where most women, the first thing they say, "Well, I was lookin' for a job when I came here and when I leave, I'll be lookin' for a job." Some of the toughest people in this city is housekeepers. We have got two to three hundred housekeepers and marched them up to the executive office, or they have did it on their own. There have been times when we've had to stop housekeepin' departments from walkin' out. I would tell 'em, "You can't do that. We have a contract there. If you walk out, they gonna lock you out and you all gonna be fired." But that's when they are tired. These are women, both black, white, and Latina; when they get tired they are tired. Most times they'll do something about it. We just have to make sure that what they do about these things are the right things. . . .

But one of the things that most workers want, they want a good contract. They want a safe environment to work in. They want that guaranteed forty-hour week. They want to hold on to that. Most of all, they want to keep that health and welfare, that insurance. They want that. They want their pension. . . .

So that was the time for me to kind of tell my story. And for the young peoples and all the peoples that read this, "Get involved. Try and get involved with somethin' that's gonna benefit your children, your grandkids." Because you know, I'm sixty-five years old and there's a possibility I'm not gonna be here sixty more years. That's a great possibility. But the things that I have done, the doors that I have caused to be opened for the young peoples that followed me, I feel really great about that today. I have not gotten sixty years old to sit down and do nothing. Most of the work that I have done for this community has been in the last eight years. So you never get too old. Don't ever get discouraged. You can never get too tired. But you gotta keep on keepin' on. That's what it's all about: just keep on keepin' on.

Hattie Canty doubted that she would be able to stand the challenges of raising her children following the death of her husband, yet she did. "I had to take care of my business," she said. "I accepted my responsibility and I took care of it." Her narrative describes the strength she found inside herself to always provide for her children. She also discovered her loyalty to the institution that made her efforts more successful—the union, that she subsequently strengthened with her dedicated efforts. As authors Susan Chandler and Jill B. Jones wrote of a group of women who joined the union in Nevada, the civil rights movement profoundly altered the way in which they saw themselves, their potential, and their ability to remedy injustice.[16] Canty worked not only for her family, but also to improve the conditions for those coming up. In doing so, she not only empowered herself, but also became a symbol of empowerment for other women.

Chapter 8

FLORENCE McCLURE

Hotel Executive Administrator and Community Activist

We were able to take every one of the unjust laws and cut it to pieces.
—Florence McClure

During the 1950s, in most US cities, the rapidly growing business and commercial sectors expanded job opportunities for women.[1] Typing, stenography, bookkeeping, clerical, and secretarial jobs attracted high school graduates or women with a few years of advanced training.[2] Definitely sex-typed and, in a majority of cases, reserved for white women, these jobs would later be known as the *pink-collar* ghetto because of the lack of advancement opportunities for women.[3] In Las Vegas women's participation in sales and office work nearly doubled over fifty years from 34 percent of all workers in 1940 to 65.9 percent in 1990. The rapid increase leveled off by 1970 and then stabilized within a few percentage points over the next decades as other areas of employment opened up as a result of the passage of antidiscrimination laws.[4]

Florence McClure followed the advice given to women of her generation and learned office skills. She grew up in downstate Illinois during the 1920s and 1930s. Her father, a World War I veteran, lived in a veterans' home out of town, so Florence and her sister were raised by three generations of women—her mother, grandmother, and great-grandmother. As a child, she loved to read and almost went to the University of Illinois. Instead, her mother convinced her to attend the local MacMurray College for Women and live at home. After one and a half years Florence switched to study at a business school and to learn tools she would use for the rest of her career. She completed her studies two months before the United States entered World War II after the bombing of Pearl Harbor.

McClure used her typing, shorthand, and keen sense of organization for the war effort in Ypsilanti, Michigan. At the age of twenty-one she worked on legal briefings for the judge advocate general. She moved to Miami Beach in 1944 and continued to support the war effort in the intelligence division of the Army ground and service forces. She met her husband, First Lieutenant James McClure, in Miami, and they married in 1945. The couple moved frequently with the Air Force from Florida to Texas, California, Japan, and back to Florida. They had two children, James and Carolyn. Florence worked when she could and on a return stay in Florida (1963–1965) she took her first job in the hotel industry at the Fontainebleau Hotel in Miami Beach. This began her association with the hotel and tourism industry. Her office skills, no-nonsense style, and impeccable manners contributed to her high recommendations and move up to the executive offices. When the McClures moved back to California, Florence went to work at the International Hotel in Los Angeles. That job led her to Las Vegas in 1966 to open the Frontier Hotel and Casino as an executive secretary.

I met Burton [Cohen] at the International Hotel at the entrance to the airport in Los Angeles. He was the nephew of Sol Cohen who I had been working for at the hotel. . . . Burton came in and took over the operation of the corporation and I became his administrative assistant. I kept track of everything that was going on—the billings and the paperwork—like I had at the Fontainebleau.[5]

As much as the McClures liked California, the smog was a problem for Florence's husband's health. They had explored moving to a desert city when an opportunity arose.

We were going for his health, but in the meantime Burton Cohen said that he wanted to talk to me. He said, "I'd like for you and Jim to go with me to Las Vegas. They want me to come there and work on the construction and operation of a hotel," and he laughingly said, "They won't take me unless you come, too." So, I talked to Jim about it and I said, that is a desert and Burton says that the climate will help you even more than Tucson or Phoenix and he said he wants you to get ready and go and try it out for your health. . . . I said, "Gambling?," because I come from the Bible Belt of southern Illinois. Five days a week my mother took me to church, you know, this sort of thing, and I never did learn how to gamble. I never really cared. I wouldn't put my mind to it. . . .

In 1966 the McClure's made a final move to Las Vegas and Florence started her job at the Frontier Hotel and Casino. By the spring or early summer of 1967 the property was completed and opened its doors.[6] After its completion, the Howard Hughes Corporation bought it. Hughes received credit for transforming the culture of Las Vegas gambling to corporate gaming through the purchase of numerous hotel properties and the implementation of legitimate business practices. Hughes had purchased the Desert Inn located across from the Frontier and he lived on the eighth floor. The purchase brought a change of venue for Cohen and McClure as they moved to the administrative offices of the Desert Inn.

I handled what some people might consider crank calls, because the executives that were around Howard Hughes did not want to talk to them. Somebody could have invented a part for an automobile or something and they needed backing and they would call in and say, "I want to talk to Howard

Hughes about this invention I've made. It will make millions for us," and this sort of thing. So, I would take their name and address and so forth, but politely get rid of them. That was the idea. . . .

[There were not many women in management on the Strip in the 1960s.] And women were not allowed to deal on the Strip. The sheriff, Ralph Lamb, said that women were not going to deal on the Strip. It was, more or less, "over my dead body." No women dealers down here. Now they had a few women dealers downtown, but none out here in the county and he was the county sheriff. . . . They didn't want women in that type of operation.[7] I saw women go in, finally, into managing a cage, a cashier's cage, but they were usually at the smaller places. They were usually men who had been credit managers in other big operations that learned the casino business and then came in as casino cage operators and managers. . . . When we opened that Frontier Burton Cohen put a woman in charge of conventions. Burton has been very open about [hiring] women. . . .

Cohen moved on to work with Jay Sarno who was building Circus Circus, but McClure decided to stay at the Desert Inn a while longer. After two years she was ready for a change.

I stayed with the Howard Hughes organization. I was office manager of the executive office at the Desert Inn. But there were a lot of people that were put in the Hughes organization that really [did not know hospitality]. They'd been working in federal offices like the Small Business Administration [SBA] The managing director of the DI after Burton left came from the SBA. That didn't teach them anything about hospitality work or the hotel industry or how one should run it. I thought they did a lousy job. Two men that were put in over at the Frontier, where Burton and I had been, were later brought up on government charges and they had been with the IRS. They were paper pushers; they were not hospitality industry administrators. There's a big difference. Government officials could be cold, but in the hospitality industry you had to have a special personality. Burton Cohen had it. He could be comedic; he's a joy to be around. It's these hard-nosed government pencil-pushers that use their accounting machines, who came into the Howard Hughes organization and did not know how to operate it. . . .

Well, I was forty-eight at the time [in 1969]. I'd been in the hotel business for a number of years in Florida, California, and in Las Vegas. . . . I was the first woman to take casino operation and management at UNLV. It was taught by Lou Kurtz who was the comptroller for Caesar's Palace at the time. . . . I made a good grade; in fact, the professor used my essay answers in courses that came up later on. But that was not because I knew gaming or how to play the games. It was because I'd had a number of courses in management. I had courses in personnel. I'd worked in security with the military, so I had a background for it. Whereas, the men in the class, I was the only woman, the men in the class were box men and blackjack dealers and such as that and they knew the games, but the course was on casino operation and management. [After a few more years,] I decided it was time to move on [from the hotel industry]. I had learned everything I had wanted to about hotel administration.

▨ Although her work in the hotel executive offices claimed a place for her in this collection, it paled in comparison to what would become her life's work as a community advocate for victims of crime, specifically sexual assault. McClure returned to finish her bachelor of arts at UNLV in sociology and became involved in politics through the LWV beginning in 1967. McClure loved current affairs and read avidly, but could not explore her interest in politics until she settled down in Las Vegas. The population of Las Vegas was about 125,000, she observed, and it was possible to meet and get to know your elected officials. When she started lobbying in the state legislature, she became familiar with officials across the state.

She continued in the LWV during the early 1970s and became the state president. Social and political unrest defined the 1970s, and this unrest was reflected in League meetings. Members studied, discussed, and took positions on civil rights, school desegregation, open housing, equal employment, abortion, and the Equal Rights Amendment (ERA). McClure's introduction to the issues came gradually, but eventually changed the course of her life.

I'd been reading about the [LWV] for years, when I lived in Texas and other states.[8] The League always seemed to be out there, ahead, putting out the political angle, informing the public. It was important and they knew it. My husband's military career kept us moving around all the time, so I couldn't put down roots, but one of the things I could do was keep reading. And so when I got here I could put down roots and I said, "I'm going to join the League." . . . The League is a training ground. I said that the first thing that anybody does when they move to a new town, if there's a League of Women Voters there, join it, because you will learn first-hand at the very beginning what it's all about. Like the booklets that Leagues put out, "Know Your Community," that has facts and figures in there that you can't get anywhere else, [and] "The Urban Puzzle," and "People Power" about how people can make a difference. I tell you something, we wouldn't have had all this trouble about the elections last time if everybody had read those publications of League of Women Voters.[9]

I started going to the legislature in 1969. Jean Ford [the state president of the LWV at the time] was the one that took a group of League of Women Voters up there to see how you lobby the legislature: what bills are up, what needs to be done, how important is this bill, the whole ramifications and I enjoyed it. So Jean Ford has been a mentor of mine these many years because it was at her feet that I learned a lot about politics.[10]

It took McClure about two years after she left the hotel business to complete her college degree at the UNLV. During that time she became more involved in the local LWV and held the office of secretary. Shortly after graduating with her BA in 1971, at the age of fifty years, her mentor, Jean Ford, asked her to consider running for state president of the LWV. Ford had left that position to campaign for the state assembly. The LWV faced a challenging time because the issues of abortion and the ERA created fissures in branches across the country. Ford and the state board of directors of the LWV believed that McClure could keep the League together as it met those challenges. She ran, and won the election.

This was the time of the women's movement. I had not seen any problems with the League or the other groups, but I soon became aware of two factions in the League: the pro-ERA and the anti-ERA people, the prochoice and the antiabortion people.[11] . . . Now, I am a person of strong character and I won't put up with people saying, "Oh, you can't do this or you can't do that because you're a woman." I did not feel that I had been harassed on the job, because I can have a sharp tongue if I need it. . . . I could chew up a person who was giving me a bad time by using good words that are in the dictionary. So when the women's movement started, I thought, "Why are they doing that?," because I wouldn't allow that to be done to me. But not all women are alike. Some did believe that because they were a woman, they were limited. I've never had that feeling, but I've had strong women in my family—my grandmothers, my mother, my aunts—therefore I felt like I could do anything I wanted to do. . . . We had some good women, who had been leaders in Nevada, but they were more feminist and they wanted to do away with our League rules [that] required study of an issue at meetings and then the building of a consensus on the issues we would take up. We wanted to stay chartered. If we had gone against the national procedures of the League of Women Voters, then we could have lost our charter. . . .

I went to the national convention of the League of Women Voters in Atlanta, Georgia, and I saw over two hundred women get up and move out of that meeting because they were against the League's pro-ERA position. The

National League did what our group had really wanted before: do not have a study, do not have a consensus, go straight for lobbying at the legislature on ERA. Otherwise we would be far behind. . . .

Jean [Ford] wanted to keep the League together and she came to me because of my previous work on different issues and because I am one of those people who works well with all people. I do not go into any faction against another group. I try to get them all to think about it and to take action after a concerted effort. The state board agreed to me being president, but they did not want anybody else. That was because I had not been part of the fray that had been going on. . . . After talking it over with my husband, I agreed to take it on. And so we got through, but it could have torn our group apart. . . .

McClure's involvement with the League introduced her to a host of women's rights issues, so when she read about a meeting to be held in Las Vegas to discuss the community's response to the rising number of rapes, she decided to go.

The meeting was going to be held on Sunday afternoon and I'd read about it in the newspaper. . . . After all, I'd just gotten my degree within the past few months in sociology and a lot of the courses I took were criminology, juvenile delinquency, and that sort of thing. So I went off to the meeting. . . . In fact, the North Las Vegas Library had a little balcony up there that they had set up for this meeting and when the people started coming and coming, waves of people coming to this meeting on rape, they couldn't believe it. They had to take over the whole library and people were sitting on tops of file cabinets and on the floors and everywhere. . . . It was unbelievable. That was September 23, 1973.[12]

Well, at the meeting we had a North Las Vegas police officer who spoke on how they enforce the laws and how they help victims. We had Jean Ford on the laws and the victims of sexual assault. [Ford had been elected to the state assembly.] They announced that any person who wanted to work on this horrendous crime should sign their name on a yellow tablet. About eighty people signed up. But, as you know, when you are starting a new organization, it's going to drop maybe to half and maybe at the next meeting it will drop again further. After two or three meetings, we came out with a good, hardcore group of fifteen who showed up at every meeting and said, "I want to do something."

In the early 1970s survivors of rape faced marginalization and repeated victimization after the sexual assault. Usually the one who had been assaulted was a woman; she had little assistance from community institutions including hospitals, police, and courts. This absence of response from the community to such a violent crime aroused a deep-seated sense of justice in McClure. A collection of women and men who were beginning to recognize the problems of sexual inequality began to organize. They started with the name. Some wanted to call it Women Against Rape with the acronym W-A-R. McClure felt that was too confrontational and would make the work more difficult. She wanted a name that conveyed a community united against the status quo on violence. The group finally agreed on the name Community Action Against Rape (CAAR).[13]

Mike O'Callaghan was governor of the State of Nevada at the time. He had an appendectomy at Sunrise Hospital here and he called me at home. He found out from a nurse that we were putting a rape crisis center together and he called me at home. . . . [He turned out to be a big supporter. When] the federal government funded the Law Enforcement Assistance Administration [LEAA], Governor Mike O'Callaghan told them to find the monies to put in a hot line phone for the Rape Crisis Center. See, we didn't have any money, we had no grants. I ran the center out of my home for five years. I took my den and I had my desk and everything set up. I had the telephone. We had a hotline run through an answering service. Sandi Petta started training people

Florence McClure in her home office, ca. late 1980s. Courtesy of Florence and Carolyn McClure.

[to answer the hotline] and we had a list of who was on duty with their telephone numbers. Now, if they couldn't reach [some]one for some reason, then I would always get a call. Sometimes it would be in the middle of the night. I've met many a mother and child in the emergency room. I would write a note and pin it to my pillow so when my husband woke up and I wasn't there, he would know where I was. . . . I didn't get a salary, but, that's all right. I got pleasure out of getting something done that needed to be done, right away. Of course, the early 1970s was the beginning of the so-called women's movement. This was my bit.[14]

■ McClure and CAAR cofounder Sandi Petta split up the responsibilities. Petta had a counseling degree from UNLV and wanted to deliver counseling services to the rape survivors. McClure's interests combined community organizing and politics, so she served as the advocate to community institutions. She noted that her prior experience working for the provost marshal at the Office of Special Investigation, for the judge advocate general's office in the military, and for a lawyer in California provided a set of skills that would be useful in her role as advocate.

She launched an educational campaign designed to raise people's understanding of the issues. She worked with the Clark County district attorneys' office, hospital staff, police departments, and elected officials. CAAR went into middle and high schools where ignorance about sexual health and sexual assault prevention ran high. She took her campaign to the university where rapes had occurred, but the administration had little knowledge about how to address the issue. And to build the support for such sweeping and ingrained changes in attitude, she networked with other women's organizations.

I had already been going in to the courtrooms here for say, a year. [I] sat in on all the sexual assault cases. We were just setting it up and I saw what injustices were occurring at the time and I would take notes. . . . I always look[ed] to see if a prosecutor wasn't handling [it]—as I said, I always wished I'd had a law degree—but if I saw that he wasn't approaching the case, I would say, "I want to suggest something. What do you think about this?" I never said, "Hey, you can't do that." What I said was, "I want you to consider this." . . . I worked with a lot of the prosecutors there and some of them were terrific. There are a few that were questionable, but I sat thousands of hours, I guess, in that courtroom, but that's how I learned what laws had to be changed. I wanted to see what was going on, the dynamics of that courtroom, and then go up [to the legislature] and say, this needs to be changed. . . . I had one district attorney who made the statement to an anchorman on a network television station, that "if my wife is ever raped, she needn't even bother to come home." [The anchorman] told me, "I think you should know this, Florence, so I'm telling you what he said at our station." If we have a DA with that attitude . . . that if his wife were raped, she had asked for it and, therefore, she needn't bother to even come home. That was the climate that we had started in, but it is not the climate today.

Another challenge rested with the hospitals and their responsiveness to raped patients.

The doctors had been refusing to consider a rape kit. A rape kit has all of the items enclosed that need to be done when the doctor examines the woman so it can be used in a court for evidence. Doctors, at that time, did not want to take time off from their work to appear in court, so we had to reform them. One woman was thrown from a car before daylight on Charleston, not too far from the hospital, and she was naked. Another car coming by, evidently going to a [Laundromat], he threw a sheet out of his car so she could wrap herself in it, but took off. Finally, a police car came by. . . . It took *four hours* for her to see a doctor. A woman detective . . . discovered that we had these doctors, [and] not one wanted to do it [examine the rape victim]. They passed to the next shift to do it so it would not be them. "It's got to be done, but not me" sort of attitude. . . . I got to the newspaper how they were doing it. Well, of course, [the doctors] didn't like that because it's bad publicity. Even in the court system, doctors failed to show up. We had to subpoena one doctor one time in the case of a fourteen-year-old girl and it was a woman doctor. See, it's not always the men. She didn't want to show up. She didn't want to testify. . . .

I was confrontational pretty much at the beginning. When I saw that I would go to the police departments and I'd say, "I'm here about the case on Miss So-and-So," and they'd say, "Oh, it's unfounded. She consented." I said "let's talk about it." They didn't want to talk about it. Here I was in my early fifties at the time and married many years. I had worked for the provost marshal Office of Special Investigation [OSI], in Japan; the judge advocate general's office. I could talk about sexual matters, crimes, and it would not faze me because I'm not talking about myself. . . .

One of our counselors took a victim to the Henderson police; [she] went there to help this girl. The girl had scratched the man with her fingernail and some skin was under her nails and the police officer wasn't even going to take the scrapings. [Our counselor] said, "Aren't you going to get that skin from under her fingers to have it analyzed?" See, our counselors were getting smarter than some of the police. They were overlooking it. They knew better than that, but they looked down on rape. . . .

Women did not want to report their rape. And a lot of the male officers at that point in time would rather that a woman forget it too, because it caused them a lot of trouble. We didn't have women officers that they could talk to. We had men and a lot of them were old enough to be their daddy . . . and they probably [were] thinking, "Well, if she hadn't walked down that street, she wouldn't have left herself open for this kind of attack." So, what are women supposed to do, have a curfew of maybe five or six o'clock in the evening on a winter day when it starts getting dark? So, you stay in and barricade the door? You cannot be like others. You're a woman. That is when I said, "This has got to change." . . .

People are more aware either through television [or] because we go around preaching, and they'd see it happening to people they care about and they know they didn't ask for it. In two weeks, I had four women over seventy years of age raped in their own beds in their own homes. Now, do you think that they asked for it? . . .

▦ The Las Vegas community had a number of groups that lent their support to the Rape Crisis Center. The American Association of University Women, Women's Democratic Club of Clark County, the League of Women Voters, and the Soroptimist International, as well as faith communities all supported the work. When former governor Bob Miller was district attorney in Las Vegas he started a Citizens' Committee for Victim Rights and another network took shape.

He asked me to bring the Rape Crisis Center as one element of this whole victim rights program. We had Temporary Assistance for Domestic Crisis [TADC which became SafeNest], WE CAN or Working to Eliminate Child Abuse and Neglect, and later on we got Mothers Against Drunk Drivers [MADD,] which is now known as Stop DUI, with Sandy Heaverly. I went in to help all of those organizations in their formation, sharing with them knowledge that I had from starting the Rape Crisis Center. . . . I used the information that Jean Ford had passed on to me and I passed it on to them. So, what we were doing was networking and networking is the big point. . . .

▦ McClure had prepared for her advocate's role by familiarizing herself with other states' treatment of rape. In particular, she studied California statutes and used those to convince Nevada lawmakers. One of the first areas to be addressed was a victim's right to privacy. While Las Vegas media had been respectful regarding privacy and not published the name of a raped woman, according to McClure, the same could not be said about the state's capital, Carson City.

Carson City had sixteen thousand people. This woman was sick, home sick in bed. She had the flu and so she had the day off; she was in bed sick and a man broke into her home and raped her. Her name appeared in the newspaper and his appeared in the newspaper. Now, in a sixteen thousand–population town, everybody pretty well knows each other. . . . So, I called them up. I paid for a toll call up there and said, "What did you do that for?" "Oh," [the journalist] says, "I think it makes the story." I said, "What do you think about that poor woman? She was not a kid, she was in her thirties or forties, was home sick, raped, and then you humiliate her?"

▪ A second privacy issue occurred in the courtroom. The attacked woman's sexual history could be and was used to discredit her claim of rape. In other words, a woman's sexual activity could be brought up in court to argue that she had a low moral character and consequently must have consented to have sex.

A defense attorney here in town had the right when we started the Rape Crisis Center to pull an alibi witness. Anybody in the audience that was competent could tell that they were lying. The defense attorney just went overboard and there was one in particular, and he's still here, that I wanted to see shut up. That was one of the laws that I went to Carson City on and I got the law changed [to state] that no previous sexual background of the victim would be brought out in court if it had nothing to do with the current case. . . . Now, if she went out with the rapist a number of times, then that could be brought out, but it had to be a personal connection. You couldn't go out and say Johnny Jones tells me that this alleged victim is promiscuous and that he had sex with her a number of times. You see, back in the days when I was growing up as a young person, fathers would get their sons off on this kind of suit by paying somebody to take the witness stand and go against the girl. The girl did not want to prosecute [the alleged rapist] because she knew that, often, the man's father, by paying a few dollars, could get somebody to get up on that stand. They didn't care. . . . With that law, no longer did a rape victim take the stand knowing that somebody would go back and look maybe ten, fifteen years in her past and say, "Well, she was living with a guy, therefore, she was promiscuous." . . . We changed the law; you could not go into her sexual history, unless the judge determined that there was a connection and, of course, there would be no connection. . . .

In the 1975 legislative session we started getting those changes made. Mike O'Callaghan, then governor of Nevada, told Senator Mel Close, chair for the senate judiciary and his vice chair was Richard Bryan, "I want you to help Florence get changes in the rape laws. Florence has got her data all laid out on what she wants." Now, in order to get that data, I made trips over to Sacramento, California, to the capital, the legislative building, and I got copies of all the bills that they had introduced on sexual assault or rape. I brought them home and I sat down with them and determined which ones were feasible for the state [of Nevada] and I went about it in an organized way. . . . It was Democrat-controlled at the time, which made it much easier. . . .

Richard [Bryan] was vice chair of senate judiciary and he later became attorney general and governor of the state, and now he's our US senator. But Richard, at that time, was the state senator and . . . he loves to tell the story that Mel Close said to him, "Richard, I want you to help Florence get her bills through, because this legislature will be in session forever if you don't help her. She'll be after us, she will not stop."

During the 1975 session McClure worked to change the name of the crime to better reflect the seriousness of the offense. By using the term *sexual assault* instead of rape advocates like McClure believed that rape would be associated with a violent attack rather than a crime of passion.

Richard Bryan called me up at home one night and said, "We have trouble. The committee's agreed to sexual battery," and I said, "That doesn't tell the whole truth. That kind of makes it more of a misdemeanor." I said, "It is an assault. It is not a battery. I want sexual assault and if we can't get it through this session, I'll go back next one. I want sexual assault and I don't want it downplayed. It is a horrendous crime, and Richard, I don't want to go for less." . . . I didn't want anybody downplaying it in court; if you said sexual battery instead of sexual assault the jurors could say, "Hey, it's not all that bad," and they're going by words. I wanted it to connote exactly what it was, a horrendous crime. So, I stuck to it and we passed it early on in the next session. . . .

It took a couple of sessions of the legislature [to pass marital rape laws] because, you see, the tone of the people: most of the legislators were males. Even some of the women who got elected at different times—I know one of them was older than I—and they just think that women shouldn't marry that type of guy to begin with and that it was her fault for marrying that type of guy. But of course, we don't always know who we're marrying. They turn out to be different people sometimes, especially if you get alcohol or, now, a lot of people are into the drugs. But it took a couple of times to do it. Then, it would have to go on its own merits. Just like a regular rape case. . . .

Later on, I had a number of people who helped pass legislation, like Jean Ford, Mary Gojack, [and] Sue Wagner who became our lieutenant governor. . . . They were serving together. . . . They may not have had law degrees, but boy, they were sharp. One of the things that I noticed about all of the women that served in the legislature during my tenure, that is say from '75 on, one of the things that I found is that those women went into those committee hearings better prepared than any of the men that were sitting on those committees.[15] . . .

In the early 1980s President Ronald Reagan's administration sought to have states take a greater role in funding their own programs. One consequence, according to McClure, was the reduction of LEAA funds coming into the state. McClure realized a new strategy was needed and appealed to two women in the state legislature.[16]

Karen Hayes and Sue Wagner had been working together on a bill. They wanted to place a tax on the marriage licenses for domestic crisis services— and here the funding on our program was going away. Since domestic crisis [services] has to house the women and children victims, they needed more funds than we would because we would be working out of an office, going to counsel victims and so forth. We did not have the overhead that they would. So, they set the marriage license fee at 15 percent to the Rape Crisis [Center], 85 percent to domestic violence, so they could maintain operations. So, I will always be grateful for those wonderful women legislators.[17] . . .

I had hoped, at one time, to get a law degree. We don't have a law school in Nevada yet.[18] But looking back, it's just as well that I didn't go on and get a law degree, because I think I was able to do more by being a thorn in the side of those legislators or government officials who kept ignoring the rights of people to live in peace. . . . Over the years, we were able to take every one of the unjust laws and cut it to pieces. . . .

After twelve years with the Rape Crisis Center, McClure stepped down as director in 1984. She cited medical reasons for the leave, but she also noted that she wanted someone younger in the post, someone who "could really go after them." The Rape Crisis Center continued its work at the time of publication.

McClure continued advocacy work and took up the cause of women prisoners in the 1980s. When plans for the relocation of the prison to a rural area became known, McClure and others expressed concerns that the isolated location would provide little access to trained drug rehabilitation professionals, had no adequate medical facility, and would make it diffi-cult for incarcerated women to visit with their families, especially with their children. McClure worked for eleven years to relocate the state's women's prison to North Las Vegas. Her suc-cess was recognized with the renaming of the institution as the Florence McClure Women's Correctional Center.

Many women in the oral history project on gaming changed their line of work over the course of their lives. Florence McClure's training in office work suited her well for the jobs open to women of her generation. She also shared a generational practice to volunteer her time to improve her community. Hundreds of thousands of women of all backgrounds served as volunteers in communities across the United States during the long postwar decades. Their voluntarism proved to be an essential unpaid labor force for the creation of community assets such as Girl Scouts, religious institutions, the Parent-Teacher Association, and civic organizations. McClure went a step farther than most as an advocate to reform the inade-quate and unjust practices and laws regarding survivors of sexual assault in Nevada.

As a newcomer to Las Vegas, I was often counseled to meet Florence McClure. "She is one of the city's movers and shakers," I was told. It took me a while, but we finally met in March 1995 at the official opening of the NWA. I came to appreciate McClure as the for-midable leader she was, but I also respected her for her understanding that the work she was engaged in was for a greater good, rather than for an individual gain. McClure's full oral history reveals a woman who from a young age wanted to be part of something bigger than herself. She wanted to go away to college and then to law school, but her family needed her near home. She eventually moved for the war effort and found numerous ways to make herself invaluable in work settings. But when she settled in Nevada and had the time to engage in her community, she followed her mentor's lead and used her full set of life skills and new relationships to make a positive change for the state. McClure became the state's foremost advocate for the improvement of rape laws and for education of the public about conscientious treatment for victims of violence. Her legacy (and that of her coworkers in that movement in Las Vegas) is the change made in the community's understanding of the violent crime of sexual assault as well as the protection of the rights of the assaulted.

Chapter 9

CAROL GERARDI

Craps Dealer and Floor Supervisor

This is my game.... I want it run this way.... While I'm here,
you do it the way I want it done.
—Carol Gerardi

Jobs in the Las Vegas hotel-casinos, as in many industries, were segregated by sex and race until the last decades of the twentieth century. Men and women worked on the casino floor, but women held jobs as beverage servers (previously known as cocktail waitresses) or change girls, while men held jobs as dealers, pit bosses, boxmen, and floor supervisors. Idiosyncratic variations in this historical pattern occurred in Las Vegas, as we have seen in the narratives of Claudine Barbara Williams and Sarann Knight Preddy. Nevertheless, from the end of the war in 1945, through the passage of the federal Civil Rights Act in 1964, to the 1981 Consent Decree, in which casinos agreed to open jobs to all who were qualified, a struggle took place to gain equal employment to jobs.[1]

Little is known about the individuals and organizations who paved the way to end sex discrimination in Las Vegas. Contemporary newspaper articles covered the entrance of women into dealing as an apparently spontaneous decision of properties to hire women as dealers in the early 1970s. D. D. Cotton's narrative in chapter 5 provided some insight on the activities of the NAACP. Annelise Orleck's study on Las Vegas's antipoverty activists reveals another force. Although the struggle for race equality in hiring has received some attention, a full scholarly assessment of the battle to end sex discrimination in employment still remains to be done.[2]

At the federal level, several notable events provided a structure for local change. President John Kennedy established a Presidential Commission on the Status of Women in 1961 to assess the barriers to women's full participation in American society and to suggest action steps. The Commission's 1963 report found numerous areas for concern, but featured the need for women to have equal opportunities in hiring, training, and promotion in the workforce. These steps would tap into the womanpower needed to compete in the Cold War economy and to remedy the wage gap between male and female workers that had characterized the workplace. The commission report also found an inadequate level of child-care resources available for working families, and advocated that the number of centers be increased as well as tax deductions for child-care expenses be implemented. Congress passed the Equal Pay Act the same year (1963), with the intent to provide workers who performed the same job under the same conditions the same amount of pay. The Equal Pay Act was landmark legislation. Nevertheless, the conditions of equity were hard to find in an economy defined by labor force segmentation. The following year, Congress passed the Civil Rights Act, which included a provision that made discrimination in employment on the basis of sex as well as race and national origin unconstitutional. The act established the EEOC as the compliance unit. Historians have demonstrated that the EEOC remained unresponsive to claims of sex discrimination for several years; when it did begin to investigate claims, however, the EEOC played a crucial role in challenging discrimination by race and sex in the case of Las Vegas.[3]

Women rarely held positions as bartenders, stagehands, upper-level managers, or dice dealers before the 1981 consent decree. These jobs paid higher wages than food servers, housekeeping, or other jobs reserved for women. In 1958 a group of male dealers became concerned that the downtown clubs might adopt Reno's policy to hire only women as card dealers, which would destroy the men's livelihood. The city commissioners decided to hear both sides of the question. Close to five hundred people attended the hearing at which protesters complained that women would work for lower wages and create bad publicity for the

Lee Irwin dealing cards at the Monte Carlo Club in downtown Las Vegas in 1954. This club hired twenty women to deal cards, which alarmed male dealers, who convinced the city commissioners in 1958 to prohibit women from dealing downtown. Courtesy of Las Vegas News Bureau.

"Women Dealers Vanish from Downtown," *Las Vegas Sun,* November 5, 1958. Courtesy of *Las Vegas Sun.*

Women Dealers Vanish From Downtown

Women dealers vanished from downtown Las Vegas yesterday afternoon under circumstances that suggested heavy pressure had been put on one or more of the casino owners who had employed ladies to handle "21" or roulette games for them.

One owner begged not to be quoted and it was learned that he had been threatened. It could not be learned who made the threats — and he wasn't talking. Police Chief Ray Sheffer said he was investigating the situation and had heard of the meeting.

About 25 women dealers lost their jobs, it was determined, and will be replaced by men.

The final decision to fire the

city. Women dealers spoke in defense of their right to earn a living and support their children, but to no avail. The city fathers voted to protect public morals and banned women dealers. The ban stayed in effect in Las Vegas until 1970. Women were still able to deal cards in communities nearby that did not adopt such a ban. However, the casinos on the Las Vegas Strip, which developed rapidly during the 1950s and 1960s, refused to open these jobs to women.[4]

Casinos and unions began to feel the pressure from the federal EEOC throughout the 1970s as lawsuits challenged discrimination by race, sex, and ethnicity in hiring and promotion. In 1971 casino operators agreed to hire and unions agreed to refer applicants for jobs regardless of race in what has been viewed as a local, civil rights milestone. The federal EEOC acted again in 1975. This time it sought to prohibit discrimination on the basis of sex and national origin. Over the next six years, the agency proceeded to document bias in hiring and promotion within the casino. For example, while women held almost all the jobs as maids, clericals, and front desk workers, men dominated in occupations such as bartenders, parking attendants, and baccarat dealers, and in management positions.[5] The division of labor had real economic outcomes because the highest-paid and highest-tipping jobs went to men. In 1981 the casinos and unions settled with another consent decree in which they promised to remove barriers to future employment for women and those of all ethnicities.

Carol Gerardi benefited from the legal efforts to end job discrimination. Her path to dealing in Las Vegas was exceptional for the period in which she started. The former dental assistant dealt dice at the craps table on the Strip. Both the particular game of craps and the Las Vegas Strip casinos were the last areas to open up dealer jobs to women.

Though others had taken down the first barriers, her narrative offers an interesting view into the second generation of women, those who worked in nontraditional areas of the hotel-casino. Of the narrators included in this volume, she is chronologically the youngest and the most recent to enter casino work. She did not move to Las Vegas until 1980. The narrative provides an on-the-ground view of the implementation of the policy. It also demonstrates that, despite equal employment law, juice remained an important aspect of securing a job.

Gerardi said she never experienced harassment on the job by either customers or coworkers. She presented herself as one who would take care of any problem herself should any occur. The theme of self-reliance arose in numerous interviews of the first generation of women who worked in the casinos, and contrasts with other published reports of women casino workers.[6] Thus, while Gerardi's narrative cannot be seen as a typical experience of women dealers, it does present an important perspective on the integration of women into nontraditional jobs in the casinos.

What really brought me here—first of all, I have family that lives here and one of my uncles was a musician with Louis Prima for seventeen years.[7] He settled out here. My grandparents moved out here in the 1960s to retire. When I turned twenty-one I came for my first vacation out here to Las Vegas and I visited and had just a great time. Prior to that, I didn't know anything about Las Vegas at all. So I came and I visited and subsequently I came again and again. My younger brother moved out here. . . . I came to visit him, I think it was in 1979, and I just decided that I needed a change from Rhode Island. . . . It was very easy for me to do this, because I had a support group here. I had family. I had him [my brother]. And I came out here with every intention of becoming a twenty-one dealer. I had no inclination at all about being a dice dealer. I didn't know anything about the game at all. One of my uncles was a keno manager at the former MGM, before it burned down, and he took me aside and he kind of pointed me in the right direction. He said, "If you're going to become a dealer you should really think about going into dice and becoming a craps dealer because there aren't that many women in the profession." . . . In the early days you never ever saw a woman craps dealer. It was always men. It was just the end of the 1970s and into the 1980s that women started coming into this field. And he thought, "Take a shot. Go for it. Go for the better job. There are better tips in dealing craps." You could go anywhere from—if you had a bad night, you could make nothing in tips. The next night you could make $1,000. . . . So I said, "Okay, fine." He made a phone call to someone that he knew that ran a school. So I arrived here in March of 1980 [and] a couple of weeks later I started dealing school. . . .

Although a casino floor may look like it is in a jumble on a busy evening, there is a clear hierarchy and order in place. Most table games have one dealer, but craps has four people on the game. Of the four, one is a boxman, one a stickman, and two are base dealers. The boxman is in charge of the bankroll, exchanges cash for chips, and oversees the entire table. On either side of the boxman are base dealers who collect and pay bets. The stickman takes bets, calls out the dice roll, and returns the dice to the player. All the activity at a table is watched by the floor supervisor. The floor supervisors are overseen by the pit boss or manager. The shift manager has responsibility for all activities during the shift and the casino manager has full oversight for all the activities.

I went to school about three months. Ninety percent of the craps game, dealing it, is your hands. You may not know the payoffs and there is always somebody to help you with that. But if you can't do what they call "get around the layout" and deal the game, you have a problem. You have to be able to get around the layout, deal to eight, sometimes nine players . . . and the whole layout could be filled with bets. If you don't know what you're doing, it can be chaos. In those days you could concentrate on learning one game. Now, they—meaning the hotels—want you to know more than one game. In other words, twenty-one, roulette, craps—at least two games they want you to know before they even think about hiring you. But in those days, I concentrated on craps and that's all I know. . . .

For three months I went in there and I learned how to deal, I learned payoffs, procedures, and got my hands in shape. The nails that I have now, I would never have been able to deal the game because you have to cut checks, you have to hand off bets, and it's virtually impossible to do it with any kind of nails at all.[8] . . . You have to be almost ambidextrous, with both hands, whereas you can't just concentrate on your right hand or your left hand. That's the first thing you learn, how to manipulate the checks and how to cut one, cut two, and then size into it so that you have a row of two, a row of three, etcetera. You don't go any higher than five. And then there's another thing they taught where you pick up the checks and you drop one, you drop two, three, etcetera, until you learn how to do this and you build up your fingers. So that's the start of school. . . .

There are different odds for every bet on the table. You have downtown odds and you have Strip [or uptown] odds. I broke in downtown; I learned downtown odds. For example: you can bet $1.00 on eleven and it's a one-roll bet and downtown it pays sixteen for one, uptown it pays fifteen for one. So of course if you have dollar-eleven, that's $15 and you're up to win again. All those bets they leave. If you hit a bet, they leave you up to win again. . . . Okay. That's just in the middle. Now you have the numbers on the other side. The pass line is an even-money bet. So if you bet $5.00, you win $5.00. The don't pass is the same thing, even money. You bet five, you win five. It's the odds that you have to calculate. For each set of numbers the odds are different. Four and ten pay two to one, five and nine pay three to two, six and eight pay six to five. I'm giving you a background in all of these because this is what they teach you. . . .

The Barbary Coast was part of the school. What they did was they allowed you to go for live training when you were ready or when they thought you were ready. . . . So, after my three months I started going to live training. Here you get hands-on [training], and you learn to deal with the public. It was very, very nerve-racking for me. I was scared to death. . . . I was twenty-nine years old and prior to that I was a dental assistant. As I said, I came out here on vacation. I had played roulette. . . . I had no idea what to expect. It's one of the toughest games on the Strip to deal because of the different odds that are involved. As I said, you have line bets, pass-line with odds, then you have don't-pass with odds, then your come-bets which are the same as line bets as far as the odds go. You have don't-come bets, which is the same as the don't-pass. Then you have place bets on all the sets of numbers. Those odds are totally different. Not to mention the hands. I don't mean to belittle a twenty-one dealer, believe me, you learn how to pitch and you learn how to pay, but you could have eight people on one number with eight separate bets that you have to get out there and you have to pay and you have to move around the lay-out. That's why I said—they stressed it and it was—practice, practice, practice. . . .

There're only three dealers on the table at one time. The fourth, they work an hour on and twenty minutes off. So that's the rotation. Most of the [other dealers] were very helpful, because they had to be. Their floor supervisor was also my teacher. This was an ongoing thing, having students come in for live training, so they couldn't be rude or obnoxious. And they weren't. That came later when you went out for a real job with real dealers. . . .

When I got my first job at the El Cortez—and back then it was considered one of the best break-in houses for any dealer—you dealt in $0.25 chips and if you can deal *that* game, you can deal anywhere. . . . At the El Cortez there were not many women breaking in when I was breaking in. There were some. I worked eighteen months down there and I had one of the floor supervisors tell me, "We can't teach you anything more here. It's time for you to move on." . . . Another uncle [said], "Go talk to this man. See if he can help you get a job." I went to look for the gentleman. I walked in, I walked over to the dice pit, I asked for the gentleman in question. [He said], "What is it in regards to?" [I said], "A dealing job." [He said], "You're a crap dealer?" I said, "Yeah." [He said], "Do you see any women around these tables, women dealers?" I said, "No." In other words, he didn't come right out and say it, but, "We don't hire [women]." I'm looking for a craps job. "Do you see any women here?" I got the message. This was not the man that I was told to go see, but this was the attitude. "We're not looking for women dealers."

[At school] it was equal opportunity for everybody. They never said, "You're a woman, you can't do this." If anybody said that to me now I'd have a few choice words to say to them. I was new, I was green. But still, you know, I don't go for that. Of course, in seventeen years I've matured a little bit more and I've taken my licks. . . . [I] never felt anything because I was a woman. [The people at the El Cortez] didn't make me feel that I was inferior to anybody else. However, there was one floor supervisor that was a real, pardon my expression, but a real hard-ass. Not just to women, but just to everybody in general. If you did something, he would scream in your ear—rant and rave. The only man in seventeen years, or the only *person* in seventeen years, to ever make me cry. I got off the game and went on my break and for twenty minutes I cried. He really did a number on me. . . .

In the hotel that I work in now, the Hilton, day shift can run anywhere from nine to five, ten to six, eleven to seven, twelve to eight at night. At the El Cortez, day shift was ten to six. If you were a day shift dealer, in other words, they may have had, I can't remember, four or five different crap games. If you were working days, you worked from ten to six. So, all these people are working the same shift. There's no alternating or coming in at different times. So we were all ten to six and we all socialized in the break room, on your break or in the cafeteria. And you got to know people. You got to know them on your shift and it was nice, it was great. After work we were allowed to go to the back, in the bar, and we would have a drink and socialize. . . .

█ Depending on the type of table game dealt, a dealer's pay could vary. The tips on a craps game usually ran higher than other games.

As far as the hotel base salary, it's a stepping-stone until you reach a max[imum], which I can't tell you what that is. For dealers, I don't know. But dice dealers at one point, especially when I broke in during the early 1980s, were going what they called table for table. You have four dealers that work a table. Whatever money they make they split four ways, anywhere from $4.00 to $4,000, depending on how much money they make. It could be more if they have what they call [a] *George*. That's a person that bets for them and tips them. If they have a real super George on the game, they could make $5,000 apiece. That's tips only. Their base salary, they don't really care about that. They're in it for the money, for the tips, more than anything else. . . . Each table splits the tokes [tips]. It goes through the cage. They get it on a paycheck and they have their taxes. That's now. Back then, it didn't work that way. The government didn't know really what they were making except for what they declared. . . . Downtown it is not that way. Downtown is a pool. It's a twenty-four-hour split. That's what they did at the El Cortez. Tokes went in a common box, all three shifts, and every day it was divided up and you got paid. Everybody made the same amount of money in tips. . . .

My first Strip job was the Sahara. I worked there for six months or so. I was on the extra board. That's where I had my first encounter with prima donna craps dealers. They didn't like women, especially coming from the El Cortez. Some of them were great. I made a friend down there that's still my friend today. . . . Others tried to intimidate. So I just stuck to my guns and I wouldn't let them do it. By the same token, I was still very nervous working at the Sahara. As I said, I was on the extra board, which means I could work anywhere from seven to eight days in a row or once a week, depending on when they needed me. So it was a table-for-table job. I did make some, what I call nice scores, but it never lasted as long as some of them who started earlier. I was there about seven or eight months and then new management came in and of course, last hired, first fired. I was out of work.

I was out of work for about six weeks and I went out pounding the pavement looking for another job. Someone who I met at the Sahara told me to go to the Dunes. They were hiring. They had just built the Oasis Casino. They were looking for dealers. . . . At the time, the Dunes was dealing silver, actual silver dollars, which is a lot harder to deal. I set up an appointment. I immediately went out and bought $20.00 worth of silver and started practicing with that. So then I could at least give a decent showing in my audition. . . .

A lot of times, and you must know this, it's not what you know but who you know, especially to get into a Strip hotel. That's the goal for any dealer, whether they be twenty-one or craps, because that's where the money is. Now to get into Caesars [Palace], that's a great job. They do not have a table-for-table split, but they still make very good money. When they did have a table-for-table split you couldn't get a job in there unless you knew God. And that's the way it is. But with this equal employment, it doesn't matter. If they're minorities or whatever, then they will hire you to fill their quota. . . . If there is an opening for a dealer, they'll go to the applications and they'll give them an audition and they'll rate their audition. If one of those people is a friend of a friend that pushes that person a little more, they'll more than likely get in, get the job. But if they're just looking for someone to fill the position, they're looking for a dealer, period, they're naturally going to look at the ability and see if this person can deal this game. If they can't deal the game, then they won't get hired. . . .

I never really had anybody come on to me, whether bosses or [others], in a derogatory manner. I was there. I did my job. I dealt the game. Sometimes you took some flak from prima donna dealers, male prima donna dealers. But I never really had the sexual innuendo or the grabbing. Nobody really ever did that to me, which I'm grateful for. Because sometimes they may think that [since] you're a woman, "Ooh, let's see how far we can go."

In 1982 Carol Gerardi went to work at the Dunes and stayed for about seven years. She began working as a dealer, but decided to try out other jobs that would move her up the ranks.

I became a box person and right before I left [the Dunes] I was a floor supervisor. I'd worked my way up into a floor supervisor position. And it was good. I never got, "You can't do this because you're a woman." . . . I don't know how it is in a lot of other hotels but at the Dunes, at the time I wanted to move up, I told them, "I'd like to go into management. I'd like to be considered for a box job. I don't want to deal anymore." And when the opportunity came, the opening came, I took it. After that I expressed a desire to move up to the floor. They realized that I could handle it, so when the opportunity came again, I got it, right before the Dunes really went downhill, right before they closed.

When the Dunes closed in January 1993, Gerardi used her network to secure her next position at the Hilton Hotel and Casino. As the Hilton expanded its properties, more jobs opened and dealers moved around. She applied after hearing from a friend that some of the jobs opening up would be box positions. Her former floor supervisor at the Dunes also had moved to the Hilton and put in a good word for her. She got the job and worked on the box and later as a floor supervisor. She moved between these two jobs as needed, something the casino referred to as dual-rate.

I stayed in that position as a dual-rate for about three years because there were just no openings. People did not leave that hotel; you talk to people who've worked there fifteen years, eighteen years. It's a good job. It's the only hotel in town that gives their employees a retirement. Not the 401(k). They have that, but they give their employees a retirement policy. . . . I got along well with my bosses and all my coworkers and when the position came available on the floor, out of all the dual-rates, and there were three on swing shift, two or three on day shift, one or two on graveyard, they evaluated everybody. It's not just because she was a woman that she should get it. They thought I was capable and they gave me the floor job.

[A floor supervisor is] the person that stands behind the game and watches everything. I give markers to the players. I sign them up. I rate players. I rate their play. Each hotel has a rating system. Each customer has a preferred customer card. The rating system all goes toward what the hotel will comp different players. Whether it be rooms or meals or airfare, along those lines. So I do that and I watch the dealers. I watch the payoffs. I watch the players. I watch just about everything. Not that I'm superwoman. I don't mean to give that impression, but if I have a dealer on one end that I know is a little weak, that's the end I watch. It could be the dealer's end. The stickman watches one end, the boxman watches another end. And I watch whatever I want to watch. For example, if [on] one end of the table, a lot of money, big checks are out, $500 checks, $1,000 checks, that's the end I'm going to watch. I'm going to make sure that dealer pays the right amount of money to the player. Nobody makes a mistake on that.

The pit bosses [watch the floor supervisors]. At the Hilton, there are three on my shift. They watch whatever they want to watch. They walk up and down the pit. They'll stop at one game if there's a big hand going on, or a lot of money on the table, they'll watch. [I am responsible for] one table. I could be responsible for more than one. You have sixteen players on a full table and that's enough.

We can work up to two hours and forty minutes at one stretch. Sometimes it doesn't always go that way. But worst-case scenario is, between my breaks, I could do two hours and forty minutes at one table, watching one game. Then I go on a break and then I take the next person out who is on a different game, and I'm on a different game doing the same thing.

If you have a game where the dice are passing, number after number after number, winner after winner after winner, and I have seen forty-minute hands, one-hour hands, where the dice just keep throwing out the numbers and you've got a table full of people and you've got every possible inch of that table filled with people's bets, this is where good dealers come in handy. They keep track of everything and they know. It gets intense. It does. I want to make sure I have enough checks on the game. I want to make sure everybody's doing their job. Then you have the boss. You've got a hand like that going on and now you've got pit bosses watching, without a doubt, making sure everything is going [okay], then they'll walk away. . . .

There are certain rules and procedures that you follow and I think they're universal in any hotel as far as the dealing of the game and customer satisfaction. Customers are number one. You go out of your way to be nice and polite and service them, answer questions. A far as that goes, I think that's universal in any hotel. I don't really see the Hilton corporate end of it. I'm in the casino. I'm in the dice pit. I'm there to do my job. . . . I do know that at times if a player wanted to give you a gift, you could take a gift of any denomination. I do know that the Hilton employees are *not* allowed to. I've had players wanting to give me a $1,000 check and I can't take it. I said, "I'm sorry, I can't take monetary gifts." . . . I've had players wanting to give me cash. [I would have to say], "No, thank you very much, I'm not allowed to take anything." Because my job is worth more than [a] $1,000 chip, you know what I mean? That's a one-time thing. I need my job, period. They have rules and regulations about that. . . .

It's the era of the corporation. Of course, all of these [television] specials and movies portray the crime and how Las Vegas was built, but that's part of Las Vegas's history. No more. I don't think it exists. Maybe on a very select level. But I don't see it. As far as the prostitution, that's what makes Las Vegas, Las Vegas. It still goes on. I know that if there are hookers in the Hilton, they are escorted out unless they are brought in by a patron. How that goes on, I don't know. I have no inkling to find out. It's there. I understand it's there [but] I don't have anything to do with it so I don't really pay attention to it, except to make a comment that I can't see how anybody would want to do that, especially in this day and age. But it exists and I know it does and okay, fine. As long as it doesn't touch me, I don't really care. [Prostitution has] always been there. I just take it for granted. It's always been there. That's part of the allure of Las Vegas for a lot of people. . . .

The first few years I was just trying to get on and trying to establish myself and let people know that I can deal this game. I'm not just a woman who knows somebody that got this job and can't do the job. For a long time, it was proving myself, that I can handle this job just as much as this guy can handle this job. And because he's a guy doesn't make him a better dealer or a better person than me. And then, after a while, people knew, my superiors knew that I could do it, and therefore that's how I got promoted when I expressed a desire to move into the management end of it.

To this day, I will not let anyone jeopardize my job, in other words. Certain things I expect on my game. I will not tolerate what they call crossfire, dealers talking to each other, to the boxman, while there is a live game going on. I won't tolerate that and they know it. I tell them, "We have a game. We have players on the game." I don't care if there is one player on the game, I won't tolerate that. I will not let anybody put me in the middle or jeopardize my job, whether it be somebody hustling a bet or making an off-color remark that the player hears, or whatever. So in that respect I have come a long way, but there is certain respect that I demand because I am a floor supervisor and [I make clear] to these guys, "This is my game. This is not your game. I want it run this way. I don't care how the next person wants their game run, that's their thing. While I'm here, you do it the way I want it done." And it's not that I'm asking them to do something that they shouldn't be doing anyway, per rules and regulations and Hilton policy. I feel because of the position that they should respect my wishes. . . .

The pay is very good for a single woman, or even for a man with a family. Of course, they have their wives that work too. But for myself, the job is great. The pay is wonderful. The retirement was a big incentive. The early outs: in other words, if I work six hours I get paid for eight. I don't punch in and out. I sign the payroll sheet and if I work, that's one of the perks. One of the big perks. I do not get paid time-and-a-half for overtime. If I work an hour overtime I get paid for an hour. I don't have sick days, paid sick days. But that's okay. I don't mind that because I can count on one hand the times that I really have to work overtime—New Year's, Super Bowl, different golf tournaments that they bring in players for. It's great because, like I said, the early outs that I get paid for more than compensate.

I would be happy to retire from this position, unless, of course, I just get really fed up with it, fed up with just the gaming and the dealers and the people and the public and everything. Right now, I don't see that happening. . . . I would like to move up even further. A pit supervisor. Although I don't see that coming, because nobody leaves unless they get—there's a couple that are close to retirement, but I don't know. There's a lot of people to choose from and I don't know if they would choose me. I know I could handle it. I have no qualms about my qualifications to do the job. If I could get it, it would be great. I'd like it. It's less work. The higher you go, the less work there is to do. There's still certain things to do, but a pit supervisor does not have to stand at the game and rate players and write markers and do what I do now. They have their own things. That would be the next step up. I wouldn't mind moving up the corporate ladder. . . . I can't say it's a guy's job, but people may perceive it to be a male domain. The Hilton has always been a little bit more flexible with women employees in the dice pit. I think with affirmative action now, you're going to see more of women in higher positions.

When asked if her female coworkers also had a desire to rise in the corporate ranks, Gerardi found that only a few expressed interest.

In the dealers that I work with now, no; they're happy to stay as a dealer. Because they probably make more money than I do in a year's time. I wouldn't doubt it in the least. I recall one of my pit bosses saying [that] one of the dealers [had] a mistake on her paycheck that pay period. He has a form that he has to fill out, so naturally he has to see the pay stub. And he looked at year-to-date and she had made more money year-to-date than he had. Here he's a pit boss and he makes decent—I don't know what his pay per day is, but it's decent. It's a good job. And here's a dealer making more money than he is. So what would you want to do? Unless you get tired as a dealer, . . . you can't bend over, or you're just plain fed up with it, then you want to move up the corporate ladder. Or try to. But why would they want to leave it? [Dealer jobs are] few and far between because, again, you get a job like that, you want to do everything that you can to keep it. [There is] very little turnover at the Hilton, very little. All the way up the line, really.

In several job categories of the hotel-casino work, unions have played major roles in securing better wages, health insurance, and job security. Dancers and performers had the AGVA. Housekeepers and food service workers had the Culinary. At the time of this interview, union organizers had made numerous, but unsuccessful, attempts to organize dealers. Gerardi responded that she didn't see unionization in the future for dice dealers. A similar disinterest had gripped women dealers in Reno.[9]

You can't get two craps dealers to agree on anything; very difficult to unite them. I think this goes back to the old days when they were making money, money, money, and the IRS was not thought about. Why would they want to bring a union into that? Unions make certain demands for their people. The dealers were getting everything they wanted just by making the money that they were making. You don't want to ruin a good thing. That's my opinion. I don't know if that's everybody else's opinion, but it makes sense to me.[10]

When asked about the path she took for promotions, Gerardi's straightforward response suggests knowledge of the difficulties as well as the idiosyncrasies of advancement.

If I wanted to be considered for a pit boss position, I could go to the casino manager and express my interest, that I would like to be considered for this position. Whether or not they do it remains to be seen. In the eight and a half years or so that I have been working at the Hilton, I've only seen one female pit boss, and that's Renelle. Prior to that, no. At the Dunes, absolutely not. I hadn't seen one. The opportunity could always be there, but again, politics. If they want you, yeah, sure. If you've got people pushing for you, yeah, "Let's give her a shot." Either they like you or they think you can do the work, or they're friends with you and they want to push you up the corporate ladder to where they are, or give you an opportunity. It's possible, but not as frequent as you would see with men. So the opportunity is there but not as abundantly as it is with men. . . .

[Without affirmative action] it would revert back to the 1960s. It would go right back down. Women would have to fight even harder to get in these dealing positions. I know it was a battle for me to get out there and look and go back and push and push. Affirmative action has helped quite a bit. If they didn't have it, then it would be very difficult, especially in the dice pit, because it's always been considered a man's position. And women have invaded and a lot of old-timers who are still around, you know, they have a hard time with that. Well, my reaction is, "Too bad. I have just as much right to be here as you have." That's the way I felt when I was dealing and that's the way I feel as a supervisor. I can do this job. I can do it better than some.[11] . . .

And maybe some will say, "What kind of a career is that?" Well, it is [a career]. In this town, it's a career and it's a respectable career for a woman. Just because you work in a casino, don't lump me in with hookers or anything like that. I'm proud of the job I do. I do it well. I do it better than a lot of men in there. I'm conscientious; . . . there's no animosity because I am a woman. Because, it's the 1990s, now, and women are there and they're in the field. But in the beginning it was tough. . . . It took me seventeen years to get where I am. It's easier now because there are more women involved in the dice game, but back then it wasn't so easy. You can't walk into this kind of job. I don't mean to make myself sound holier than thou or anything like that, but it took me seventeen years. I paid my dues. . . . I took the yelling and the screaming and the rude players, and I don't think I would be here now if I didn't have family that I could count on back then.

Carol Gerardi took pride in her skilled work as a dealer, the advancement she earned, and the independence she had because of her work. Nevertheless, it was not a choice she would want her young female relatives to take. The work could be done handily by any woman; it wasn't that. Rather, it was a long, hard road to achieve what she had. She wished that education would smooth the way for her younger relatives more than it had for her.

Gerardi's sentiments are familiar to others who were among the first to take a job in a field that had been closed to women. She entered the previously male-only field of casino floor gambling. In the early 1980s, she took that job believing, "I have just as much right to be here" as did the male dice dealers. Twenty-some years earlier, when women dealers appealed to the city commissioners to keep their card-dealing jobs, they lost that battle. They lost because the country still allowed jobs to be categorized by race and sex, rather than solely by skill. In those intervening years, a revolution in laws and ideas had changed the labor force. The change took place at the federal level, but it also took place at the local level with individuals and groups willing to challenge the status quo.

CONCLUSION

New Narratives—Social and Economic Change in Women's Lives

Las Vegas greets its visitors with the "Welcome to Fabulous Las Vegas" sign. Brilliant in its simple diamond design, primary colors, and single ascendant star, the sign quickly became ubiquitous in all forms of advertising and souvenirs. Designed by Betty Willis in 1959, the welcome signage symbolizes for me the contrasts that exist in the history of women in this city: present everywhere, yet virtually unknown.[1] Tourists do not know about the creative Willis, or the entrepreneurial Williams and Preddy. They do not think about the workers behind the scenes. Nor do they think about the entertainers as regular employees. Rather, the image of the showgirl came to define women in Sin City. Taken to its pinnacle in the 1970s, the showgirl promised to fulfill a man's desire, if only in his mind. By the 1990s the topless, feather-and-rhinestone mannequins of decades earlier appeared tame compared to the strippers and lap dancers of the so-called gentlemen's clubs. Yet, the image of easy women and accessible sex continued to play as Las Vegas sold itself as the place where anything goes. These constructed images powerfully shaped visitors' perceptions and dominated the narrative of women's lives in Sin City, obscuring the varied experiences of women in the city's history. *Changing the Game* has brought working women's lives into focus alongside the familiar commercial images. In doing so, it has expanded our understanding of women at work in the second half of the twentieth century.

Legal gambling existed in Nevada and Las Vegas well before the beginning of this study, yet it is difficult to imagine the rapid growth and popularity of Las Vegas without specific characteristics of the postwar culture. Increased discretionary income and leisure time for American families facilitated the development of tourism starting in the 1950s. The existence of both, although unevenly distributed to workers and between races, contributed to Americans'

173

sense of their country as a global power. Many Americans celebrated by vacationing with Hollywood stars and business elite at the tables in Las Vegas. Workers and middle-class homemakers could watch the same entertainment revues, dine at the same restaurants, gamble at the same tables, and thereby assume the facade of the good life during their vacations. The hotel-casinos facilitated these fantasies with inexpensive rooms and meals subsidized by gambling. Illegal in other jurisdictions, gambling produced a destination that democratized entertainment and fulfilled the postwar economic goal of consumerism—not of goods, but of services.[2] A second less well known postwar characteristic also helped Las Vegas to boom. More women entered the labor force, and their workforce participation increased steadily through the end of the century.

The great vacation play land that presented Liberace, the Rat Pack, and Elvis to consuming tourists also employed thousands of workers in a variety of jobs. The focus on Las Vegas's gambling tourism oddly has obscured the fact that the city is a city of workers, half of whom are women. Postwar mobility brought them to Las Vegas for the jobs the industry offered. In the earliest decades covered in this book, women worked in a narrow spectrum of occupations, limited by gender and race segregation, in sales, office, and service jobs. Race limited further the occupations that women of color held, reserving service jobs for all but the entrepreneur. In the greater Las Vegas economy, professional work included nursing and teaching. A few women struck out on their own as business owners. Today, employed women are an increasingly diverse group, not only of racial and ethnic backgrounds, but also in the jobs that they do.

Employment in the hotel-casinos did not demand advanced education but rather the ability to do the job. Most of the narrators finished high school and a few went beyond. Williams left school in the tenth grade to work, dancers moved into their craft following school, Jaeger and McClure finished college after raising their families. Each of them remarked on their belief in a job well done, their own hard work, and belief in meritocracy despite the years of racial and sexual discrimination in employment. In the years prior to equal employment protection, they found work through their personal relationships (family, friends, and friends of friends). For those who sought entry-level jobs, the Culinary Union opened more doors than juice did.

Three major findings about women's employment emerged from the Las Vegas Women Oral History Project, presented through the eleven narratives in this book. First, over four decades (1950 to 1990), the percentage of women employed in greater Las Vegas surpassed that of the country as a whole. Many migrated to this city specifically for work. They reflected all marital statuses: single, married, divorced, with or without children. Their engagement in the labor force illustrated their need for or their commitment to work, despite mainstream admonitions that wage earning was inconsistent with traditional female roles. In greater Las Vegas more than one third of women over the age of sixteen held jobs in 1950. That proportion grew steadily until 1990, when nearly 60 percent of women worked. The area's rapidly expanding tourism industries combined with a growing population base contributed to steady job growth. As the city grew, so did the business community and the demands for labor in new sectors of the economy.

Most of the women included in this book have worked throughout their lives. The second finding of the study, therefore, is that narrators blended child rearing with employment. Twentieth-century commentators problematized the dual duties of working mothers asking, Was she neglecting her primary duties to house and home? That angst rarely came up in the narratives. Instead, the women combined those duties into one whole. How women accomplished that task varied tremendously. Williams hired domestic help. Preddy, Cotton, Canty, and Bryant largely relied on family members. McQuary shared or paid for home child care. Jaeger, Kravenko, and McClure spaced their employment around their child rearing. LeCoque and Gerardi had no children. By the mid-1960s the availability of birth control pills gave women greater choice over whether they would have children and, if so, when and how many to have. These arrangements remained private matters, yet the topic of combining work with family remained central to women's lives.

Third, women used different strategies to overcome barriers in the workplace. In the context of the times, when job segregation was a legal and accepted practice, a woman who wanted secure employment needed to be creative. This book illustrates the varied paths taken by women in the hotel-casino industry. The entrepreneurial women in the business of gambling, Claudine Barbara Williams and Sarann Preddy, made a way out of no way to develop their respective gambling businesses. For a small number of professionals in office management or in dance individual actions took precedence. They negotiated their business relationships as they kept up their skill sets to move up in their positions. In service work, where women held approximately one-half of the service jobs over the period of the study, back-of-the-house jobs offered (and continue to offer) a pathway for workers with limited education or language skills. Service workers had the least ability to negotiate independently and found their greatest job security and support in collective action through unions and civil rights groups.

During the decades covered in *Changing the Game,* the workplace changed from one that divided jobs by gender, race, and ethnicity to one that incorporates equal employment laws. Title VII of the federal Civil Rights Act of 1964 prohibited employment discrimination on these criteria, yet it took lawyers and activists working on the local level to challenge continuing discrimination. With the support of the US EEOC, nondiscrimination activists won eventual agreements from several properties and trade unions through two consent decrees, one in 1971 and one in 1981. Respectively, they opened jobs by race, and gender, and ethnicity.[3] To the extent that the narrators discussed this transition, women of color clearly understood the importance of civil rights advocacy on the basis of race, but rarely recognized the impingement of sex discrimination. Preddy and Cotton worked with the local NAACP to challenge racial discrimination in hiring. Bryant and Canty gave credit for job expansion to UNITE HERE (the Hotel Employees and Restaurant Employees) Local 226, known to members simply as the Culinary. Canty noted that she could not separate labor rights from civil rights. Yet, race discrimination was not the only barrier to better-paying jobs as Preddy, Cotton, and Gerardi found out. Separate legal challenges to end sex discrimination were needed to open floor jobs, bartending jobs, and other nontraditional categories of work to women. Furthermore, professional and management women attributed their progress in the workplace to their individual merit and skills. Few mentioned the larger context of the gender equity laws that eventually opened jobs to all qualified women. The exception in this study is Carol Gerardi, the worker who sought to enter a previously male-only field of dice dealing. The study is too small to make any claims about gender consciousness among women, but it raises serious questions about the invisibility of gender equity struggles.

While significant for Las Vegas history, the contribution of *Changing the Game* goes beyond the gambling center. The Las Vegas case demonstrates that the experiences of women in the area's employment not only shared, but also anticipated, major trends in post-1945 labor history. Women's participation in the migration of workers during and after the war, their increased portion of the labor force for subsequent decades, the combination of employment with family life, and the unionization of service workers all offer rich veins for future local studies. How did other urban centers with different local economies incorporate the influx of women? Does the evidence of diverse workplace strategies found in Las Vegas exist in more-diversified local economies? How does the variety of strategies explain support for or opposition to collective activities such as labor organizing or the women's movement? Historians have provided significant contributions in understanding gender and labor in the context of policy and unions. More remains to be done in other areas of labor force participation.

Another contribution of *Changing the Game* is in understanding the ways in which oral history enables historians to reevaluate commonly shared but narrow perceptions of American life. Oral histories provided the richest source from which to fill out the contours of women's work experiences. Not because oral sources gave the true facts about an event or a particular period, but because they offered new forms of insight for this study: context and meaning. The federal census analysis provided a framework from which to understand the trends in labor force participation. Yet, the census, manuscripts, newspapers, and other commonly used historic sources could not go beyond that framework. For example, local newspapers covered the points of conflict for workers: strikes, marches, legal action. It could not cover the way in which those events impacted workers, or what workers thought about the situations they faced. Oral history drew out the complexity of lives as it revealed why these women came to town, why they took the jobs they did, and how they understood their choices within the context of their time. Their understanding of their context and the ways in which they conveyed it made accessible the meaning that work held for them. I have honored the narratives as they were told in each chapter, yet the meaning derived as well as their place in US women's history is based entirely on my own analysis. Interpreting the meaning is a dialogic process, much like oral history as a methodology. Both the narrator and the historian participate in creating meaning from information shared. Three examples from this research help to clarify how oral histories present collaborative new meanings.

Old-timers who worked in the hotel-casinos in the early years, including some in this book, would say, "The town was better when the mob ran it." To me, this statement contains contradictions that need a translation. How could the mob have made anything better, I wondered? How could employment in a sex- and race-segregated workplace be better than equal opportunity? When asked to clarify what they meant, some workers emphasized that they could increase their wealth through the tips in a service economy. Baggage handlers, dealers, waitresses, hairdressers, and beverage servers relied on customers' tips to increase their wages. For several decades tips went underreported until corporate practices formalized reporting. In addition, narrators sympathetically shared examples of the owners' and managers' paternal assistance when a worker needed help with a family emergency, a sick child, or death in the family. Over time and many conversations, I began to understand that when men and women said, "The town was better when the mob ran it," they meant the town was smaller and the hotel-casino was less formal. Specifically, business was well organized, but not yet corporate; properties were smaller than today's hotel-casinos; workers and owners recognized each other by name; money was looser and perks were greater. Furthermore, tourism and jobs expanded, which resulted in a growth cycle that continued until the Great Recession of 2008. In short, workers perceived that more people shared in the wealth.

The second example highlights the ways in which the narrators negotiated their economic existence within the gaming culture. With the hindsight of several years, our narrators remembered both how they thought about their earlier work experiences as well as how they reinterpreted those experiences with their familiarity of more contemporary views on gender or race bias. Not all of the narrators expressed these ideas, but the meaning drawn from the examples needs consideration in studies of the late twentieth century.

Entertainers and other earners understood that skill and merit counted, but so did appearance in a world of limited opportunities. These women read the mid-century cultural signals about gender and race and knew the playing field had different rules for men and for women. Rather than reject or attempt to change the sex-gender system that promoted stereotyped portrayals of women, as many women did in the 1970s, they cultivated the gender norms. Operating as individuals in a competitive workplace, they started with merit and utilized appearance and networks to get them to their goals. Several of the narrators who worked as dancers and showgirls reported that they enjoyed being treated like celebrities. They saw the opportunity to be in show business as a dream come true, and frequently, while still in their teen years, jumped at the chance. The fact that they rehearsed without pay, sometimes worked weeks on end without a day off, and were asked to dress up the casino with their presence in between shows did not stop them; they did not complain about overwork and abuse. The entertainment persona with its trappings of luxury and glamour epitomized capitalism's consumer dreams. Women of color could not access those dreams as readily, but they participated in a parallel world of entertainment until desegregation of the showrooms and hotel-casinos opened up access to them.

Individualism also characterized narrators' responses to sexual harassment. No name for this behavior, so well-recognized today, existed before the mid-1970s when it was legally recognized as a form of sex discrimination. While the interviewers made a point to ask about sexual harassment, our narrators did not see the behavior they experienced in those terms. Instead, they emphasized with pride their ability to take care of troublesome customers independently. They "knew how to deal" with such customers, they "would give them a clue," or they "handled it" without intervention. Presumably, women who didn't want to work in that atmosphere left the job and we do not have their accounts. One might also assume that workers did not want to give management the impression that they could not handle the job, therefore they found individual solutions. By the 1980s hotel-casino human relations offices and legal counsels gave greater attention to the practice because of the rise in lawsuits.

The topic of women's individual action as an economic strategy has not been considered in women's postwar labor history. The reasons are apparent. Historians of women and labor have given greater attention to the collective actions that have significantly changed employment opportunities for all women. These include, but are not limited to, the role of organized labor in bringing early lawsuits for workplace equity, national women's organizations that successfully challenged and changed sex-discrimination laws, and small women's groups whose agenda for cultural change raised the consciousness of a generation to the presence and damages of racism and sexism. Nevertheless, workers who did not take collective action, but who remained a presence in the workforce, garnered attention for needed change by their presence.

The third example of oral history's ability to understand context and meaning addresses the difference between the way in which our narrators represented their experiences and the way in which women workers have been portrayed. One might expect women who worked in Sin City's temples of extravagance to have quite a lot to say about sex and the sexualized environment of the industry, especially in the years of this study. That is, of course, the image that is portrayed by the master narrative: women as the objects of male desire. Contemporary research has analyzed casino dress and appearance codes, sexual harassment, and sex work.[4] Yet not only could we not find women involved in sex work for our oral history project, but also among our narrators only a few took the opportunity to discuss sex in the workplace. LeCoque, Jaeger, and Kravenko mentioned prostitution and focused on the house girls of their time. Each expressed a matter-of-fact understanding of the economics of prostitution in the lives of women in the sex industry who supported their families. In addition, LeCoque challenged the idea that the seductive posture of the showgirl and her public display of nudity was degrading to women. She emphasized that the performers retained the power in the situation and portrayed an ideal of beauty. McQuary adamantly protested the unfair representation of dancers and showgirls as prostitutes. She and her circle of friends were too busy to be romantically involved, and too protected by management to be harassed in the 1950s and 1960s. The narrators' interpretation of their work emphasized hard work, professionalism, and pride.

Yet the cultural representation of women in Las Vegas as sex objects has had a remarkably long life and wide appeal. During the decades preceding the revolution in attitudes about sex, women who worked in mostly rhinestones and feathers were viewed and promoted as sexual beings. Male writers, filmmakers, headliners, and advertising departments perpetuated the image. It bled over to characterize dancers, cocktail waitresses, and secretaries as promiscuous—ready and available. Even in 1996 when Annie Liebowitz published her photos in *The New Yorker,* many were shocked at the normal lives behind the spectacular costumes. Why would the sexualized portrayal of women workers have such longevity and why did the descriptions of their lives differ so greatly between the narrators and the observers?

Several answers present themselves. First, narrators may have shared a generational resistance to put personal issues in public. If gender norms of the 1950s portrayed a dualistic split between "good girls" and "bad girls," no cultural space for variation existed. It could be that the subjects consciously shaped their narrative for wider appeal. As Luisa Passerini and her coeditors have written, "Memories supportive of the maintenance of existing power structures are usually assured wider social space and easier transmission."[5] A second explanation finds its basis in historical periods of change in the workplace. Women have often had to defend their reputations from charges of immorality by those who opposed their presence in the workplace. In the nineteenth century, when white women entered manufacturing, they were called prostitutes. African American women and working-class women have a legacy of impugned sexual reputations. Twentieth-century mill workers who went out on strike were called communists and whores. The presence of women as cocktail servers, waitresses, and dancers were not a change in the workplace, however, but rather a continuation of gender-typed work.

I suggest a third explanation. The conflicting descriptions of women in the workplace symbolized the growing tensions in gender dynamics as women became a larger part of public life in the fifty years after World War II. By tension, I do not mean microlevel tensions such as those between individuals. Rather, I mean macrolevel tensions, those unspoken contests that may be unconscious, but nevertheless are present in the public workplace. Evidence of the tensions may be found in the variety of narrators' actions within a segregated labor system, such as running their own businesses, individual workplace strategies (working the postwar sex-gender paradigm), civil rights campaigns, expanded unionization, and a nascent politicized women's movement.[6] Gender itself is not fixed, but evolves from social contradictions. As women moved into jobs at a greater pace from the 1950s forward, women's actual practice contradicted the dominant ideological roles. The tensions illustrated the inherent changeability of gender as it responds to and is acted on by other forces.[7] Although most of the jobs continued to be segregated by race and sex through the 1970s, the desire for greater occupational choice and better-paying jobs on the part of women was evident and resisted. Those who maintained conventional race and gender roles viewed the gradual movement of people of color and women into new types of jobs as a threat to the status quo and their relative positions. Women viewed their opportunities for employment as a measure of fulfillment of needs, independence, and a testimony of skill. They revealed impatience with the limits of the status quo. Most importantly, they revealed the weakness of the master narrative's sexualized and dismissive portrayal of women.

The process of transforming gender continues into the twenty-first century, although not in a progressive line. The challenges of employment desegregation by race and sex have lessened. The commodification of women's bodies in the casinos and entertainment continues. Working women have a wider range of jobs in the Las Vegas economy than they had during the years covered by this study. The dichotomy presented in the portfolio of photos by Annie Leibovitz that opened this book has less shock value in 2013 than it did when it first appeared.

In the end what makes these narratives significant to our understanding of history is not how special one woman was, or that she was the first to do something. These are important, to be sure. Yet, what establishes a place in the broad sweep of history is how actions of an individual or group help us look at something we've seen many times before and see it anew. May the readers of this book understand women who lived and worked in Las Vegas in the last half of the twentieth century as they never have before—as actors in the larger story of women's employment in the United States.

Notes

Introduction | Discovering Women in Post-1945 Las Vegas

1. Annie Leibovitz and Stephen Schiff, "Showgirls," *New Yorker*, January 29, 1996, 69–77.

2. The population figures come from the US Census, http://quickfacts.census.gov /qfd/states/32/32003.html. The following provide a scholarly introduction to the history of Las Vegas and its economic foundation in the gambling industry: James P. Kraft, *Vegas at Odds: Labor Conflict in a Leisure Economy, 1960–1985* (Baltimore: Johns Hopkins University Press, 2010); Hal K. Rothman and Mike Davis, *The Grit Beneath the Glitter: Tales from the Real Las Vegas* (Berkeley: University of California Press, 2002); Eugene P. Moehring, *Resort City in the Sunbelt: Las Vegas, 1930–2000* (Reno: University of Nevada Press, 2000); Hal K. Rothman, *Devil's Bargains: Tourism in the Twentieth Century West* (Lawrence: University Press of Kansas, 1998); John M. Findlay, *People of Chance: Gambling in American Society from Jamestown to Las Vegas* (New York: Oxford University Press, 1986). On the economic development of Las Vegas, see Moehring, *Resort City;* and Hal K. Rothman, "Colony, Capital, and Casino: Money in the Real Las Vegas," in Rothman and Davis, *Grit Beneath the Glitter,* 307–34. On the development of race and ethnic communities, see Jerry L. Simich and Thomas C. Wright, eds., *The Peoples of Las Vegas: One City Many Faces* (Reno: University of Nevada Press, 2005). On social activism, see Annelise Orleck, *Storming Caesars Palace: How Black Women Fought Their Own War on Poverty* (Boston: Beacon Press, 2005); Elmer Rusco, "The Civil Rights Movement in Nevada," *Nevada Public Affairs Review: Ethnicity and Race in Nevada* vol. 2 (1987): 75–81; Earnest N. Bracey, "Ruby Duncan, Operation Life and Welfare Rights in Nevada," *Nevada Historical Society Quarterly* 44, no. 2 (2001): 133–46. The first work to examine the lives of working women in Las Vegas was the documentary film *Stripped and Teased: Tales from Las Vegas Women,* directed by Amie Williams (Bal-Maiden Films, 1998 [DVD released 2002]).

3. The impact of the Playboy empire on the American consciousness is explored in Elizabeth Fraterrigo, *Playboy and the Making of the Good Life in Modern America* (New York: Oxford University Press, 2009).

4. Las Vegas showroom entertainment featured two forms of nudity. LeCoque referred to the first, the showroom spectacles that came to Las Vegas via European troupes that played at the Stardust Hotel and Casino ("Lido de Paris") and the

Tropicana Hotel and Casino ("Folies Bergere") during the 1950s. These shows described their nudity as an artistic presentation of the beauty of the female body. The women who worked as showgirls reinforced that view in their oral histories. The second form, burlesque, had a time-honored appeal and featured individual strippers. They later developed into full-featured stage shows. Fluff LeCoque's statement came from "A Life in Dance: Interview with Fluff LeCoque," by Lon Gordon [videotape] (UNLV, 2002).

5. Until recently, Las Vegas residents on vacation from the city would often be asked, "Does anyone really live there?" This book has benefitted immensely from three important studies that offer substantial information on women hotel-casino workers in Las Vegas: Susan Chandler and Jill B. Jones, *Casino Women: Courage in Unexpected Places* (Ithaca, NY: Cornell University Press, 2011); Kraft, *Vegas at Odds;* and Orleck, *Storming Caesars Palace.* Two additional references that focus on the contemporary service worker experiences are Jill B. Jones and Susan Chandler, "Connecting Personal Biography and Social History: Women Casino Workers and the Global Economy," *Journal of Sociology and Social Welfare* 28, no. 4 (December 2001): 173–92; and Kit Miller, *Inside the Glitter, Lives of Casino Workers: Photographs and Interviews* (Carson City, NV: Great Basin Publishing, 2000).

6. Earlier explorations of these ideas appeared in Joanne L. Goodwin, "Mojave Mirages: Gender and Performance in Post-war Las Vegas," *Women's History Review* Special Issue: *US Women and the Performing Arts* 11, no. 1 (Spring 2002): 115–31; and Joanne L. Goodwin, "'She Works Hard for Her Money,' A Reassessment of Las Vegas Women Workers, 1940–1980," in Rothman and Davis, *Grit Beneath the Glitter*, 243–59.

7. Susan G. Davis argues that the commercialization of leisure after World War II needs greater attention on the workers of a tourist economy in her historiographic essay on leisure and tourism in the postwar economy. See Susan G. Davis, "Time Out: Leisure and Tourism," in *A Companion to Post-1945 America*, ed. Jean-Christophe Agnew and Roy Rosenzweig (Malden, MA: Blackwell, 2006), 64–77.

8. Jacqueline Jones, "Shifting Paradigms of Black Women's Work in the Urban North and West: World War II to the Present," in *African American Urban History since World War II*, ed. Kenneth L. Kusmer and Joe W. Trotter (Chicago: University of Chicago Press, 2009), 295–315, here 296.

9. The Nevada Test Site was the US mainland location for above- and below-ground nuclear tests. Locals and tourists watched the predawn above-ground tests as a demonstration of US military strength. The experiences of many involved with the Test Site have been documented in the Nevada Test Site Oral History Project, which may be accessed at digital.library.unlv.edu/ntsohp/.

10. Las Vegas is a new city. Born of the railroads, kept alive with Hoover Dam and World War II military spending, it matured as a metropolis after 1950 with gambling and tourism. Thus, many of its historical actors lived into the twenty-first century.

Historians of established cities do not have the opportunity to witness a city as it develops, but historians who lived in Las Vegas in the past fifty years have experienced the boomtown and talked with its mid-century actors.

11. Moehring, *Resort City,* 18–20, 31–37.

12. US Census Bureau, *Census of Population,* Decennial (1940–1980): Counties, minor civil divisions, and places of less than a hundred thousand [for 1940 & 1950]; Summary of Population Characteristics, for the State, by Size of Place, 1960; Large Metropolitan Areas—Population, 1960–1980; and Summary of General Characteristics, 1970. These patterns are discussed in greater detail in Goodwin, " 'She Works Hard for Her Money.' "

13. For full academic studies on women, see Kraft, *Vegas at Odds;* Chandler and Jones, *Casino Women;* and Orleck, *Storming Caesars Palace.*

14. Recent histories of specific communities are conscious to include some material on Las Vegas women. For example, see Trish Geran, *Beyond the Glimmering Lights: The Pride and Perseverance of African Americans in Las Vegas* (Las Vegas: Stephens Press, 2006); Simich and Wright, *The Peoples of Las Vegas;* Moehring, *Resort City;* Rothman and Davis, *Grit Beneath the Glitter;* and Eugene P. Moehring and Michael S. Green, *Las Vegas: A Centennial History* (Reno: University of Nevada Press, 2005).

15. For an account of the creation of the NWA and the Las Vegas Women Oral History Project, see Joanne L. Goodwin, "Revealing New Narratives of Women in Las Vegas," in *Contesting Archives: Finding Women in the Sources,* ed. Nupur Chaudhuri, Sherry Katz, and Mary Elizabeth Perry (Urbana: University of Illinois Press, 2010), 177–91. For coverage of individual women and organizations in southern Nevada during the first half of the twentieth century, see Anita Ernst Watson, *Into Their Own: Nevada Women Emerging into Public Life* (Reno: Nevada Humanities Committee, 2000). A selection of biographical portraits exist. For example, see M. A. Duval, ed., *Skirts That Swept the Desert Floor: One Hundred Biographical Profiles of Nevada Women in History,* vol. 1 (Las Vegas: Stephens Press, 2006). Notable additions to the history of women after 1945 are Orleck, *Storming Caesars Palace;* and Claytee D. White, " 'Eight Dollars a Day and Working in the Shade': An Oral History of African American Migrant Women in the Las Vegas Gaming Industry," in African American Women Confront the West: 1600–2000, ed. Quintard Taylor and Shirley Ann Wilson Moore (Norman: University of Oklahoma Press, 2003), 276–92.

16. Quote in Ned Day, "The Selling of Las Vegas," *Las Vegas Magazine* (August 1984): 78.

17. Chandler and Jones discuss "the lucrative marriage of gaming and sexual stimulation," in Gabriel Vogliotti's and Mario Puzo's work of the mid-1970s. Today they find the linkage between women's bodies and access to sex focused on the cocktail servers. See Chandler and Jones, *Casino Women,* 31–33; quote p. 32. Annelise Orleck discusses

the sexualized environment in which hotel-casino employees worked, and quotes Dorothy Sue Cobble on the connections between sexual teasing and service workers' interactions in the 1960s (Orleck, *Storming Caesars Palace,* 53–54, 323 n35).

18. William Chafe, *The American Woman: Her Changing Social, Economic and Political Roles, 1920–1970* (New York: Oxford University Press, 1972).

19. Elaine Tyler May, *Homeward Bound: American Families in the Cold War Era* (New York: Basic Books, 1988), 198–200.

20. Barbara Bergmann, *The Economic Emergence of Women* (New York: Basic Books, 1986), 3. See also Nancy MacLean, "Postwar Women's History: The 'Second Wave' or the End of the Family Wage?," in Agnew and Rosenzweig, *A Companion to Post-1945 America,* 235–59.

21. For a diverse sample of the many works, see Stephanie Gilmore, *Groundswell: Grassroots Feminist Activism in Postwar America* (New York: Routledge Press, 2013); Joanne Meyerowitz, ed., *Not June Cleaver: Women and Gender in Postwar America, 1945–1960* (Philadelphia: Temple University Press, 1994); and Susan Lynn, *Progressive Women in Conservative Times: Racial Justice, Peace, and Feminism, 1945 to the 1960s* (New Brunswick, NJ: Rutgers University Press, 1992). Nancy MacLean reassesses the postwar period as one in which the constraints of the family wage began to be dismantled providing an essential context for advancement for women. See MacLean, "Postwar Women's History," 244–54.

22. This area of women's history is one of the richest and deepest. The classic study on the history of women's labor force participation is Alice Kessler-Harris, *Out to Work: A History of Wage-Earning Women in the United States* (New York: Oxford University Press, 1982 (20th anniv. ed. 2003) For an analysis of census and other documentary materials that changed our understanding of patterns of women's work, see Claudia Goldin, Understanding the Gender Gap: An Economic History of American Women (New York: Oxford University Press, 1990). The breadth of the field and its impact may be found in several publications, for example Dorothy Sue Cobble, *The Other Women's Movement: Workplace Justice and Social Rights in Modern America* (Princeton, NJ: Princeton University Press, 2005); Alice Kessler-Harris, *Gendering Labor History* (Urbana: University of Illinois Press, 2006); Ruth Milkman, "New Research in Women's Labor History," *SIGNS* 18, no. 2 (Winter 1993): 376–88; and Ava Baron, ed., *Work Engendered: Toward a New History of American Labor* (Ithaca, NY: Cornell University Press, 1991). The majority of twentieth-century scholarship examines labor organizing in manufacturing industries. A subset of that group focuses on women's entrance into wartime industries. A growing number of studies explore women workers in service and pink-collar industries, particularly in the postwar years. See Mary Romero, *Maid in the USA* (New York: Routledge, 1992); Dorothy Sue Cobble, *Dishing It Out: Waitresses and Their Unions in the Twentieth Century* (Urbana: University of Illinois Press, 1991);

and Kathleen Barry, *Femininity in Flight: A History of Flight Attendants* (Durham, NC: Duke University Press, 2007). On the topic of legislative inroads for workplace equality, see Nancy MacLean, *Freedom Is Not Enough: The Opening of the American Workplace* (Cambridge, MA: Harvard University Press, 2006).

23. The data included in this and the following two paragraphs are from *Historical Statistics of the United States,* Table Ba561–570 (accessed July 10, 2010), "Female Labor Force, by Race and Hispanic Origin: 1954–2000"; and US Department of Commerce, Bureau of the Census, *Twentieth Census of the United States,* Population Characteristics: 1980, vol. 1, pt. 30, Las Vegas Standard Metropolitan Statistical Area SMSA.

24. John P. Tuman, David F. Damore, and Maria Jose Flor Agreda, "Immigration and the Contours of Nevada's Latino Population," *Brookings Mountain West* (June 2013). This study illustrates a similar pattern of worker migration to Las Vegas, although it focuses on Mexican and Central American immigrants to the city from 2000 to 2010. The authors found that immigrants came for better economic opportunities, particularly as their home economies shrank. A significant portion of immigrants in this study (37 percent) worked in entertainment, recreation, accommodation, and food services—all of which cover the hotel-casino. Their immigration was fostered by social capital, including migration networks and the Catholic Church. Similar to the narrators in this book, they took jobs that had low requirements for education and many of those jobs were unionized by the Culinary Workers Union, Local 226 of UNITE HERE, formed when the Union of Needletrades, Industrial and Textile Employees (UNITE) merged with the Hotel Employees and Restaurant Employees (HERE) unions. The authors noted that Latinos made up approximately 45 percent of that union's membership in 2008.

25. US Census Bureau, *Census of Population,* Decennial (1940–1980): Counties, minor civil divisions, and places of less than a hundred thousand [for 1940 & 1950]; Summary of Population Characteristics, for the State, by Size of Place, 1960; Large Metropolitan Areas—Population, 1960–1980; and Summary of General Characteristics, 1970. These patterns are discussed in greater detail in Goodwin, "'She Works Hard for Her Money.'"

26. According to authors Sally Denton and Roger Morris, Benjamin Siegel received two loans from out-of-state banks for the Flamingo. See Denton and Morris, *The Money and the Power: The Making of Las Vegas and its Hold on America, 1947–2000* (New York: Alfred A. Knopf, 2001), 55.

27. Moehring, *Resort City,* 52–55; chap. 3 for the development of Strip properties; 115–19 for the second wave of hotel-casino building in 1960s.

28. Other recognizable corporate names such as Barron Hilton and Dell Webb supported the efforts to liberalize licensing that would enable the corporation to invest. Greater detail on the operations of organized crime in the development of the gambling

industry may be found in Denton and Morris, *The Money and the Power;* Kraft, *Vegas at Odds,* 14–31; and Rothman, "Colony, Capital, and Casino." For the mob's influence on the development of the Las Vegas valley, see Moehring, *Resort City,* 78–87, 242–44.

29. For details on this era of labor unrest, see Kraft, *Vegas at Odds,* chap. 7. For the role of Al Bramlet in building union membership and negotiating agreements between 1954 and 1977, see Chandler and Jones, *Casino Women,* 50–55; and Moehring, *Resort City,* 86.

30. Authors Chandler and Jones offer a portrait of this wave of new immigrants to casino work and the way in which the Culinary Workers Union incorporated them. Chandler and Jones, *Casino Women,* chap. 5, p. 60, nn 57 and 58. On the organizing campaigns of the union, the authors cite Dorothee Benz, "Labor's Ace in the Hole: Casino Organizing in Las Vegas," *New Political Science* 36 (2004): 525–50; and Courtney Alexander, "Rise to Power: The Recent History of the Culinary Union in Las Vegas," 145–75, in Rothman and Davis, *Grit Beneath the Glitter.*

31. Dr. James B. McMillan arrived in Las Vegas in 1955 and opened a dental practice. In 1960 McMillan, president of the NAACP Las Vegas branch, challenged the casino owners by promising a march on the Las Vegas Strip unless public accommodations were opened to blacks. For his account of the Moulin Rouge Agreement, see Robert Thomas King, Gary Elliott, James B. McMillan, *Fighting Back: A Life in the Struggle for Civil Rights* (Reno: University of Nevada Oral History Program, 1997), 91–98, 101.

32. Moehring, *Resort City,* 189–90, 199; and Kraft, *Vegas at Odds,* 132–35. McMillan's oral history, *Fighting Back,* takes a personal and very comprehensive account of all forms of segregation that the NAACP worked to end.

33. On sex discrimination and barriers to employment, see Moehring, *Resort City,* 201; Kraft, *Vegas at Odds,* 135–36; Orleck, *Storming Caesars Palace,* 232–33, 239, 246–49.

34. For additional information on the Consent Decree, see Nevada Advisory Committee to the US Commission on Civil Rights. "The Impact of Two Consent Decrees on Employment at Major Hotel/Casinos in Nevada," June 1989, 6, 10, 40–45.

35. Luisa Passerini, "Work, Ideology and Consensus under Italian Fascism," *History Workshop Journal* 8, no. 1 (1979): 84.

36. Alessandro Portelli, *The Death of Luigi Trastulli and Other Stories: Form and Meaning in Oral History* (Albany: State University of New York Press, 1991), 50.

37. The call for a critical examination of personal narrative and, as a part of that, the need to contextualize one's narrative, experience, or autobiographical writing, has been met by scholars in many disciplines. On autobiography, see Julia Watson and Sidonie Smith, eds., *Women, Autobiography, Theory: A Reader* (Madison: University of Wisconsin Press, 1998). For a poststructuralist critique, see Joan Scott, "Experience," *Critical Inquiry* 17 (Summer 1991): 773–98. The latter generated a spirited discussion on accessing history of marginalized people. For example, see Shari Stone-Mediatore, "Chandra Mohanty and the Revaluing of Experience," Hypatia 13, no. 2 (Spring 1998): 116–33.

38. Joanna Bornat and Hanna Diamond, "Women's History and Oral History: Developments and Debates," *Women's History Review* 16, no. 1 (2007): 19–39.

39. Sherna B. Gluck, "What's So Special about Women? Women's Oral History," in *Women's Oral History: The Frontiers Reader*, ed. Susan H. Armitage with Patricia Hart and Karen Weathermon (Lincoln: University of Nebraska Press, 2002), 3–17 (quote p. 3). This article was originally published in *Frontiers: A Journal of Women's Studies* 2, no.2 (Summer 1977): 2–14.

40. "To Our Readers," Frontiers: A Journal of Women Studies 7, no. 1 Women's Oral History Two (1983): iv. See also Susan H. Armitage, "The Next Step," *Frontiers: A Journal of Women Studies* 7, no. 1, Women's Oral History Two (1983): 3–8.

41. Susan Armitage and Sherna Berger Gluck, "Reflections on Women's Oral History: An Exchange," *Frontiers: A Journal of Women Studies* 19 no. 3 (1998): 1–11; quote p. 7.

42. The following works have influenced my use of oral histories as historical sources. Alessandro Portelli, *They Say in Harlan County: An Oral History* (New York: Oxford University Press, 2011); Fran Leeper Buss, ed., *Forged Under the Sun/Forjada Bajo el Sol. The Life of Maria Elena Lucas* (Ann Arbor: University of Michigan Press, 1993); and Jacquelyn Dowd Hall et al., *Like a Family, the Making of a Southern Cotton Mill World* (Chapel Hill: University of North Carolina Press, 1987).

43. Joyce Marshall, Claytee D. White, and Myoung Ja Lee Kwon worked with me on the Las Vegas Women in Gaming and Entertainment Oral History Project. As the project expanded in later years, its name changed to the Las Vegas Women Oral History Project.

44. Joanne L. Goodwin, "From the Ground Up: Building Archival Sources for the History of Women in Las Vegas," *Nevada Historical Society Quarterly* 49, no. 4 (Winter 2006): 273.

45. The term *juice* refers to influence, in this case the influence to recommend to a superior that an individual should be considered for a job.

46. Sidonie Smith, "Who's Talking/Who's Talking Back? The Subject of Personal Narrative," *SIGNS* 18, no. 2 (1993): 392–408. In the context of her review, Smith identifies three frameworks found in analyzing subjects and the way each framework results in a different understanding of the subject.

47. All of these oral histories have been collected by the Las Vegas Women Oral History Project, a history project of the WRIN and the history department at UNLV. Full citations including the interviewers are listed in the notes of each chapter.

48. Jeannette M. Oppedisano, *Historical Encyclopedia of American Women Entrepreneurs, 1776 to the Present* (Westport, CT: Greenwood Press, 2000), xi.

1 | Claudine Barbara Williams, Casino Owner

1. This chapter contains selections from the original publication, "Claudine Williams: A Life in Gaming," interview conducted by Joanne L. Goodwin (Women's Research Institute of Nevada, UNLV, Las Vegas, 2007).

2. Texas gambler Lester Ben (Benny) Binion had several gambling clubs in Texas from the late 1930s until 1946 when he moved to Las Vegas. He opened Binion's Horseshoe on Fremont Street that operated from 1951 to 2004. See "Lester Ben 'Benny' Binion: Some Recollections of a Texas and Las Vegas Gaming Operator," conducted by Mary Ellen Glass on May 22 and 23, 1973 (University of Nevada Oral History Program, 1976). *The Las Vegas Review Journal* described Jake Friedman as a "Houston hotelier and prodigious gambler." He built the Sands Hotel and Casino in 1952, and its entertainment, led by Jack Entratter, became a draw when the Rat Pack performed and played there. Quoted from Warren Bates, *Las Vegas Review Journal,* May 17, 1996, 2A.

3. In addition to Sarann Knight Preddy, the subject of chapter 2, four other women had leadership roles in casinos during the 1960s and 1970s: Judy Bayley, Magaret Elardi, Jeanne Hood, and Mitzi Stauffer Briggs. Bayley came to Las Vegas in 1956 with her husband "Doc" Bayley to open the Hacienda Hotel. While she was known as the first lady of gambling, she did not have the background or intimacy with casino games that Williams and Preddy had. Margaret Elardi received her license in 1988 to open the Frontier on the Las Vegas Strip. In 1991 the Culinary Union went out on a strike that lasted six and a half years and ended with the sale of the property. Jeanne Hood had been managing hotels since 1958, but took over as the chief executive of the downtown property, the Four Queens, following the death of her husband in 1977, and remained its president until 1993. Stauffer Briggs, an heiress to the Stauffer Chemical fortune, held a majority ownership stake in the Tropicana Hotel and Casino in the mid-1970s. Unfortunately, some among her staff worked for the Civella mob family of Kansas City. Their skim drained her fortune.

4. For a brief and yet thoughtful response to the impact of gender analysis on business history, see Joan W. Scott, "Comment: Conceptualizing Gender in American Business History," *Business History Review* 72 (Summer 1998): 242–49. The two entrepreneurs in this study do not appear in women and business histories, nor do they fit the characteristics of historical female entrepreneurs according to Virginia Drachman. She argued that women often entered business to continue the family's interest after losing a husband. This was the case of a contemporary of Claudine Williams, Katharine Graham, who became editor of the *Washington Post.* Nor did they follow the pattern of starting businesses focusing on women's conventional needs or interests (family, fashion, children, beauty products) as did another contemporary, Mary Kay Ash, who started a cosmetic company. They do, however, make Drachman's larger point that women were not only consumers in the twentieth-century consumption and leisure

economies, but also helped to build that economy. See Virginia G. Drachman, *Enterprising Women: 250 Years of American Business* (Chapel Hill: University of North Carolina Press, 2002); Philip Scranton, ed., *Beauty and Business: Commerce, Gender and Culture in Modern America* (New York: Routledge, 2001); and Mary A. Yeager, ed., *Women in Business,* 3 vols. (Northampton, MA: Elgar Reference Collection, 1999).

5. Claudine Barbara Williams was born on March 17, 1921, to Robert E. and Hazel O. Williams. Additional biographical information may be found in Goodwin, "Claudine Williams"; and Carole Bellmyer, ed. *Distinguished Women of Southern Nevada* (Las Vegas: Distinguished Publishing, 1995), 184. See also Phil Hevener, *Las Vegas Sun,* November 4, 1991, 2D.

6. Chuck-a-luck is a game played with three dice. The dice remain in an hourglass wire cage that is turned end over end. Players bet on the numbered dice that they think will appear.

7. Carey Estes Kefauver served in both the US House of Representatives and US Senate from Tennessee. Williams is referring to his role as chair of the Senate's Special Committee to Investigate Organized Crime in Interstate Commerce. The committee held hearings across the country between 1950 and 1952. The hearings and their publicity raised Americans' awareness about the presence of organized crime in businesses. It led to local crackdowns of gambling establishments throughout the country and the subsequent migration of gamblers to Las Vegas.

8. Abe Weinstein and his brother Barney owned nightclubs in Dallas and Houston. He opened Abe and Pappy's with Pappy Dolson in both cities. The clubs were renown for burlesque and contemporary bands. Apparently it also followed Jim Crow policies of the era with its black entertainers. One of its matchbooks advertises "Red Hot All-Colored Revue," and featured images of black-face caricatures on one side and a seminude dancer on the other (http://www.flickr.com/photos /christianspenceranderson/6879113086/).

9. Williams clarified that she kept a small apartment in Dallas, but considered Houston her home. She drove there on her days off. Jake Friedman became a partner in the Las Vegas Sands.

10. The buffet holds an iconic place in mid-century Las Vegas history. The first buffet on the Strip has been awarded to the El Rancho Vegas, although Williams distinguished between their chuck wagon and her property's buffet. For more on dining history in Las Vegas, see http://gaming.unlv.edu/dining/early.html.

11. Williams consistently used the name Holiday Casino to refer to the property although it was incorporated as the Riverboat Casino, Inc. Holiday Inns, Inc. of Memphis, Tennessee ran the hotel that accompanied the casino. In 1979 Holiday Inns, Inc purchased 40 percent ownership in property and in January 1983 bought the remaining 60 percent. Two years later the corporation changed the name to Holiday Corporation.

In April 1992 the Harrah's purchased the property. Goodwin, "Claudine Williams," 24–26, 29.

12. Irwin Molasky became a Las Vegas real estate developer. "The Developer's Developer," in *The First 100: Portraits of Men and Women Who Shaped Las Vegas,* ed. A. D. Hopkins and K. J. Evans (Las Vegas: Huntington Press, 1999), 258–61.

13. Shelby and Claudine Williams's Holiday Casino opened on July 2, 1973.

14. Liberal slots refers to slot machine settings that pay out a higher percentage of the time. High limits refers to the amount that a player can bet on a game.

15. The entertainment director arranged for the acts in the casino lounges and showrooms. The Sennett brothers, Rocky and Frank, would arrange for entertainment in numerous clubs around the country, for example the Lookout House in Kentucky, and at clubs in Los Angeles and Las Vegas.

16. Williams referred to the people and incidents recorded in the book *Casino* by Nicholas Pileggi and the film of the same name directed by Martin Scorsese.

17. Williams named the founders of the UNLV Foundation as Claudine Williams, Irwin Molasky, Tom Wiesner, Art Ham, and Pat Goodall (who was the university president at the time). In addition to those listed by Williams, Perry Thomas and Jerry Mack started the land foundation that acquired the land for the original buildings. The UNLV Foundation was incorporated in 1981. I am grateful to Lucy Klinkhammer, previously with the UNLV Foundation, for providing the names of additional trustees who served with the first five on the original Foundation Board. They were Ernest Becker, James Cashman Jr., Michael Gaughan, Sig Rogich, and Grant Sawyer.

2 | Sarann Preddy, Casino Owner

1. This narrative is an edited selection from the original transcript "An Interview with Sarann Preddy: An Oral History," conducted by Claytee D. White (Las Vegas Women in Gaming and Entertainment Oral History Project, UNLV, 1998). Similar topics were discussed during different sessions of the interviews. Consequently, segments in this chapter may appear in an order different from the transcript. I have taken the utmost care to preserve the author's intent and meaning.

2. Moehring, *Resort City,* chap. 6.

3. In addition to the references on women entrepreneurs in chapter 1, note 4, historical studies of African American entrepreneurs have focused on individuals such as Madame C. J. Walker and Mary Ellen Pleasant. For a multidisciplinary collection of interviews and historical profiles, see Cheryl A. Smith, *Market Women: Black Women Entrepreneurs, Past, Present, and Future* (Santa Barbara, CA: Greenwood Publishing Group, 2005). Also, see Oppedisano, *Historical Encyclopedia.*

4. For information on civil rights and the history and significance of the Moulin Rouge in Las Vegas, see Moehring, *Resort City*; Dr. William H. "Bob" Bailey, *Looking Up! Finding My Voice in Las Vegas* (Las Vegas: Stephens Press, 2009); McMillan, *Fighting*

Back, chaps. 10–14; Earnest N. Bracey, "The Moulin Rouge Mystique: Blacks and Equal Rights in Las Vegas," *Nevada Historical Society Quarterly* 39, no. 4 (1996): 272–88; and Bracey, "The Political Participation of Blacks in an Open Society: The Changing Political Climate in Nevada," *Nevada Historical Society Quarterly* 42, no. 3 (1999): 140–59. The University of Nevada Oral History Program produced additional oral histories on African Americans in gaming and politics in Nevada.

5. The original Cotton Club building burned down and the place was rebuilt.

6. Hawthorne is approximately three hundred miles north of Las Vegas and the site of a large military depot.

7. Preddy lived in Hawthorne from 1950 to 1957. It would not be unusual to express the fear of having her home shot into because civil rights activists in several Southern states during the 1950s had their lives threatened and homes attacked. Although Nevada was not formally considered the South, African Americans frequently referred to patterns of behavior in southern Nevada and Las Vegas specifically as the Mississippi of the West.

8. The individuals named here were professionals who moved to Las Vegas in the mid-1950s and became leaders in the local civil rights movement. The original research on the role of the black middle class in the development of civil rights in Las Vegas was conducted by Claytee D. White. Her master's thesis, articles, and oral histories, located in the Special Collections Department of UNLV, provide an excellent background to this discussion. Additional biographical material may be found in McMillan, *Fighting Back*; and Bailey, *Looking Up!*

9. Prior to 1958 a few women worked as dealers in downtown, North Las Vegas, and Westside casinos. Reno had left the job of card dealing open to women, but job competition in Las Vegas led a group of male dealers to successfully persuade the city commissioners to ban women's employment as dealers. This mandate stayed in effect until 1970, when the city lifted the ban. Contingent cities had varied policies. It took federal and state intervention to end employment discrimination by sex, which opened a variety of jobs, including dealing cards and dice, to all who were qualified. The section on D. D. Cotton in chapter 5 and all of chapter 9 focus on the history of opening jobs more specifically.

10. I have searched for published information on the Chinese in Reno gambling clubs without success. For another mention of the Chinese in Reno, see "Clarence Ray: Black Politics and Gaming.in Las Vegas, 1920s–1980s: An Oral History," interview conducted by Helen M. Blue and Jamie Coughtry (University of Nevada Oral History Program, Reno, 1991), 39.

11. She operated a clothing cleaner and then a clothing store next door to it. She described both ventures as short term.

12. Both women achieved professional status and worked with the NAACP to end race discrimination. Johnson was the first black nurse in Clark County and Hoggard

was the first black teacher in Las Vegas. See "Lubertha Johnson, Civil Rights Efforts in Las Vegas: 1940s–1960s: An Oral History," interview conducted by Jamie Coughtry and edited by Jamie Coughtry and R. T. King (University of Nevada Oral History Program, Reno, 1988); and "Our Histories: Profiles of Nevada Women," http://wrinunlv .org/research/our-history-profiles-of-nevada-women/mabel-hoggard/.

13. The Gamma Phi Delta sorority is a national organization of professional and business women from the African American community. It was founded in Detroit in 1943 with the purpose of aiding young people in education and in their vocational careers. It supports charities with similar goals. See their home page at http://www .gammaphideltasorority.com/.

14. The Women's Auxiliary started at the national level and could be found in many chapters. Preddy began the Las Vegas group.

15. Also see "An Interview with Alice Key," interview conducted by Claytee D. White (Las Vegas Women in Gaming and Entertainment Oral History Project, Las Vegas, 1998).

16. Jeffrey J. Sallaz, "Civil Rights and Employment Equity in Las Vegas Casinos: The Failed Enforcement of the Casino Consent Decree 1971–1986," *Nevada Historical Society Quarterly* 47, no. 4 (2004): 283–302. The author is currently revising for publication an article-length manuscript that explores the 1981 Consent Decree and the varied initiatives that brought it into being.

17. The 1971 Consent Decree was a federal court document signed by eighteen major hotel-casinos and labor unions agreeing to hire blacks in positions other than race-typed jobs. Lubertha Johnson recounted a similar story of the Sal Sagev owner and his reaction to the 1960 desegregation plan to open public accommodations through the Moulin Rouge Agreement. See Coughtry, "Lubertha Johnson," 64–65. For a discussion of the meeting that brokered an end to this form of segregation in Las Vegas and the consent decree, see Moehring, *Resort City*, 173–202; and McMillan, *Fighting Back*, 91–98.

18. Jerry's Nugget is located in North Las Vegas. That municipality did not have the same ban on women dealers as the city of Las Vegas. Some downtown Las Vegas clubs rehired women dealers during the 1970s, but the Las Vegas Strip casinos, which are located in a different jurisdiction, Clark County, maintained their sex discrimination (with a few exceptions) until a second consent decree, this one in 1981, compelled properties to open all jobs to people qualified regardless of sex or national orgin.

19. On African American women owning casinos in Las Vegas, see "An Interview with Anna Bailey: An Oral History," interview conducted by Claytee D. White (Las Vegas Women in Gaming and Entertainment Oral History Project, UNLV, Las Vegas, 1997).

3 | Bernice Jaeger, Assistant General Manager

1. This chapter is based on "An Interview with Bernice Jaeger: An Oral History," interview conducted by Joanne L. Goodwin on July 25, 1997; July 30, 1997; and February 3, 1998 (Las Vegas Women Oral History Project, UNLV, Las Vegas, 1998). I have paid great attention to conveying the meaning intended by the narrator when I edited and combined segments of the transcript.

2. Since the late 1990s this relationship has shifted as hotel-casinos brought in restaurateurs and retail to enhance the experience of tourism and broaden sources of revenue.

3. Northern Kentucky gambling has drawn the attention of numerous popular and academic articles. For example, see David Wecker, "Before There Was Vegas, There Was Newport," *Cincinnati Post*, September 4, 2004, A1; Robert Geoielli, "Suburbs vs. Slot Machines: The Committee of 500 and the Battle over Gambling in Northern Kentucky," *Ohio Valley History* 5, no. 2 (Summer 2005); Hank Messick, Syndicate Wife (New York: MacMillan, 1968); Bryan Meade, "Gangsters in Our Own Back Yard: 'Little Mexico' a.k.a. Newport, KY," *Better Living Magazine* [online] last update April 4, 2005, http://newporthighschool.org/gangsters.htm.

4. The greater Las Vegas area despite experiencing major growth was still a medium-size city at that time. The US Census recorded the population of Las Vegas city at sixty-four thousand in 1960. The greater surrounding area had nearly twice as many people recorded. As important, the population of the city had jumped two and a half times since the previous census. US Department of Commerce, Bureau of the Census, *Eighteenth Census of the United States*, 1960, Population and Housing, Table 32. "Summary of Social Characteristics."

5. The pit is the area of the casino that holds the table games: twenty-one, poker, roulette, and craps, for example. A very large casino may have several pits. The entire pit is supervised by the pit manager, often called the pit boss. The floor man or floor person keeps the games balanced and resolves disputes. Each table game has a dealer, except for craps which has four: A boxman is in charge of the money and supervises the craps game table. On either side, a base dealer collects and pays bets. A stickman takes bets, calls out the dice roll, and returns the dice to the player. The pit clerk records information on the players. The cage is located on the floor but outside the pit and is the area of exchange for cash and chips. All these positions had been traditionally male jobs.

6. When Jaeger started at the Riviera, Ed Torres had just sold it to Meshulam Riklis. Riklis was born in Istanbul in 1922 and lived in Tel Aviv before going to college in the United States. He made millions of dollars in business by leveraging business takeovers. His acquisitions included Fabergé, Samsonite, and the Riviera Hotel and Casino. He had just married actress and singer Pia Zadora when he purchased the Riviera from Torres, according to Jaeger. Torres agreed to stay on as manager for five years after the sale.

7. The narrator has conducted numerous interviews with old-time gamblers in an effort to capture the stories of their work and lives. In collaboration with her nephew, she produced a video documentary, which has never been released publicly.

8. Jaeger is referring to the 1981 Consent Decree, which enforced equal opportunity for women and people of Hispanic lineage in all casino jobs. Following the 1971 Consent Decree, which focused on race discrimination, women still experienced segregation into what were known as women's jobs. After a series of legal actions at the federal, state, and local levels, a second consent decree was applied to hotel-casino jobs. For more on the consent decrees, see Sallaz, "Civil Rights and Employment Equity." See also Kraft, *Vegas at Odds*.

9. In 1985 Jaeger received her bachelor of arts in women's studies from the UNLV. She changed careers after receiving her master of arts in counseling from the UNLV in 2003.

10. Lester "Benny" Binion brought his gambling expertise from Texas to Las Vegas in the mid-1940s.

4 | Ffolliott "Fluff" LeCoque, Company Manager

1. This chapter is based on "An Interview with Ffolliott LeCoque: An Oral History," interview conducted by Joyce Marshall on May 5, 1997 (Las Vegas Women in Gaming and Entertainment Oral History Project, UNLV, Las Vegas, 1998).

2. Donn Arden, a choreographer, producer, and director, who was best known for his spectacular showroom productions, worked for sixty years in showrooms around the globe. He began as a dancer in Prohibition-era clubs, became a lead dancer with a Fanchon and Marco troupe, and produced his first show at age eighteen. During World War II he produced shows for Allied troops, and in 1948 began a lifelong working relationship with Margaret Kelly and her Bluebell Girls in Paris. In Las Vegas he produced shows for the Desert Inn beginning in 1950 and brought the "Lido de Paris" show to the Stardust in 1958. In 1978 Arden innovated again with his extravagant production show "Hallelujah Hollywood" at the MGM Grand. "He dared to do things that had never been tried on a stage before," like sinking the Titanic, revving airplane engines, and recreating the burning Hindenburg, said LeCoque. These shows shifted from the star format that had dominated showroom entertainment and toward a format in which the show itself became the star. In 1981 "Jubilee!" opened at the MGM with million-dollar stage sets, Bob Mackie–designed costumes, and showgirls and dancers that captured the aura of Las Vegas during the 1970s when the showgirl and spectacle entertainment dominated the stage. For more, see Michael Paskevich, "Donn Arden (1917–1994) Master of Disaster," in *The First 100*, 255–57.

3. LeCoque quoted in Paskevich, "Donn Arden," 256. Florenz Ziegfeld, Jr. has been credited with creating the iconic American showgirl in the early twentieth century. See Michael Lasser, "The Glorifier: Florenz Ziegfeld and the Creation of the American

Showgirl," *The American Scholar* 63, no. 3 (Summer 1994): 441–48. For Earl Carroll, see Ken Murray, *The Body Merchant: The Story of Earl Carroll* (Pasadena CA: Ward Ritchie Press, 1976).

4. Fanny "Fanchon" Wolff and Mike "Marco" Wolff produced acts and managed dance troupes in theaters throughout the West Coast during the 1930s and 1940s. This brother and sister team began as cabaret dancers and moved into production. Several of the dance narrators in the Las Vegas Women Oral History Project worked on the West Coast circuit for one of the duo's troupes. For histories of women in Butte, see Mary Murphy, *Mining Culture: Men, Women and Leisure in Butte, 1914–1941* (Urbana: University of Illinois Press, 1997); and Janet L. Finn and Ellen Crain, eds., *Motherlode: Legacies of Women's Lives and Labors in Butte, Montana* (Livingston, MT: Clark City Press, 2005).

5. The entertainment format LeCoque described was characteristic of that found in thousands of clubs across the country during the 1940s and 1950s. The larger showroom spectacles began to replace that format in the late 1950s.

6. Located across the river from Cincinnati near Covington, Kentucky, the Lookout House was originally a supper club owned by Bill Hill, but it became a private gambling club in 1933 when Jimmy Brink bought it. Brink agreed to collaborate with the Cleveland syndicate and sell the club in exchange for retaining the position of manager and a small interest in the property. Thus Sam Tucker was most likely in charge of operations when Arden brought his entertainment to the club. Matthew DeMichele and Gary Potter, "Sin City Revisited: A Case Study of the Official Sanctioning of Organized Crime in an "Open City," *Justice and Police Studies,* Eastern Kentucky University, [no date], http://www.rootsweb.ancestry.com/~kycampbe/newportgambling.htm. Also see Bernice Jaeger's contribution to this volume (chapter 3).

7. Margaret Kelly, also known as Madame Bluebell, was born in Ireland and introduced to dance at a young age. She worked at the Folies Bergère in Paris during World War II. She became renowned for hiring tall dancers known as the Bluebell Girls. The Bluebell Girls were thought to be French, but many were Australian, American, and British. French girls were not tall enough. LeCoque recalled that American dancers would go to Europe to rehearse and be hired by Bluebell. Years later, Arden and Kelly brought the "Lido de Paris" show to Las Vegas and introduced European shows with nudity to the Strip. For a biography of Margaret Kelly, see George Perry, *Bluebell: The Authorized Biography of Margaret Kelly, Founder of the Legendary Bluebell Girls* (New York: Harper Collins, 1986).

8. The Desert Inn, which opened in 1950, was conceived and built by Wilbur Clark and financed with assistance from Moe Dalitz and other investors. Before coming to Las Vegas, Dalitz had built up a portfolio of properties and businesses financed from the profits of bootlegging and racketeering. John L. Smith, "Morris B. "Moe" Dalitz," in *The First 100,* 165–68. Also see the oral history of Toni Clark, Wilbur Clark's widow: "An

Interview with Toni Clark: An Oral History," interview conducted by Joanne L. Goodwin (Las Vegas Women Oral History Project, UNLV, 1997, rev. 2006). The Desert Inn was razed in 2000 to make way for the construction of Wynn Las Vegas.

9. The theater and its namesake have their own interesting entertainment history. Carroll built his first theatre on Broadway near Seventh Avenue and 50th Street in 1922. He produced shows called *Vanities*, which combined comedy and chorus girls, to compete with Florenz Ziegfeld. He rebuilt a more lavish building in 1931, but could not sustain the enterprise. Ziegfeld purchased the property, and Carroll moved west and built his theatre again in Hollywood on Sunset Boulevard. It opened in 1938 and became an entertainment palace. Across the entrance to both theatres, Carroll had the words, "Through these portals pass the most beautiful girls in the world." Carroll died in a plane crash in 1948 and the property changed hands. In 1953 it began to operate as the Moulin Rouge. In a funny twist of popular entertainment, the Moulin Rouge became the site for the recording of a popular television show that ran from 1955 to 1964 called "Queen for a Day." The entertainment value of that show was the competition between housewives whose down-on-their-luck stories were rated by an audience with an applause-o-meter. The one who received the highest rating won her wish as Queen for a Day. For more on the television show, see Georganne Scheiner, "Would You Like to Be Queen for a Day? Finding a Working Class Voice in American Television of the 1950s," *Historical Journal of Film, Radio and Television* 23, no. 4 (October 2003): 375–87.

10. The production opened seven months later than expected after a catastrophic fire swept through the hotel-casino, killing eighty-seven people; it also destroyed all the costumes and sets for the show. The MGM Grand changed ownership and its name to Bally's in 1985.

11. La Verne Lignon was one of those dancers. She auditioned at the MGM Studios in Culver City, CA, was hired for Arden's production "Hallelujah Hollywood" in November 1973, and became the dance captain. She said that she was the first African American dance captain on the Las Vegas Strip. "Las Vegas African American Community Conversations," Episode 3, http://www.vegaspbs.org/tv-programs/local/african-american-conversations/. Anna Bailey recounted that she was the first African American dancer to perform in an integrated line at the Flamingo, in around 1960 or 1961. Pearl Bailey insisted on having African American dancers integrated into her line when she performed in Las Vegas. According to Anna Bailey, Pearl Bailey insisted that they wear dark makeup so the bright lights would not conceal the fact that they were black. "An Interview with Anna Bailey: An Oral History," interview conducted by Claytee D. White (Las Vegas Women in Gaming and Entertainment Oral History Project, UNLV, 1997), 33, 52.

12. Fischman was vice president of entertainment at Bally's at the time.

5 | Gail McQuary, Janet Kravenko, and D. D. Cotton, Dancers

1. I am grateful to Brigid Kelley who interviewed several dancers for the larger project and commented on this chapter. The classic historical work on showroom dancers for the early twentieth century is Susan A. Glenn, *Female Spectacle: The Theatrical Roots of Modern Feminism* (Boston: Harvard University Press, 2000). Also see Lewis A. Erenberg, *Steppin' Out: New York Nightlife and the Transformation of American Culture, 1890–1930* (Chicago: University of Chicago Press, 1981), esp. chapter 7; and Linda Mizejewski, *Ziegfeld Girl: Image and Icon in Culture and Cinema* (Durham, NC: Duke University Press, 1999). For an analysis that finds empowerment and independence in the dancers of the postwar era, see Wendy Buonaventura, *Something in the Way She Moves: Dancing Women from Salome to Madonna* (Cambridge, MA: DaCapo Press, 2004); and Becki Ross, *Burlesque West: Showgirls, Sex, and Sin in Postwar Vancouver* (Toronto, ON: University of Toronto Press, 2009).

2. This specific characteristic of the showgirl can be traced back to early-twentieth-century European clubs and cabarets. *Nevada Magazine* 38, no. 2 (1978): 44; quote on p. 44.

3. See Jack E. Sheehan, "In Defense of Showgirls," *Las Vegan Magazine* (August 1984): 17–23, 88–89, 92–96.

4. For a cultural analysis of the influence of African Americans on dance, see Jayna Brown, *Babylon Girls, Black Women Performers and the Shaping of the Modern* (Durham, NC: Duke University Press, 2008). For additional oral histories on African American women dancers, see the interviews conducted by Claytee D. White in the Las Vegas Women Oral History Project.

5. As a comparison, the New York City Rockettes did not integrate its chorus line with Asian and African American dancers until 1987 and 1988, respectively. Integration happened in waves in Las Vegas and there were early exceptions. Anna Bailey danced in an integrated line at the Flamingo in the early 1960s and Laverne Lignon danced in a Donn Arden production in the early 1970s. The Moulin Rouge Agreement opened accommodations to blacks after 1960. Two consent decrees, one in 1971 and one in 1981, intended to open all fields of employment to African Americans, and to all ethnicities and women, respectively. For an assessment of the 1971 Consent Decree and its failure to end race discrimination in casino hiring, see Sallaz, "Civil Rights and Employment Equity." Also, see Bracey, "The Moulin Rouge Mystique."

6. A tiller line is a chorus line that uses high kicks and precision dancing; it originated in England. John Tiller formed a troupe of precision dancers at the beginning of the twentieth century. One of his troupes appeared in the "Ziegfeld Follies" of 1922 in the United States. The New York City Radio City Hall Rockettes are the most renowned example in the United States. For more on the early-twentieth-century development of this style of dance, see Glenn, *Female Spectacle*.

7. At this stage in her career, McQuary spent less than a year in Las Vegas. She moved to the Riverside Hotel in Reno and then the Beverly Hills Country Club in Covington, Kentucky. She then returned to Las Vegas.

8. "An Interview with Gail S. McQuary: An Oral History," interview conducted by Joanne L. Goodwin (Las Vegas Women in Gaming and Entertainment Oral History Project, UNLV, Las Vegas, 2003).

9. "An Interview with Janet Kravenko," interview conducted by Brigid Kelly, August 7, 2002, unpublished transcript Women's Research Institute of Nevada, UNLV, Las Vegas.

10. Perry, *Bluebell.*

11. Initially, the contracts lasted six months after which the dancers would return to Paris or their home. However, the contract had an option for renewal, so Kravenko came back every six months for a period of one and a half years. After a while the cost of changing shows so frequently became too expensive and they kept them running for several years.

12. Ron Lewis choreographed a number of Las Vegas shows. Major Riddle operated the Dunes Hotel and Casino.

13. The rest of this paragraph has been moved here from another part of the interview where the topic was repeated.

14. Ronald Smothers, "Neighborhoods: Sugar Hill in Harlem, Once a Model of Sweet Life Has Soured," *New York Times,* October 14, 1976, 40.

15. The Links Incorporated is a national service organization that has been dedicated to serving the needs of African Americans since 1946.

16. Katherine Dunham brought to modern dance the movement styles of African and Caribbean cultures that she combined with ballet and modern techniques. She founded the Negro Dance Troupe in Chicago, the nation's first self-supporting black dance troupe. In 1939 she moved her company to New York City. In 1945 she opened the Dunham School of Dance and Theater in Manhattan, where she influenced many of the twentieth century's dancers. See Jack Anderson, "Katherine Dunham, Dance Icon, Dies at 96," *New York Times,* May 23, 2006, http://www.nytimes.com/2006/05/23/arts/dance/23dunham.html?pagewanted=all&_r=0.

17. "An Interview with D. D. Cotton: An Oral History," interview conducted by Claytee D. White on February 14, 1997 (Las Vegas Women in Gaming and Entertainment Oral History Project, UNLV, Las Vegas, 1999). Born Ethel Dolores and nicknamed Dee Dee, she went by D.D. This chapter uses only a small part of the information contained in the interview. It sheds light on the entertainment world for African Americans in the pre–civil rights years, on working in the nontraditional fields of card dealing and floor supervision, and on the work of the NAACP in moving the gaming industry into compliance with equal opportunity hiring.

18. See chapter 4 for a description of another circuit of clubs, in which Fluff LeCoque worked.

19. Singer Lonnie Sattin recorded and appeared in films. Norma Miller became known as the "Queen of Swing" and was renown for her acrobatic innovations in the Lindy Hop.

20. Murray Weinger died suddenly of a heart attack at age thirty-nine. His obituary noted his role in starting the nightclub scene in Miami. "Services Slated Today for Murray Weinger, 39," *Miami News,* January 17, 1957, 4A.

21. For more on the integration of chorus lines and shows, see the Las Vegas Women Oral History Project interviews of Anna Bailey, Fluff LeCoque, and Betty Bunch, Special Collections Department, Lied Library, UNLV, Las Vegas, NV.

22. Other narrators reported that they auditioned for shows in major cities such as New York or Los Angeles and then their troupe went on tour or came to Las Vegas.

23. Cotton is referring to the "Cotton Club Revue" that brought her to Las Vegas.

24. Cliff and Claude Trenier formed the core of this rhythm-and-blues group that sang and played in major clubs from Chicago to Los Angeles and in Las Vegas. Other musicians and relatives joined the group over time. "Claude Trenier, 84, a member of Family's Las Vegas Ensemble," *New York Times,* November 22, 2003, B7.

25. Dr. William H. "Bob" Bailey came to Las Vegas in the mid-1950s as the master of ceremonies for the revue at the Moulin Rouge. He started as a singer and became one of two featured singers in Count Basie's orchestra. Bailey stayed in Las Vegas with his wife Anna Bailey and became a real estate broker and developer. In 1964 they opened a club called Sugar Hill in North Las Vegas. He also played a role in the formation of the Voters League and the Equal Rights Commission. A. D. Hopkins, "Breaking the Color Line, Bob Bailey," *The First 100,* 204–206; and Bailey, *Looking Up!*

26. Richard Walker is one of the sons of Sarann Knight Preddy, an African American entrepreneur and club owner in Las Vegas, and the subject of chapter 2.

27. Cotton's path in casino work moved through many parts of the casino. For another narrative on dealing, see chapter 9 in this book.

28. James B. McMillan had three terms as president of the Las Vegas NAACP—1960, 1971–73, and 1977–79.

29. According to the fact-finding associated with both the 1971 Consent Decree to end race discrimination and the 1981 Consent Decree to end discrimination on the basis of sex and ethnicity, this strategy was used frequently to keep blacks, Latinos, and all women from holding positions. Nevada Advisory Committee to the US Commission on Civil Rights, "The Impact of Two Consent Decrees."

6 | Lucille Bryant, Housekeeper and Uniform Room Supervisor

1. The significance of the unions to the service workers in Las Vegas's hotels and casinos has been discussed most recently and completely in Kraft, *Vegas at Odds*. Also see Chandler and Jones, *Casino Women*.

2. "An Interview with Lucille Bryant: An Oral History," interview conducted by Claytee D. White on December 13, 1995 and March 1, 1996 (Las Vegas Women Oral History Project, Las Vegas, 1997).

3. The history of African American women's lives and earning continues to expand and enrich our understanding of the intersections of gender and race. For example, see Jacqueline Jones, *Labor of Love, Labor of Sorrow: Black Women, Work, and the Family, from Slavery to the Present* (New York: Basic Books, 1985, rev. 2010); Lisa Krissoff Boehm, *Making a Way Out of No Way* (Jackson: University Press of Mississippi, 2009); Gretchen Lemke-Santangelo, *Abiding Courage: African American Migrant Women and the East Bay Community* (Chapel Hill: University of North Carolina Press, 1996).

4. For a broader discussion of the migration of African Americans from the South to the West during and after World War II, see Quintard Taylor, *In Search of the Racial Frontier: African Americans in the American West, 1528–1990* (New York: Norton, 1998), esp. chaps. 9 and 10. Specific studies on African American women's experiences may be found in Taylor and Moore, *African American Women Confront the West*; Orleck, *Storming Caesars Palace*; and Lemke-Santangelo, *Abiding Courage*.

5. The transportation of African Americans from the South to Las Vegas is explored in Claytee D. White, "The Roles of African American Women in the Las Vegas Gaming Industry, 1940–1980" (master's thesis, UNLV, 1997).

6. When Lucille Bryant moved to Las Vegas in 1953, de facto segregation characterized the town. African Americans, whose proportion in the general population increased through the next decades, confronted residential segregation in the old Westside, just north and west of downtown. Jobs, schools, and recreation also followed racial segregation with few exceptions. See Moehring, *Resort City*, chap. 6; Bailey, *Looking Up!*; and McMillan, *Fighting Back*.

7. The Stardust Hotel and Casino opened in 1958 and closed in 2007.

8. Wallace Turner, "Reputed Organized Crime Heads Named in Casino Skimming Case: 15 Indicted in Las Vegas Skimming Case," *New York Times* October, 12 1983, A1. This case provided the background for Nicholas Pileggi's book *Casino*, and for the movie of the same name based on the book. The introduction to *Changing the Game* contains a fuller discussion of the transition from mob-controlled casinos to corporations.

9. On the struggle to end de facto segregation, see note 6 above. For information on the nightclubs of the African American neighborhood, see chapter 2 in this volume.

10. The union did exist, but it may not have had a contract with the first property where she initially worked.

11. On the murder of Bramlet, see Kraft, *Vegas at Odds,* 160–63.

12. Lemke-Santangelo, *Abiding Courage,* 6.

7 | Hattie Canty, Culinary Workers Union Organizer

1. This narrative is an edited selection from the original transcript, "An Interview with Hattie Canty," interview conducted by Claytee D. White (Las Vegas Women in Gaming and Entertainment Oral History Project, UNLV, Las Vegas, 1998). Hattie Canty has been featured in several popular and academic works, but this chapter is the first time that she has explained her experiences in detail and in her own words. For examples of works featuring Canty, see Jones, "Shifting Paradigms"; Steven Greenhouse, "Local 226, 'the Culinary,' Makes Las Vegas the Land of the Living Wage," *New York Times,* June 3, 2004; and Sara Mosle, "How the Maids Fought Back," *New Yorker,* February 26, 1996, 151.

2. That strike has been documented in the film *One Day Longer: The Story of the Frontier Strike* (Bal-Maiden Films, Hotel Employees and Restaurant Employees International Union, c/o Transit Media, 2000).

3. The prominence of Las Vegas as a center of union activity in the United States has been widely reported in a variety of news media from the *Wall Street Journal* to *The Nation* since 1994. For example, see Greenhouse, "Local 226"; Marc Cooper, "Labor Deals a New Hand," *The Nation,* March 24, 1997, 11–13; and Mike Davis, "Armageddon at the Emerald City: Local 226 vs. MGM Grand," *The Nation,* July 11, 1994, 46–50. Journalists and historians have referred to Las Vegas as the last Detroit or Pittsburgh in a reference to the shift from industrial workers' unions to service workers' unions. See Hal K. Rothman, *Neon Metropolis: How Las Vegas Started the Twentieth-Century* (New York: Routledge, 2002), esp. 63–88. Two important additions to the literature are Chandler and Jones, *Casino Women*; and Kraft, *Vegas at Odds.*

4. The use of collective power through unions is explored in Susan Chandler and Jill B. Jones, "Because a Better World Is Possible: Women Casino Workers, Union Activism and the Creation of a Just Workplace," *Journal of Sociology and Social Welfare* 30, no. 4 (December 2003): 57–78.

5. For an overview of the history of African Americans in the West and the Second Great Migration, see Taylor, *In Search of the Racial Frontier,* esp. chaps. 9 and 10; and Orleck, *Storming Caesars Palace,* chap. 1.

6. The original research on African American women's employment in Las Vegas may be found in White, " 'Eight Dollars a Day.' " On the Culinary Union, see Chandler and Jones, *Casino Women;* and Michael Nyre, "Union Jackpot: Culinary Workers Local 226, Las Vegas, Nevada, 1970–2000" (master's thesis, California State University, Fullerton, ProQuest/UMI Dissertations Publishing, 2001), 1404893. The most complete work on women's involvement with the Hotel Employees and Restaurant Employees Union is Cobble, *Dishing It Out.* Also see Maria Jurkovic, "Picketing in Paradise: The Garment,

Laundry, and Hotel Workers' Unions in 1950s Miami, Florida" (master's thesis, Florida Atlantic University, ProQuest,/UMI Dissertations Publishing, 1995), 1361618.

7. While Canty was on the margins of union activity, the Culinary Union Local 226 faced a crisis of leadership with the murder of one leader, Al Bramlet, and the problem-filled administration of his successor, Ben Schmoutey. See Nyre, *Union Jackpot,* chapter 3.

8. Canty's pride in her children is apparent in the original transcript. She had six sons and four daughters. Some of her children worked in the casino industry. The issue of low wages for poor, black, women workers was one of the central issues for the women of Operation Life, whose history has been written about so beautifully by Annelise Orleck. Their spokeswoman, Ruby Duncan, consistently made the connection between low-wage jobs available to black women and welfare. Orleck, *Storming Caesars Palace,* 75, 147, 233, 239, 247.

9. The swing shift included hours after noon. Canty said she always worked the four-to-twelve shift.

10. Henderson, Nevada, is a city southeast of Las Vegas.

11. In the early 1980s casino and hotel workers faced serious challenges to unions. As reported in the *Las Vegas Review Journal* at the time, the labor–management issues in Las Vegas's largest industry were similar to those taking place around the country in the early years of the Reagan administration. "It was the turn of the Las Vegas unions to face the same meat grinder that had already spit out the air traffic controllers, Greyhound bus drivers, copper miners and auto and steel workers" (cited in Nyre, *Union Jackpot,* 81). Also see Kraft, *Vegas At Odds,* 204–5.

12. Numerous national media reported on the strike. For local coverage, see *Las Vegas Sun,* February 1, 1998, http://www.lasvegassun.com/news/1998/feb/01/nations-longest-strike-comes-to-an-end/.

13. The NAACP, local antipoverty organizations, and legal aid attorneys worked during the late 1960s through the 1980s to end job discrimination by race, ethnicity, and gender. This activity resulted in several legal actions taken against the hotel-casinos as well as unions in Las Vegas. These actions are discussed in chapters 2 and 5 in this volume. For an overview of the 1971 Consent Decree that prohibited race discrimination in hiring, see Sallaz, "Civil Rights and Employment Equity."

14. For an intersectional analysis of Las Vegas hotel employees by race, ethnicity, class, and gender, see Barbara G. Brents and Melissa J. Monson, "Whitewashing 'the Strip': The Construction of Whiteness in Las Vegas," in *White Reign: Deploying Whiteness in America,* ed. Joe L. Kincheloe, Shirley R. Steinberg, Nelson M. Rodriguez, and Ronald E. Chennault (New York: St. Martin's Press, 1998), 213–28.

15. For more on the Culinary Academy of Las Vegas (formerly called the Culinary Training Center) and the success of this labor–management partnership, see its website (www.theculinaryacademy.org/); and Chandler and Jones, *Casino Women,* 71–72.

16. Chandler and Jones, *Casino Women*, 50.

8 | Florence McClure, Hotel Executive Administrator and Community Activist

1. This chapter is based on "An Interview with Florence McClure: An Oral History," interview conducted by Joanne Goodwin on January 24 and February 6, 1996, and August 2, 2001 (Las Vegas Women Oral History Program, Las Vegas, 2007).

2. The transition from a predominantly male occupation to a mostly female office workforce began in the nineteenth century. For the nineteenth century, see Carole Srole, *Transcribing Class and Gender: Masculinity and Femininity in Nineteenth-Century Courts and Offices* (Ann Arbor: University of Michigan Press, 2010). For the twentieth century, see Sharon Hartman Strom, *Beyond the Typewriter: Gender, Class, and the Origins of Modern American Office Work, 1900–1930* (Urbana: University of Illinois Press, 1992).

3. The term *pink collar* refers to jobs that have historically and traditionally been done by women. The term is a parallel construction to the blue collar jobs held predominantly by working-class men and the white-collar jobs held by those with professional training, better salaries, and a career trajectory. Credit has been given to Louise Kapp Howe for the original use of the term in her book *Pink Collar Workers: Inside the World of Women's Work* (New York: G. P. Putnam's Sons, 1977).

4. A census analysis of the female work force in Las Vegas may be found in Goodwin, "'She Works Hard for Her Money.'"

5. Cohen took major roles in building, opening, and managing several hotels, beginning with the Frontier Hotel Casino in which he had part ownership. When Howard Hughes bought the Frontier, Cohen moved to the Desert Inn, Circus Circus, and others. The Flamingo Hotel and Casino was acquired by the Hilton Corporation in 1971, and Cohen became president of that property. In 1973 he went to Caesars; he became vice president of Caesars Palace in 1977. Cohen led the financial reorganization of the Dunes Hotel Casino in 1986, increasing the property's value significantly. He returned to the Desert Inn in 1992 as president and continued there until his retirement in 1995. Mark Mayer, "Burton Cohen 'on the record,'" *Gaming Today*, September 3, 2013, http://gamingtoday.com/vegasstyle/vegas_style_GoingOut/article/43050-Burton_Cohen_on_the_record_made_Desert_an_Inn_locale#.Uv6DvvldWSo.

6. She noted that when they opened a young Steve Wynn became their slot manager. He later went on to become one of the leading casino owners in Las Vegas, creating the Mirage, the Bellagio, and most recently the Wynn and Encore Hotel-Casinos. A few owners later, the Elardi family owned the Frontier during the long strike described in chapter 7.

7. The history of women dealers working in Las Vegas and on the Strip is covered in chapter 9 in this volume.

8. The LWV evolved from the national suffrage organizations following passage

of the Nineteenth Amendment. Having succeeded with gaining the vote for women, the League's mission changed to voter education. This nonpartisan organization provided essential education in civic activities, electoral politics, and current issues of local and national interest. Many women who ran for office during the twentieth century credited the League with their initial training. During the 1960s and 1970s the mainstream LWV experienced the turmoil of social change as the organization discussed and debated numerous issues raised by the women's movement. Numerous state and local studies exist for the League. For their impact on the national scene, see Marisa Chappell, "Rethinking Women's Politics in the 1970s: The League of Women Voters and the National Organization for Women Confront Poverty," *Journal of Women's History* 13, no. 4 (Winter 2002): 155–79; Barbara Stuhler, *For the Public Record: A Documentary History of the League of Women Voters* (Westport, CT: Greenwood Press, 2000); and Louise Merwin Young and Ralph A. Young, *In the Public Interest: The League of Women Voters, 1920–1970* (New York: Greenwood Press, 1989).

9. McClure is referring to the voting problems associated with the presidential election of 2000.

10. See "Jean Ford: A Nevada Woman Leads the Way," from oral history interviews conducted and edited by Victoria Ford (University of Nevada Oral History Program, Reno, 1998).

11. In 1972 the US Congress passed the ERA and sent it to the states for ratification. The Nevada state legislature took up the issue in subsequent sessions, but failed to ratify it. The abortion issue created major rifts within the state LWV. McClure noted her relief when the US Supreme Court decided on *Roe v. Wade* (1973) and made it unnecessary for the state LWV to take up the issue. The Nevada LWV faced two other issues of national prominence and local significance while McClure was state president: welfare rights and school desegregation. The only study on Nevada's ERA campaign is Caryll Batt Dziedziak, "The Gendering of Nevada Politics: The ERA Ratification Campaign, 1973–1981" (PhD dissertation, UNLV, 2010). The best coverage on the antipoverty movement in Las Vegas is Orleck, *Storming Caesars Palace*. On the desegregation movement in general, see Ronan Matthew, "A History of the Las Vegas School Desegregation Case: *Kelly et al. v. the Clark County School District*" (PhD dissertation, UNLV, 1998).

12. News reports credit library director Thomasine Carson and her staff for calling the meeting at which an estimated four hundred people attended. Historically, the US women's movement drew public attention to previously private issues in order to help women and children. Violence against women—battering, incest, or rape—became one of several advocacy areas within local communities around the country. As scholars of the antiviolence movement acknowledged, rape and other forms of violence created a context of terror in which girls grew to womanhood. The silence and victim blaming that surrounded rape kept the entire subject in the shadows. As the people who attended this early meeting in Las Vegas indicated, the lack of adequate legal, medical,

and judicial remedies for rape was unacceptable. In fact the efforts that resulted from that meeting changed how we think about and respond to sexual violence. See Nancy A. Matthews, *Confronting Rape: The Feminist Anti-Rape Movement and the State* (New York: Routledge, 1994). No history has been written on the development of the antiviolence or antirape movement in Las Vegas.

13. The Community Action Against Rape was renamed the Rape Crisis Center on an unknown date. McClure used both names in her interviews.

14. Grants supplied some salaries at a later date. Myron Leavitt who sat on the city council at the time arranged for money from the city to be used to rent an office near the courthouse. A long-time supporter, he later became a district court judge, then a state supreme court justice.

15. Women had served in the state legislature since winning suffrage, but in limited numbers. By the mid-1970s more women from both parties sought and won political offices.

16. US Senator Paul Laxalt from Nevada chaired the federal subcommittee on LEAA in 1978. He asked McClure to testify in front of a committee hearing in Washington, DC, which she did.

17. Proposed in 1991 by state senator Sue Wagner, SB371 added a specific amount (originally $5.00) to the cost of marriage licenses in the state. These designated monies funded domestic violence shelters and the rape crisis centers in the state. "I had practically every senator on it, maybe all of them," Wagner noted in her oral history. Nevada had an advantage over other states in that it led the nation as a wedding destination site. See Sue Wagner with Victoria Ford, edited by Richard Hoaldley and Kathleen Coles, *Through the Glass Ceiling: A Life in Nevada Politics* (Reno: University of Nevada Oral History Program, Reno, 2005), 255–56.

18. The UNLV added the William S. Boyd School of Law in 1998.

9 | Carol Gerardi, Craps Dealer and Floor Supervisor

1. Studies on desegregation of the labor force have been written for several industries, for example the auto industry and mining industries, yet there is only a slim body of scholarship on women dealers. See Chandler and Jones, *Casino Women*, 109–37; Darlene B. Dunston, "Women of the Strip: A Gendered History of Las Vegas" (master's thesis, University of Hawaii at Manoa, 2002); Elaine Enarson, "Emotion Workers on the Production Line: The Feminizing of Casino Card Dealing," *NWSA* [National Women's Studies Association] *Journal* 5, no. 2 (Summer 1993): 218–32.

2. The 1971 Consent Decree prohibited race discrimination and has been discussed in more detail than the 1981 decree. For example, see Sallaz, "Civil Rights and Employment Equity"; and Kraft, *Vegas at Odds*. African American women were particularly active in the quest to open all casino jobs regardless of race and sex, according to Orleck, *Storming Caesars Palace;* and Committee of Low Income Women, "Low-Income

Women Charge Discrimination against LV Hotels," *Operation Life Community Press* 1, no. 1 (November 10, 1977): 1, Special Collections Department, Lied Library, UNLV. The author is revising for publication an article entitled "Wages, Rights, and Civic Life: Women's Lives in Las Vegas, 1940–1990," which places the efforts to end sex discrimination in employment in Nevada within a national context.

3. The classic text covering the national events is Cynthia Harrison, *On Account of Sex: The Politics of Women's Issues, 1945–1968* (Berkeley: University of California Press, 1989).

4. Reno welcomed women dealers, but these protesters thought it ruined the Reno economy and would ruin the Las Vegas economy. Greater Las Vegas had two major gambling centers: the older downtown area where the town began, and the resort hotel-casinos built on Las Vegas Boulevard (known as the Strip) in the county. All quotes are from Colin McKinlay, "City Dads Halt Gal Dealers," *Las Vegas Review Journal,* November 7, 1958, sec. 1, p. 1; Las Vegas City Commission, *Minutes,* XI, November 5, 1958, 233–35, Special Collections Department, Lied Library, UNLV. North Las Vegas passed its ban on women dealers in 1959 and repealed it in 1967. D. Berns, "Gaming Chips: New Year's Brighter for Casinos," *Las Vegas Review Journal,* January 7, 2001, 1F.

5. Sharon Spigelmyer, "Las Vegas Gaming Biased Against Women," *Las Vegas Sun,* October 1, 1977, 1, 4; "Casinos, Hotels Accused of Bias," *Los Angeles Times,* October 15, 1970, A2, ProQuest Historical Newspapers; and Kraft, *Vegas at Odds,* 133–38.

6. Chandler and Jones, *Casino Women,* 109–19. The authors found dealers to be the most highly regulated of casino employees. "Because dealers handle the money, casino owners from the beginning have left nothing to chance in their relationship with these employees. . . . At the heart of their strategy is absolute control" (110). Their interviews with women dealers in Reno found concerns about health, job pressures, and speed-ups created a negative work environment. An earlier study of women dealers in Reno casinos also found that women reported an unhealthy work environment filled with noise and smoke pollution. Elizabeth Bernheimer and Ruth Tsukada, "Health Problems of Women Casino Dealers: A Pilot Study," *Nevada Public Affairs Review* 1 (1982): 52–57.

7. From the transcript, "Interview with Carol Gerardi," interview conducted by Joanne Goodwin at the UNLV on December 4, 1996 (Las Vegas Women in Gaming and Entertainment Oral History Project, UNLV, Las Vegas, 1996).

8. Cutting checks refers to stacking chips. Dealers start by cutting them in piles of one chip and then move up to larger stacks. The process is referred to as sizing in.

9. According to Chandler and Jones, dealers also feared for their job security and benefits. For a discussion of the effort to start dealers' unions in Las Vegas, see Chandler and Jones, *Casino Women,* 119–21; Kraft, *Vegas at Odds,* 78–91; and Christina Binkley, "Show of Hands: In Drive to Unionize, Casino Dealers Defy a Las Vegas Tradition—Their Old Bosses Took Care of Them; Then, Sin City Became a Corporate Town—Less 'Juice' and Fewer 'Tokes,'" *Wall Street Journal,* March 6, 2001, A1, ProQuest 398786702.

10. Since the interview, dealers in two Las Vegas properties have unionized and signed contracts with Local 721 of the Transport Workers Union of America (TWU). See, *Las Vegas Sun,* November 2, 2010 and *Las Vegas Review Journal,* July 11, 2012.

11. This interview took place in the year prior to the interview with D. D. Cotton (chapter 5). Although they had different positions on the floor, both had moved up from dealer.

Conclusion | New Narratives—Social and Economic Change in Women's Lives

1. Willis never copyrighted the design for the sign and it remains in the public domain. The physical sign, installed at the southern end of old Highway 91 (known as the Las Vegas Strip) belongs to Young Electric Sign Company, which leases it to Clark County. In 2009 it was approved for the National Register for Historic Places. Willis also designed the signage for the Moulin Rouge Hotel and Casino. Although that property burned down, the signage has been preserved in the Neon Museum in Las Vegas. Like all the women portrayed in this book, Willis worked for a living. Like some, she worked in a field dominated by men. Unlike any other woman included here, though, Willis spent her life in Las Vegas because her parents arrived in 1905, the year that real estate lots for the new town were auctioned for sale. For more information on Willis, see http://www.pbs.org/wgbh/amex/lasvegas/peopleevents/p_willis.html, and http://www.nps.gov/nr/feature/weekly_features/2009/LasVegasSign.pdf. The participation of women in the growth of this metropolitan area has yet to be written in full. *Changing the Game* has built on earlier works on employed women such as Chandler and Jones, *Casino Women;* Kraft, *Vegas at Odds;* Orleck *Storming Caesars Palace;* and Goodwin, "'She Works Hard for Her Money.'"

2. Atlantic City legalized gambling in the late 1970s. Since then, municipalities have added gambling in an attempt to replace declining revenues.

3. I am grateful to Annelise Orleck for bringing to my attention this important effort to connect antipoverty efforts with expanded opportunities in employment for women. A sample of the continuing campaign to open jobs to African Americans, Latinos/as, and all women may be found in Ruby Duncan and Rev. Albert Dunn, "Et tu Caesar," *Las Vegas Voice,* September 2, 1976, 8–9.

4. Chandler and Jones included Darlene Jespersen's lawsuit against Harrah's Entertainment, Inc.'s appearance requirements in Chandler and Jones, *Casino Women,* chap. 6. On brothel prostitution outside Clark County, see Barbara G. Brents, Crystal A. Jackson, and Kathryn Hausbeck, *The State of Sex: Tourism, Sex and Sin in the New American Heartland* (New York: Routledge, 2010).

5. Selma Leydesdorff, Luisa Passerini, and Paul Thompson, eds., "Introduction," *Gender and Memory* (New Brunswick, NJ: Transaction Publishers, 2005), 8.

6. Kessler-Harris, *Out to Work.* A significant portion of historians' work on women in the labor force during the postwar years is on labor unions. For one example that

argues for the combination of social citizenship rights alongside women's right to work, see Eileen Boris and Sonya Michel, "Social Citizenship and Women's Right to Work in Postwar America," in *Women's Rights and Human Rights: International Historical Perspectives* (New York: Palgrave, 2001), 199–219.

7. Scott, "Comment."

Index